D0475207

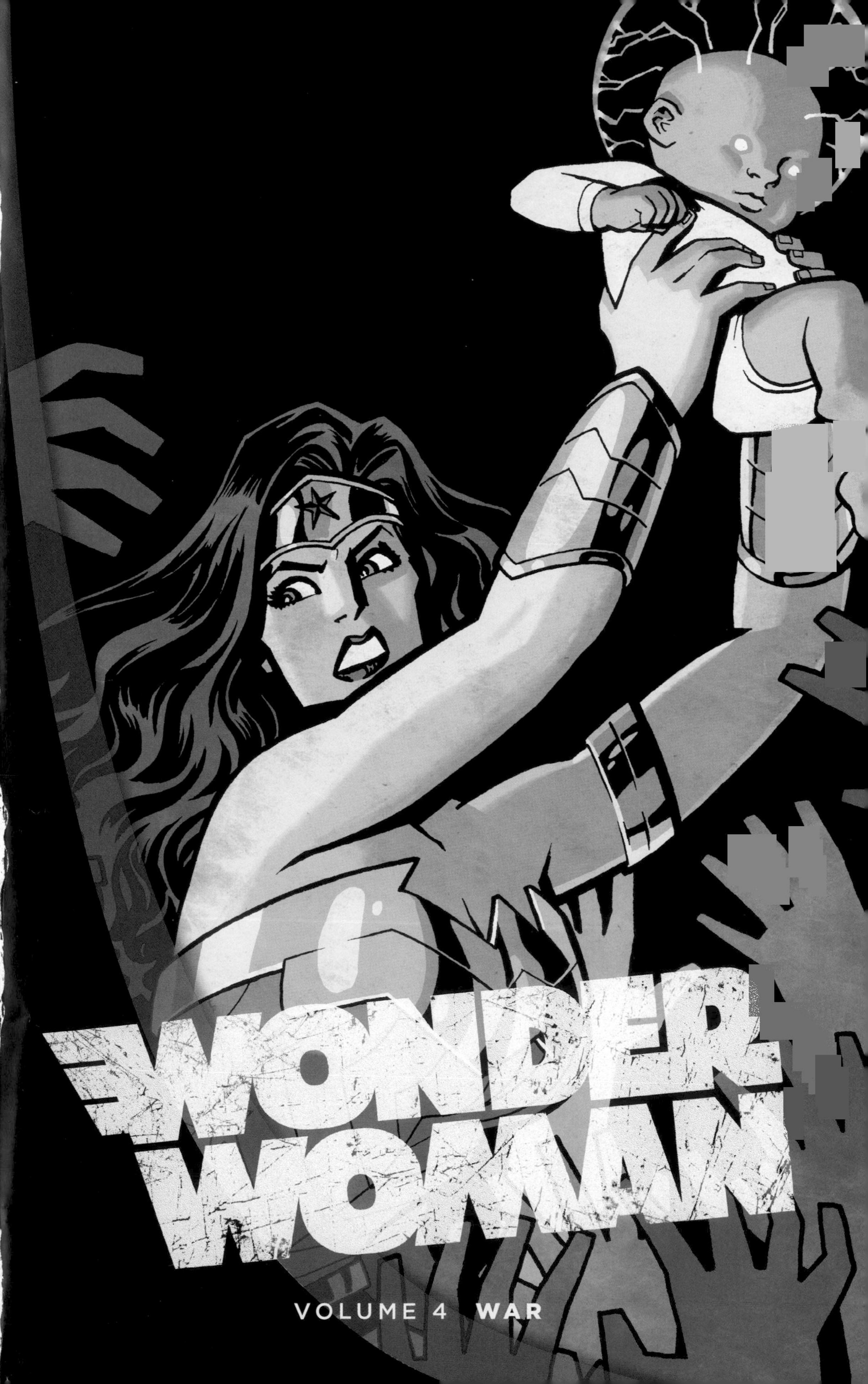
WONDER WOMAN

VOLUME 4 WAR

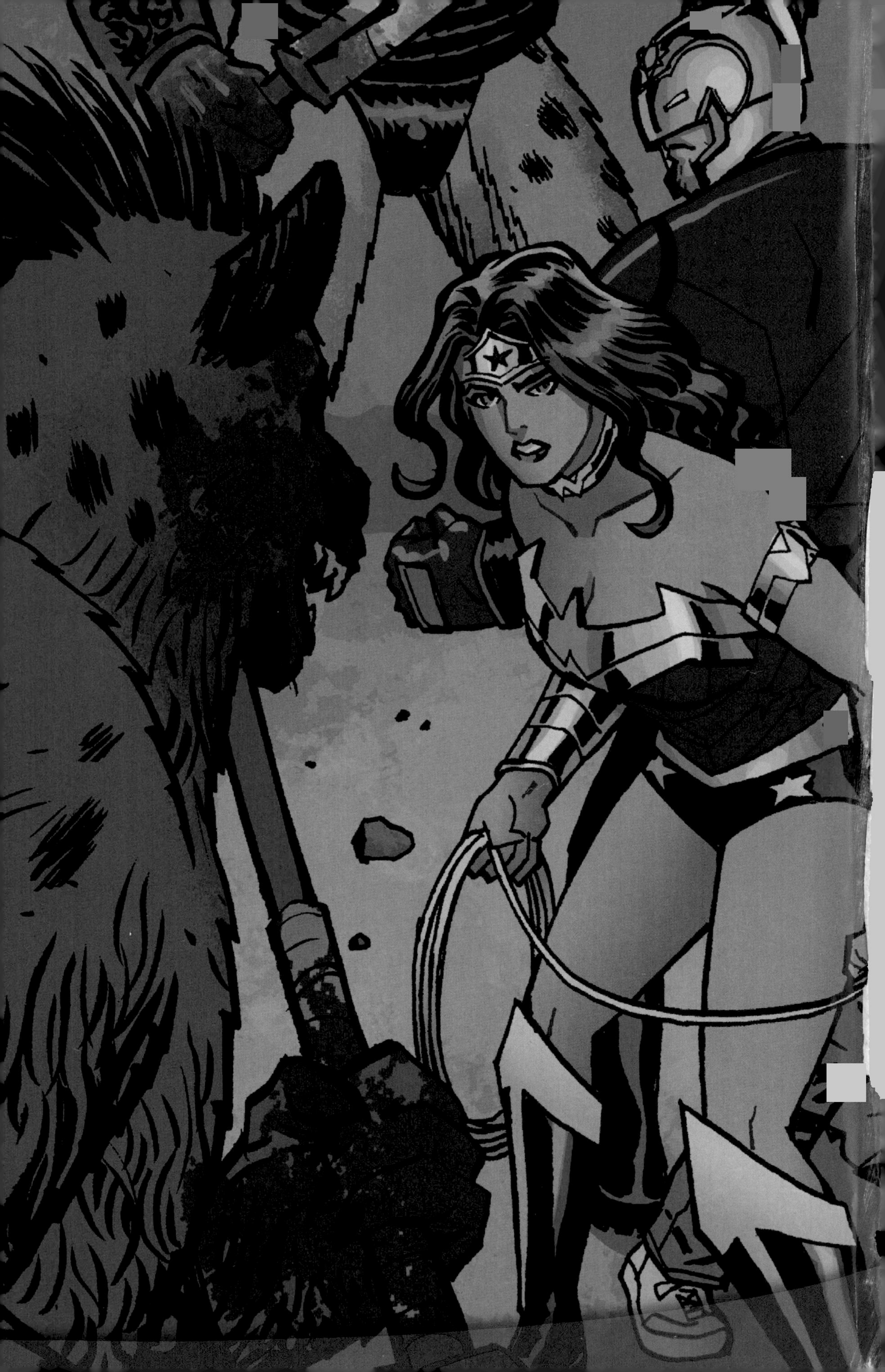

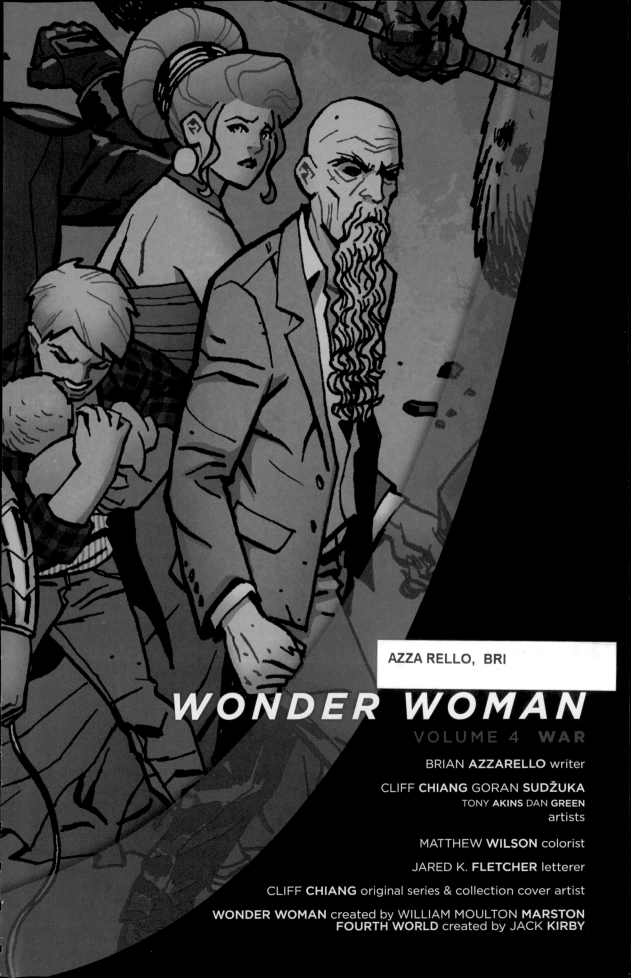

AZZA RELLO, BRI

WONDER WOMAN
VOLUME 4   WAR

BRIAN **AZZARELLO** writer

CLIFF **CHIANG** GORAN **SUDŽUKA**
TONY **AKINS** DAN **GREEN**
artists

MATTHEW **WILSON** colorist

JARED K. **FLETCHER** letterer

CLIFF **CHIANG** original series & collection cover artist

WONDER WOMAN created by WILLIAM MOULTON **MARSTON**
FOURTH WORLD created by JACK **KIRBY**

MATT IDELSON Group Editor – Original Series CHRIS CONROY Associate Editor – Original Series
RACHEL PINNELAS Editor ROBBIN BROSTERMAN Design Director – Books
ROBBIE BIEDERMAN Publication Design

BOB HARRAS Senior VP – Editor-in-Chief, DC Comics

DIANE NELSON President DAN DIDIO & JIM LEE Co-Publishers
GEOFF JOHNS Chief Creative Officer
JOHN ROOD Executive VP – Sales, Marketing & Business Development
AMY GENKINS Senior VP – Business & Legal Affairs NAIRI GARDINER Senior VP – Finance
JEFF BOISON VP – Publishing Planning MARK CHIARELLO VP – Art Direction & Design
JOHN CUNNINGHAM VP – Marketing TERRI CUNNINGHAM VP – Editorial Administration
ALISON GILL Senior VP – Manufacturing & Operations HANK KANALZ Senior VP – Vertigo & Integrated Publishing
JAY KOGAN VP – Business & Legal Affairs, Publishing JACK MAHAN VP – Business Affairs, Talent
NICK NAPOLITANO VP – Manufacturing Administration SUE POHJA VP – Book Sales
COURTNEY SIMMONS Senior VP – Publicity BOB WAYNE Senior VP – Sales

WONDER WOMAN VOLUME 4: WAR

DC Comics, 1700 Broadway, New York, NY 10019
A Warner Bros. Entertainment Company.
Printed by RR Donnelley, Salem, VA, USA. 2/7/14. First Printing.
ISBN: 978-1-4012-4608-2

SUSTAINABLE FORESTRY INITIATIVE
Certified Chain of Custody
At Least 20% Certified Forest Content
www.sfiprogram.org
SFI-01042
APPLIES TO TEXT STOCK ONLY

Library of Congress Cataloging-in-Publication Data

Azzarello, Brian, author.
Wonder Woman. Volume 4, War / Brian Azzarello ; [illustrated by] Cliff Chiang, Tony Akins.
pages cm. — (The New 52!)
Summary: "Wonder Woman's world is shocked to its core when her eldest brother, the First Born, is freed from his slumber. Now, with her family in ruins and her friends scattered, she must turn to Orion and the New Gods of New Genesis to save herself and Zola's newborn from the First Born's wrath! Collects Wonder Woman #19-23"— Provided by publisher.
ISBN 978-1-4012-4608-2 (hardback)
1. Graphic novels. I. Chiang, Cliff, illustrator. II. Akins, Tony, illustrator. III. Title. IV. Title: War.
PN6728.W6A994 2014
741.5'973—dc23
2013046159

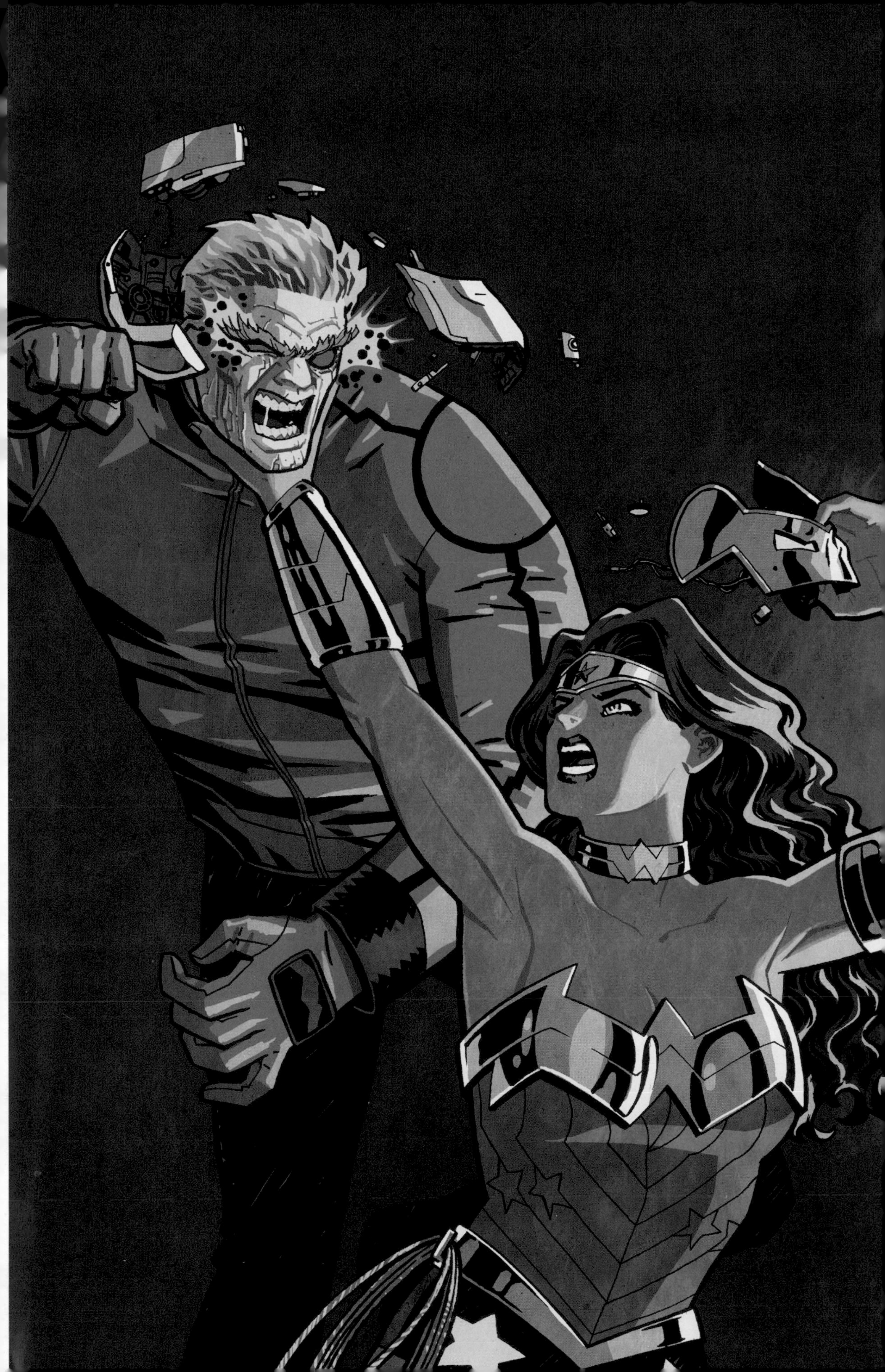

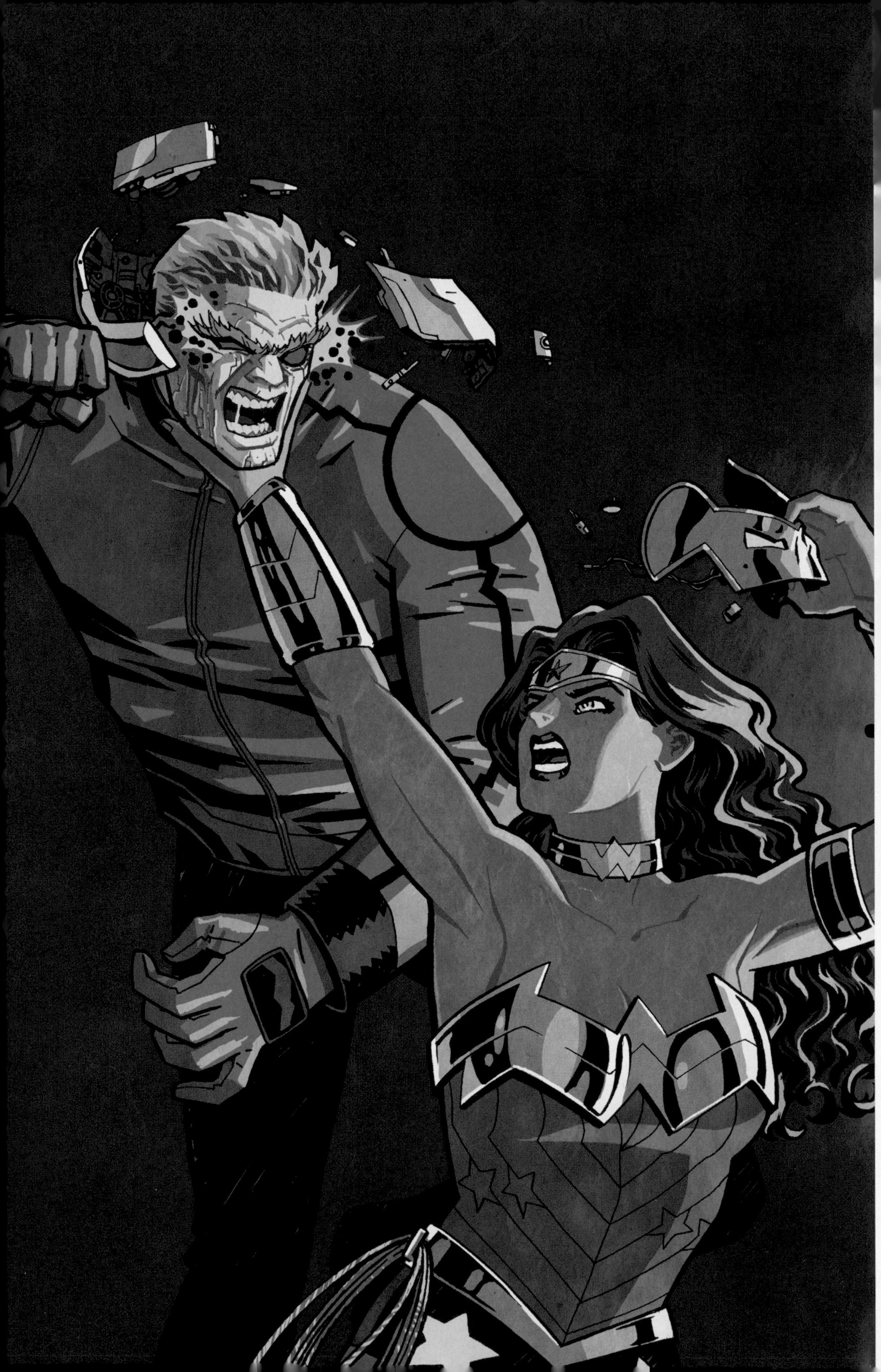

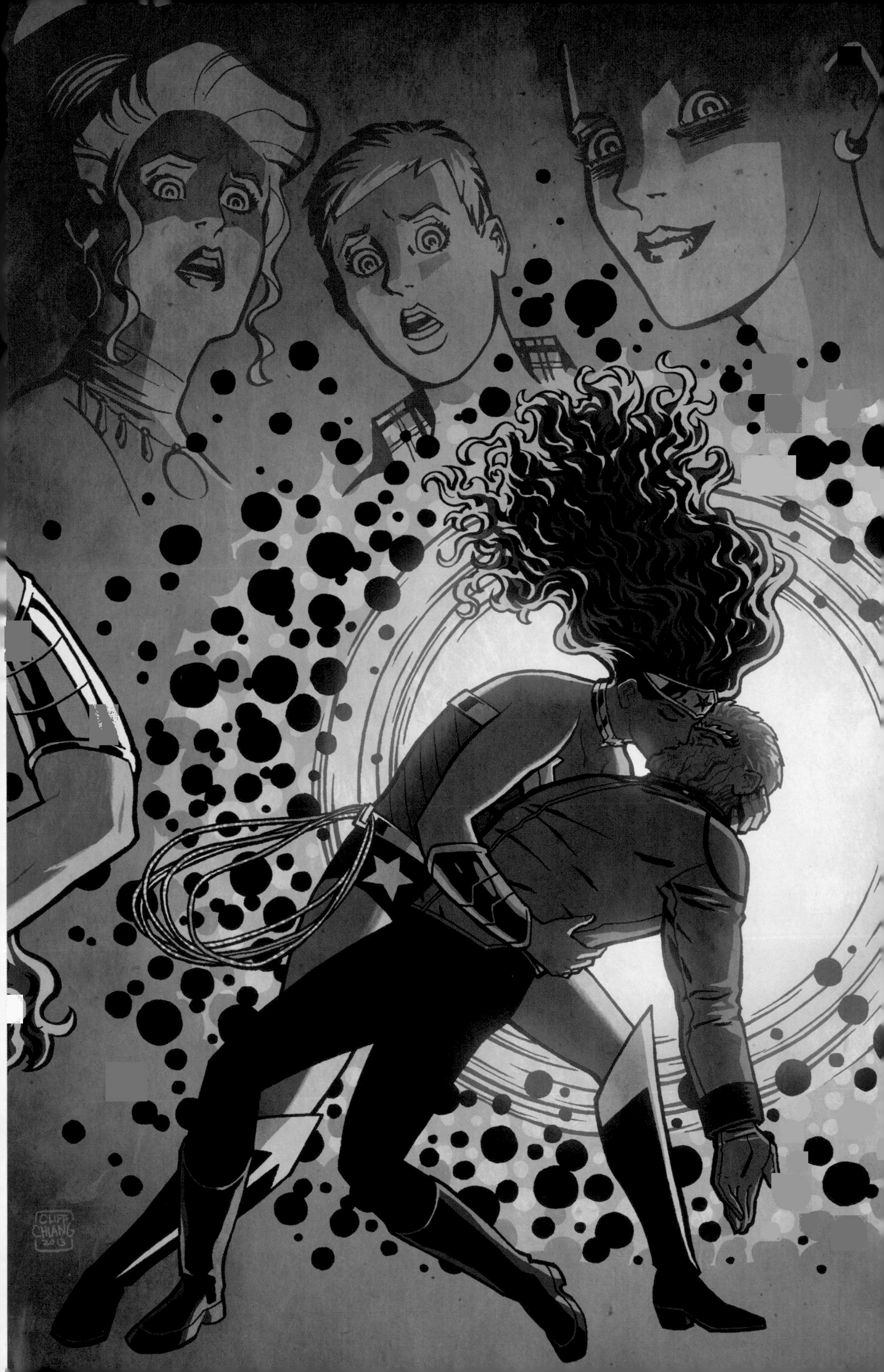
CLIFF CHIANG 2013

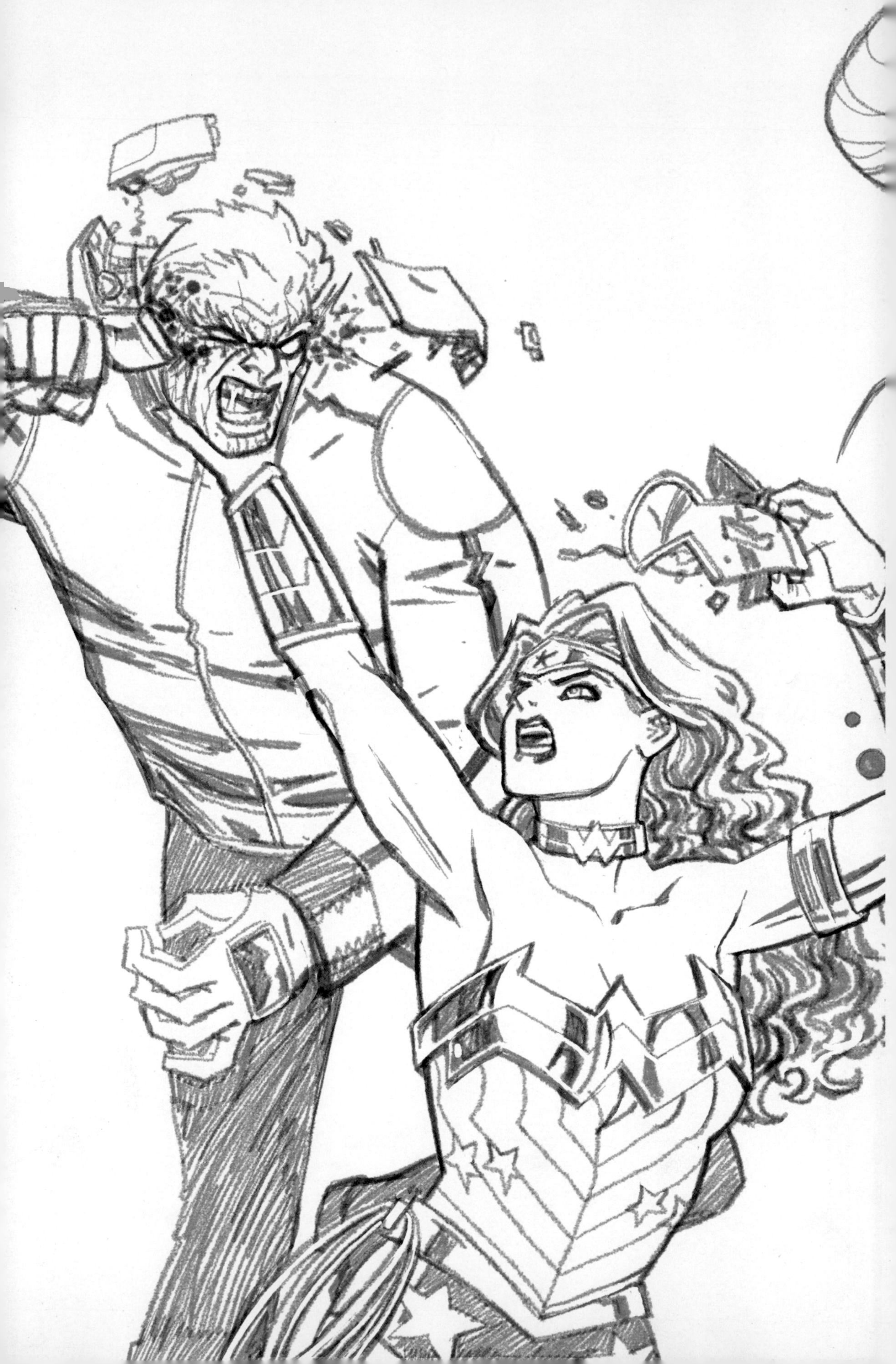

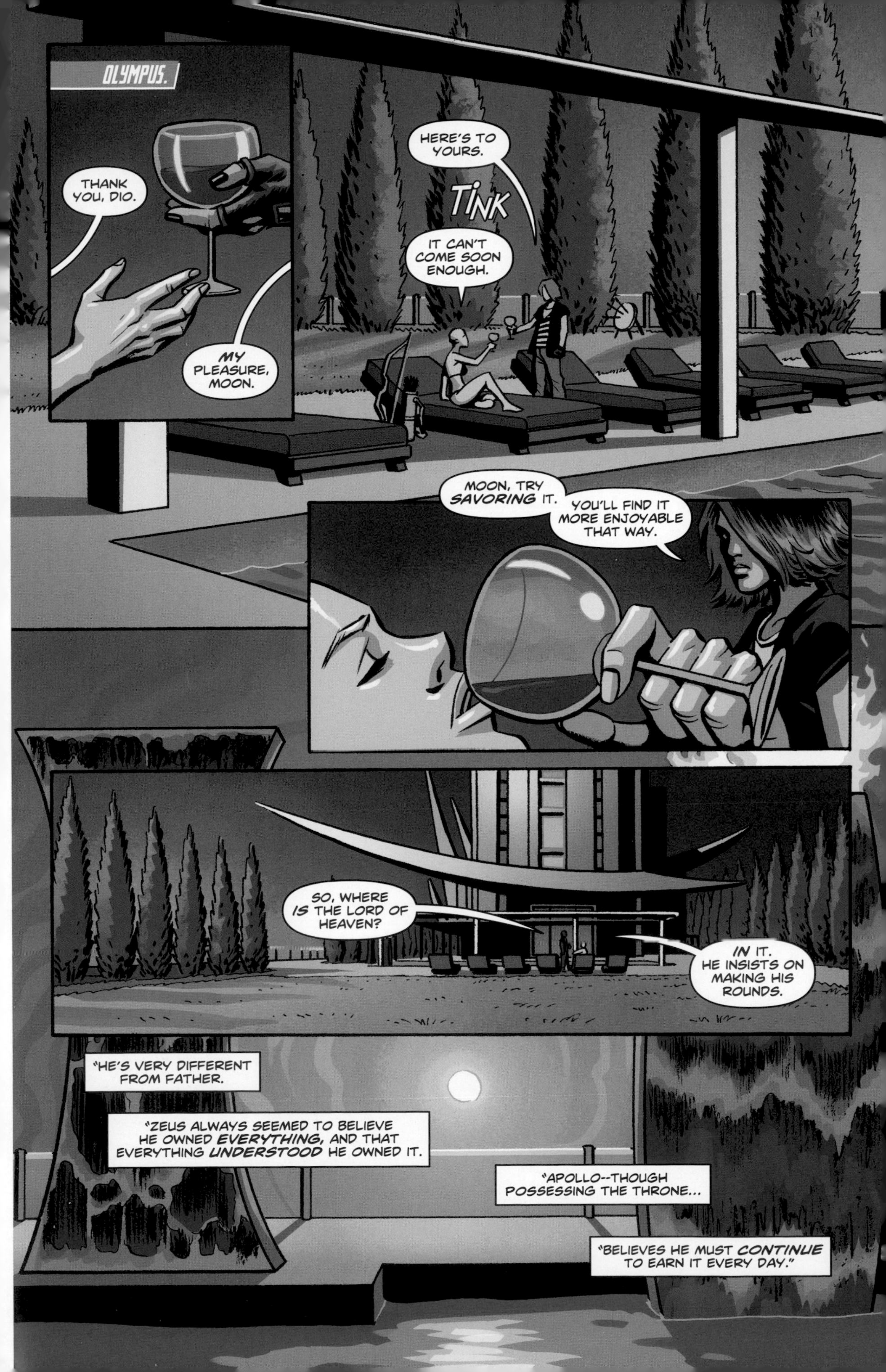
OLYMPUS.
THANK YOU, DIO.
MY PLEASURE, MOON.
HERE'S TO YOURS.
TINK
IT CAN'T COME SOON ENOUGH.
MOON, TRY SAVORING IT.
YOU'LL FIND IT MORE ENJOYABLE THAT WAY.
SO, WHERE IS THE LORD OF HEAVEN?
IN IT. HE INSISTS ON MAKING HIS ROUNDS.
"HE'S VERY DIFFERENT FROM FATHER.
"ZEUS ALWAYS SEEMED TO BELIEVE HE OWNED EVERYTHING, AND THAT EVERYTHING UNDERSTOOD HE OWNED IT.
"APOLLO--THOUGH POSSESSING THE THRONE...
"BELIEVES HE MUST CONTINUE TO EARN IT EVERY DAY."

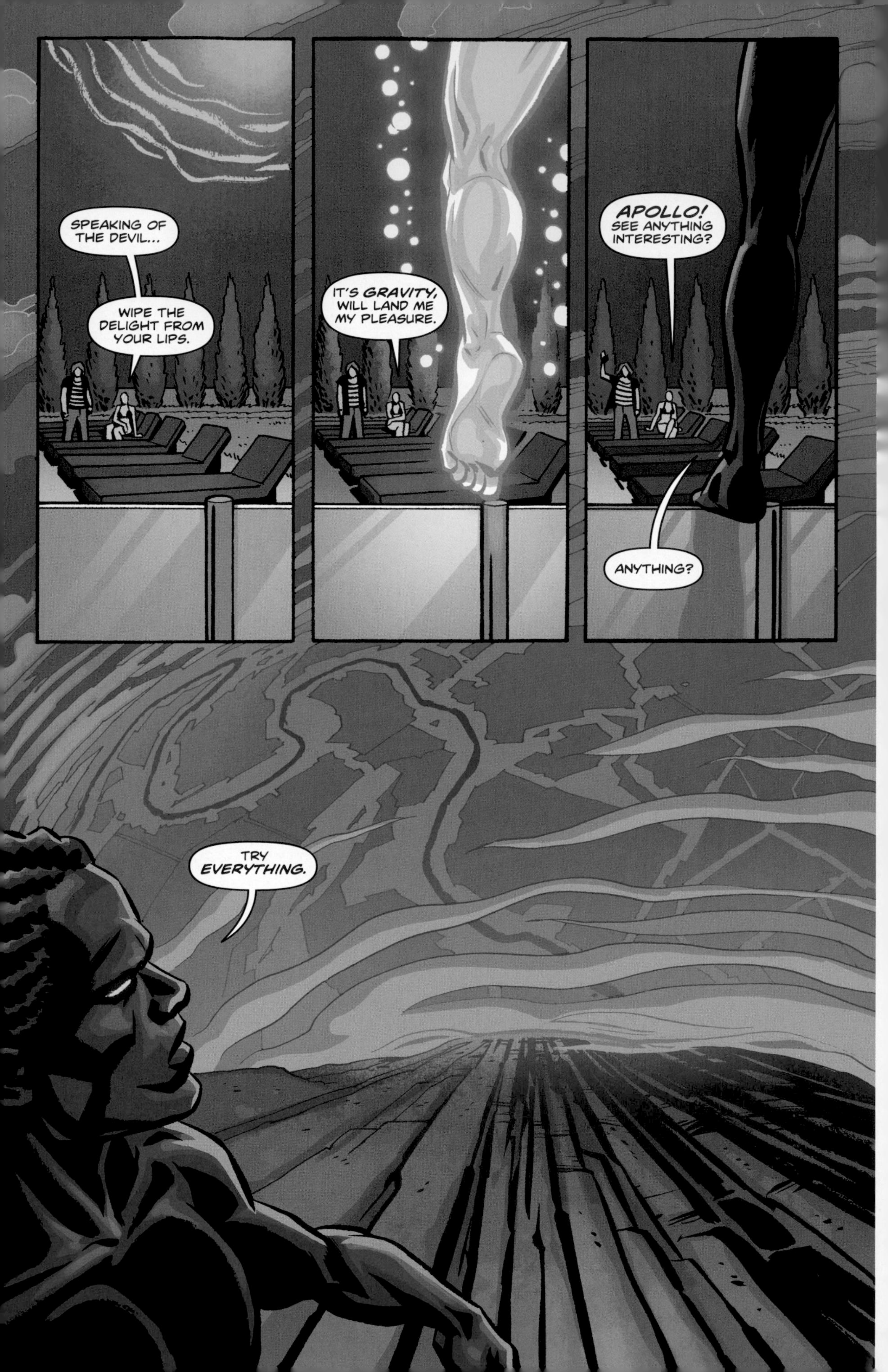
SPEAKING OF THE DEVIL...
WIPE THE DELIGHT FROM YOUR LIPS.
IT'S *GRAVITY*, WILL LAND ME MY PLEASURE.
APOLLO! SEE ANYTHING INTERESTING?
ANYTHING?
TRY *EVERYTHING.*

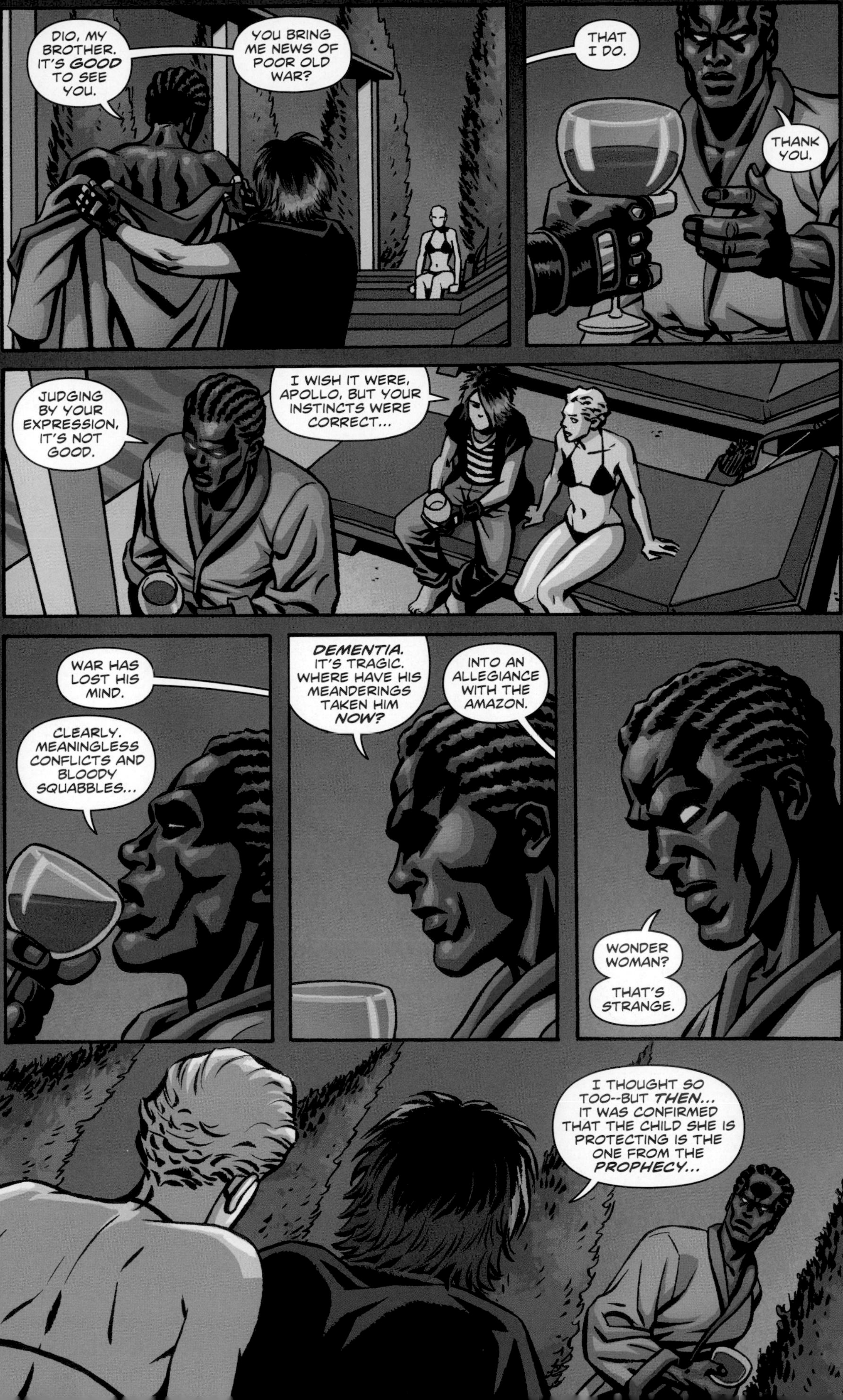
DIO, MY BROTHER. IT'S GOOD TO SEE YOU.
YOU BRING ME NEWS OF POOR OLD WAR?
THAT I DO.
THANK YOU.
JUDGING BY YOUR EXPRESSION, IT'S NOT GOOD.
I WISH IT WERE, APOLLO, BUT YOUR INSTINCTS WERE CORRECT...
WAR HAS LOST HIS MIND.
CLEARLY. MEANINGLESS CONFLICTS AND BLOODY SQUABBLES...
DEMENTIA. IT'S TRAGIC. WHERE HAVE HIS MEANDERINGS TAKEN HIM NOW?
INTO AN ALLEGIANCE WITH THE AMAZON.
WONDER WOMAN?
THAT'S STRANGE.
I THOUGHT SO TOO--BUT THEN... IT WAS CONFIRMED THAT THE CHILD SHE IS PROTECTING IS THE ONE FROM THE PROPHECY...

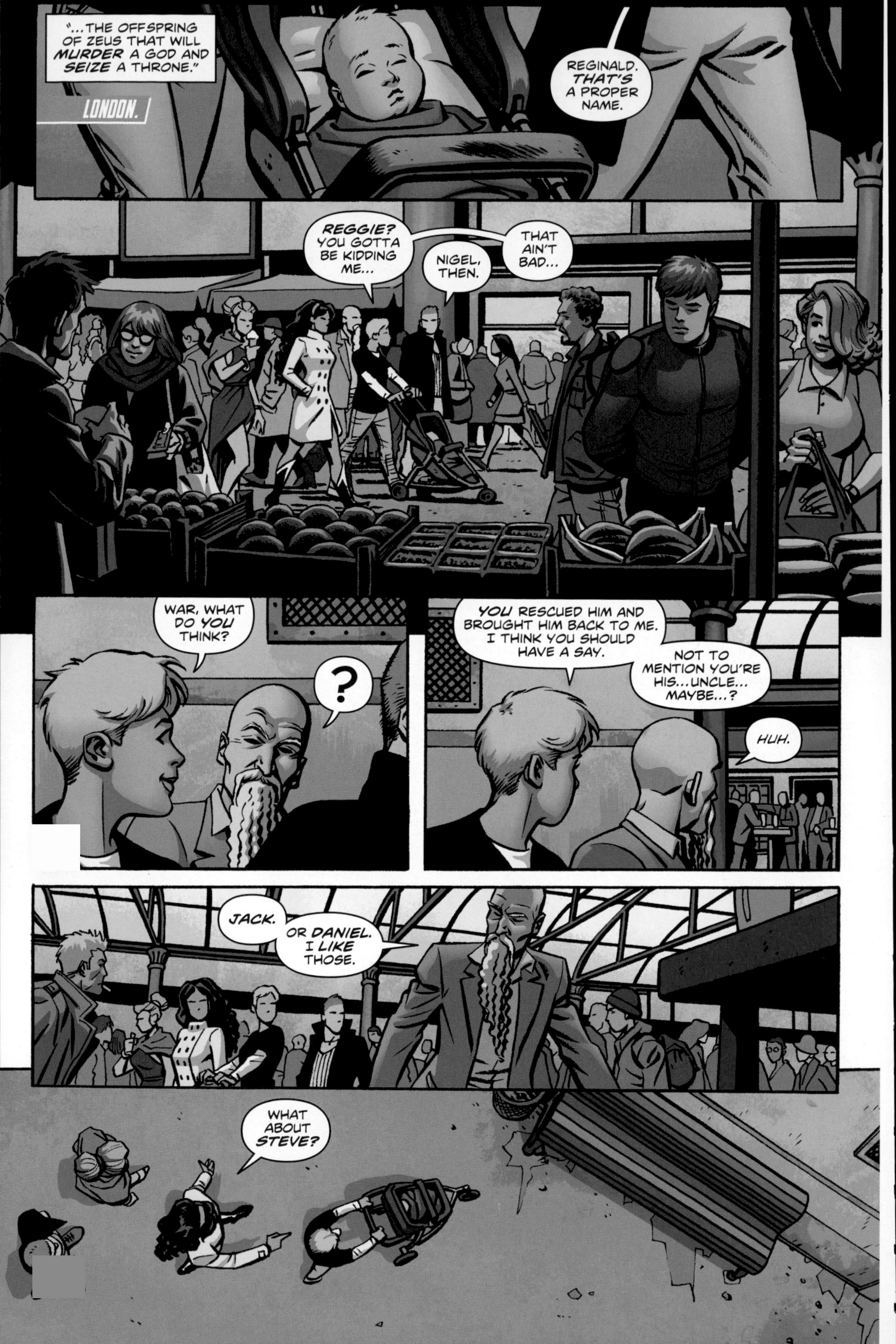
"...THE OFFSPRING OF ZEUS THAT WILL MURDER A GOD AND SEIZE A THRONE."
LONDON.
REGINALD. THAT'S A PROPER NAME.
REGGIE? YOU GOTTA BE KIDDING ME...
NIGEL, THEN.
THAT AIN'T BAD...
WAR, WHAT DO YOU THINK?
?
YOU RESCUED HIM AND BROUGHT HIM BACK TO ME. I THINK YOU SHOULD HAVE A SAY.
NOT TO MENTION YOU'RE HIS...UNCLE... MAYBE...?
HUH.
JACK.
OR DANIEL. I LIKE THOSE.
WHAT ABOUT STEVE?

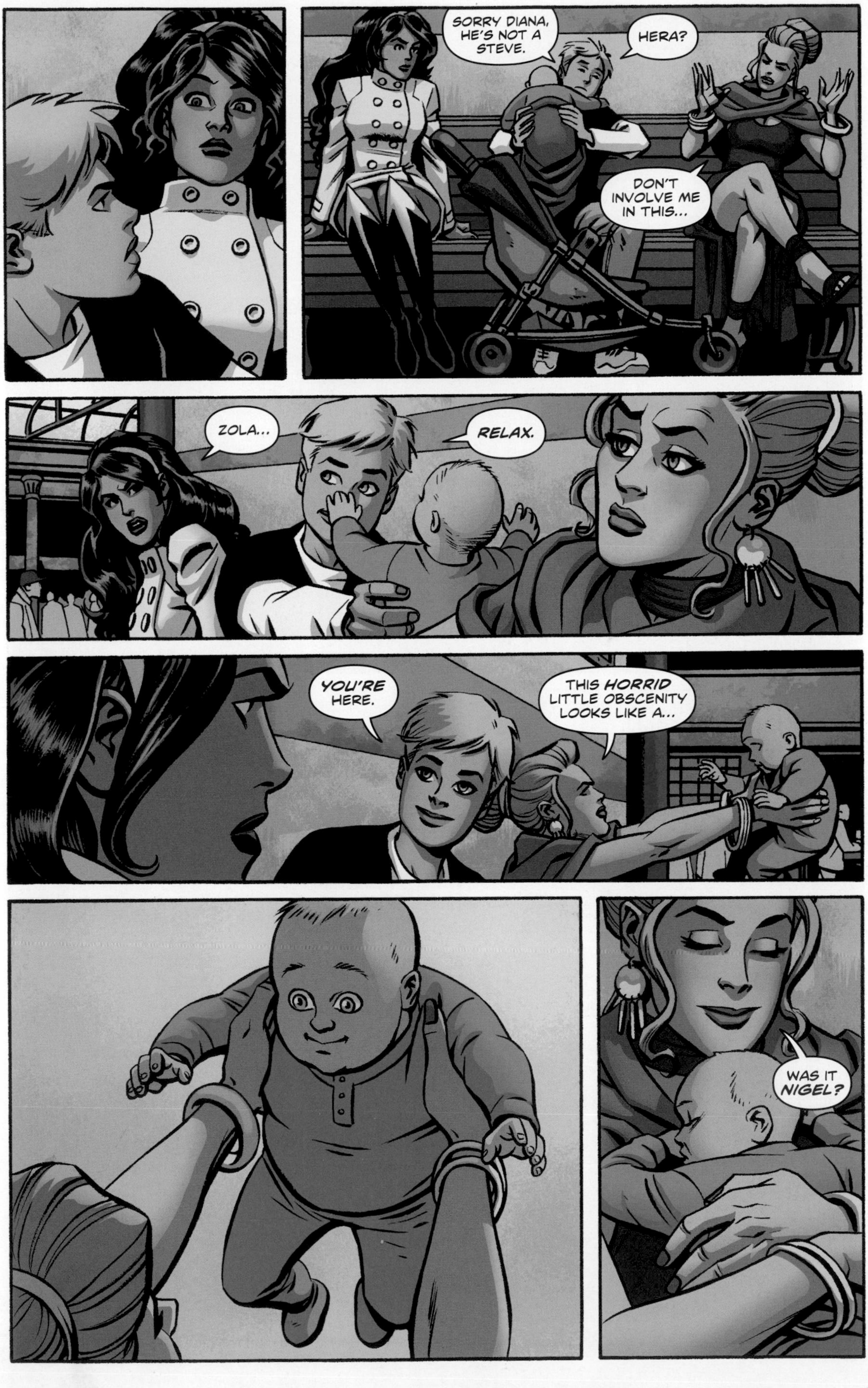
SORRY DIANA, HE'S NOT A STEVE.
HERA?
DON'T INVOLVE ME IN THIS...
ZOLA...
RELAX.
YOU'RE HERE.
THIS HORRID LITTLE OBSCENITY LOOKS LIKE A...
WAS IT NIGEL?

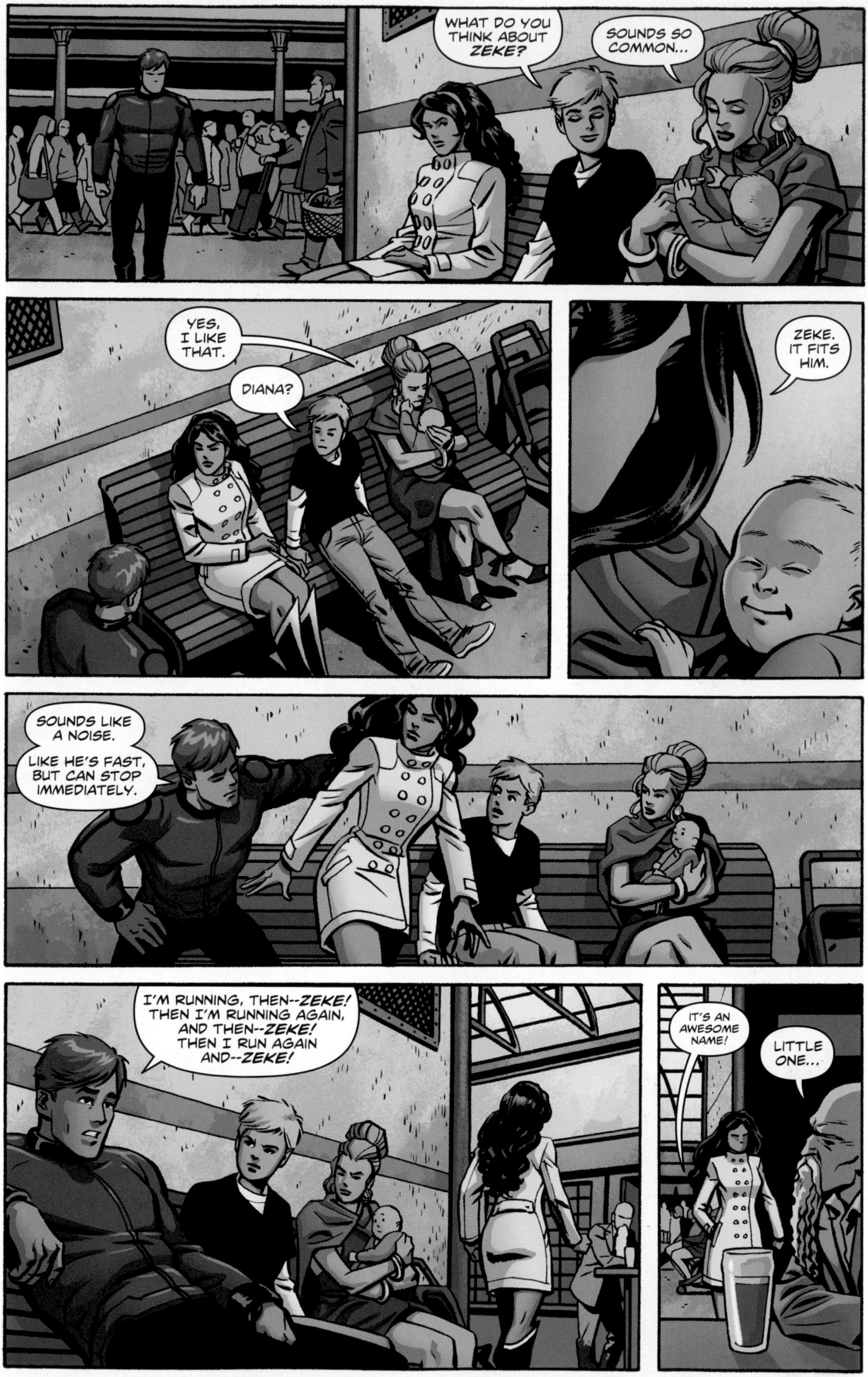
WHAT DO YOU THINK ABOUT ZEKE?
SOUNDS SO COMMON...
YES, I LIKE THAT.
DIANA?
ZEKE. IT FITS HIM.
SOUNDS LIKE A NOISE.
LIKE HE'S FAST, BUT CAN STOP IMMEDIATELY.
I'M RUNNING, THEN--ZEKE! THEN I'M RUNNING AGAIN, AND THEN--ZEKE! THEN I RUN AGAIN AND--ZEKE!
IT'S AN AWESOME NAME!
LITTLE ONE...

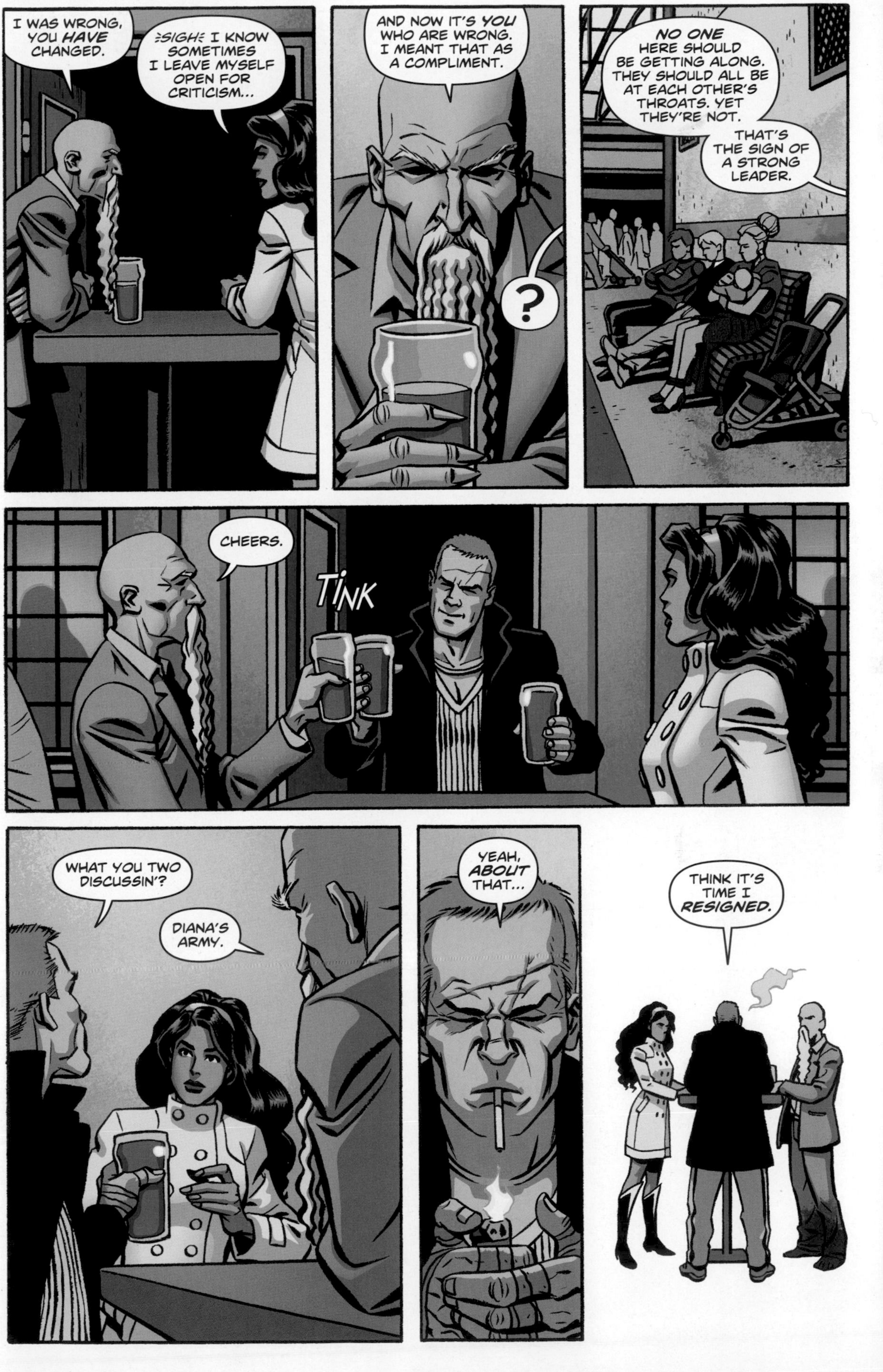
I WAS WRONG, YOU HAVE CHANGED.
SIGH I KNOW SOMETIMES I LEAVE MYSELF OPEN FOR CRITICISM...
AND NOW IT'S YOU WHO ARE WRONG. I MEANT THAT AS A COMPLIMENT.
?
NO ONE HERE SHOULD BE GETTING ALONG. THEY SHOULD ALL BE AT EACH OTHER'S THROATS. YET THEY'RE NOT.
THAT'S THE SIGN OF A STRONG LEADER.
CHEERS.
TINK
WHAT YOU TWO DISCUSSIN'?
DIANA'S ARMY.
YEAH, ABOUT THAT...
THINK IT'S TIME I RESIGNED.

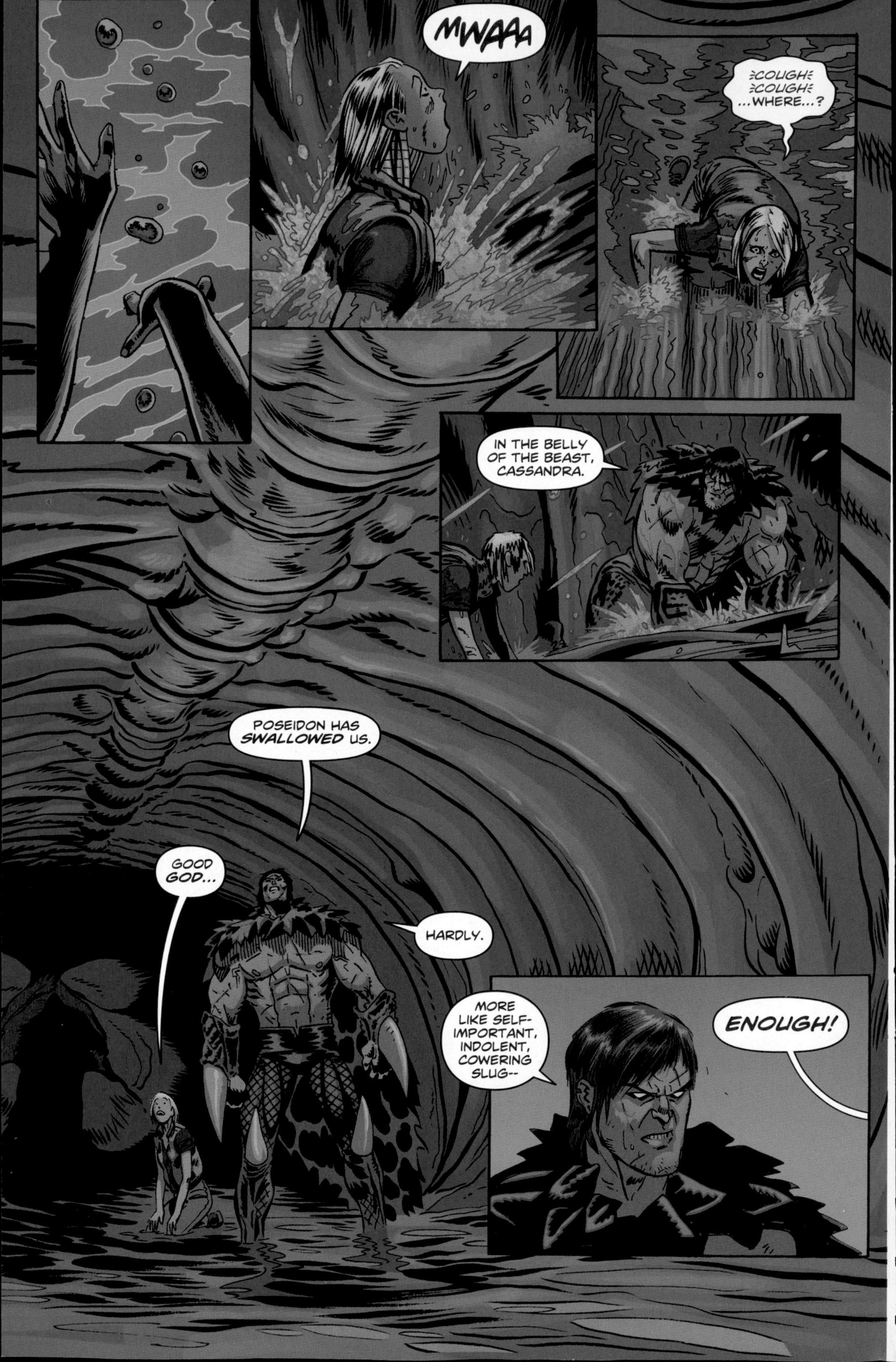
MWAAA
COUGH COUGH ...WHERE...?
IN THE BELLY OF THE BEAST, CASSANDRA.
POSEIDON HAS SWALLOWED US.
GOOD GOD...
HARDLY.
MORE LIKE SELF-IMPORTANT, INDOLENT, COWERING SLUG--
ENOUGH!

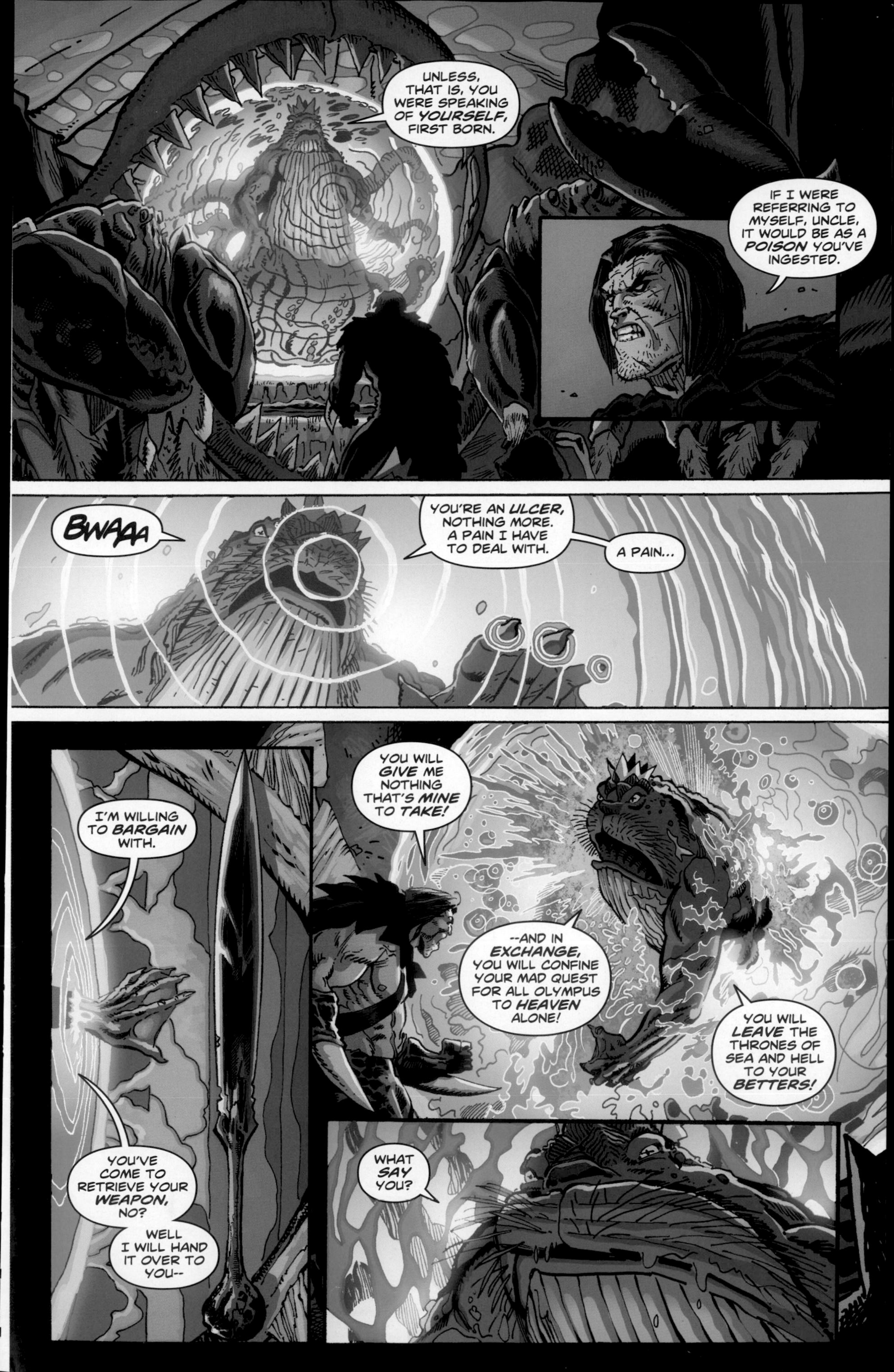
UNLESS, THAT IS, YOU WERE SPEAKING OF YOURSELF, FIRST BORN.
IF I WERE REFERRING TO MYSELF, UNCLE, IT WOULD BE AS A POISON YOU'VE INGESTED.
BWAAA
YOU'RE AN ULCER, NOTHING MORE. A PAIN I HAVE TO DEAL WITH.
A PAIN...
I'M WILLING TO BARGAIN WITH.
YOU'VE COME TO RETRIEVE YOUR WEAPON, NO?
WELL I WILL HAND IT OVER TO YOU--
YOU WILL GIVE ME NOTHING THAT'S MINE TO TAKE!
--AND IN EXCHANGE, YOU WILL CONFINE YOUR MAD QUEST FOR ALL OLYMPUS TO HEAVEN ALONE!
YOU WILL LEAVE THE THRONES OF SEA AND HELL TO YOUR BETTERS!
WHAT SAY YOU?

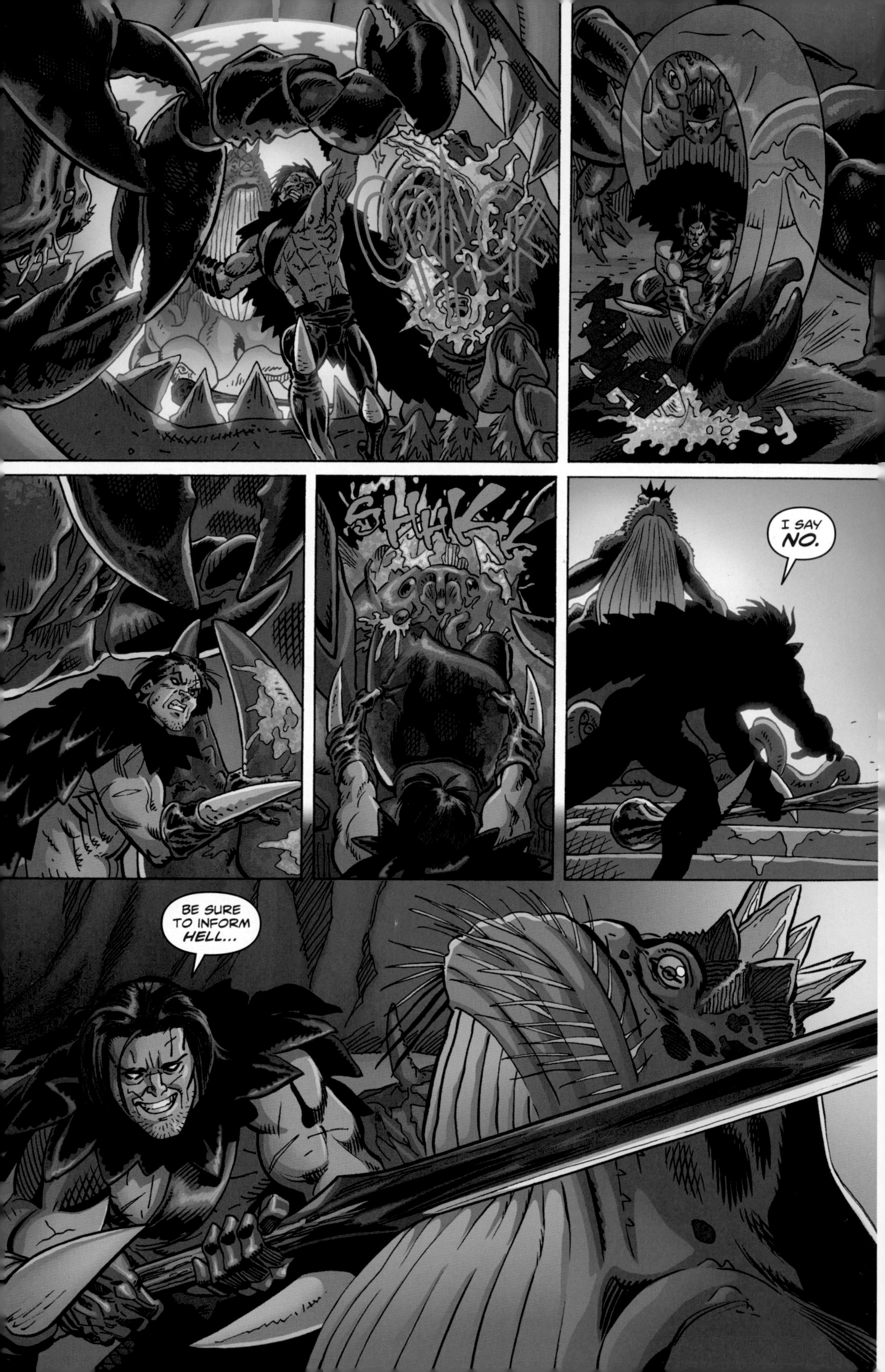
CRUNCK
SHUK
I SAY NO.
BE SURE TO INFORM HELL...

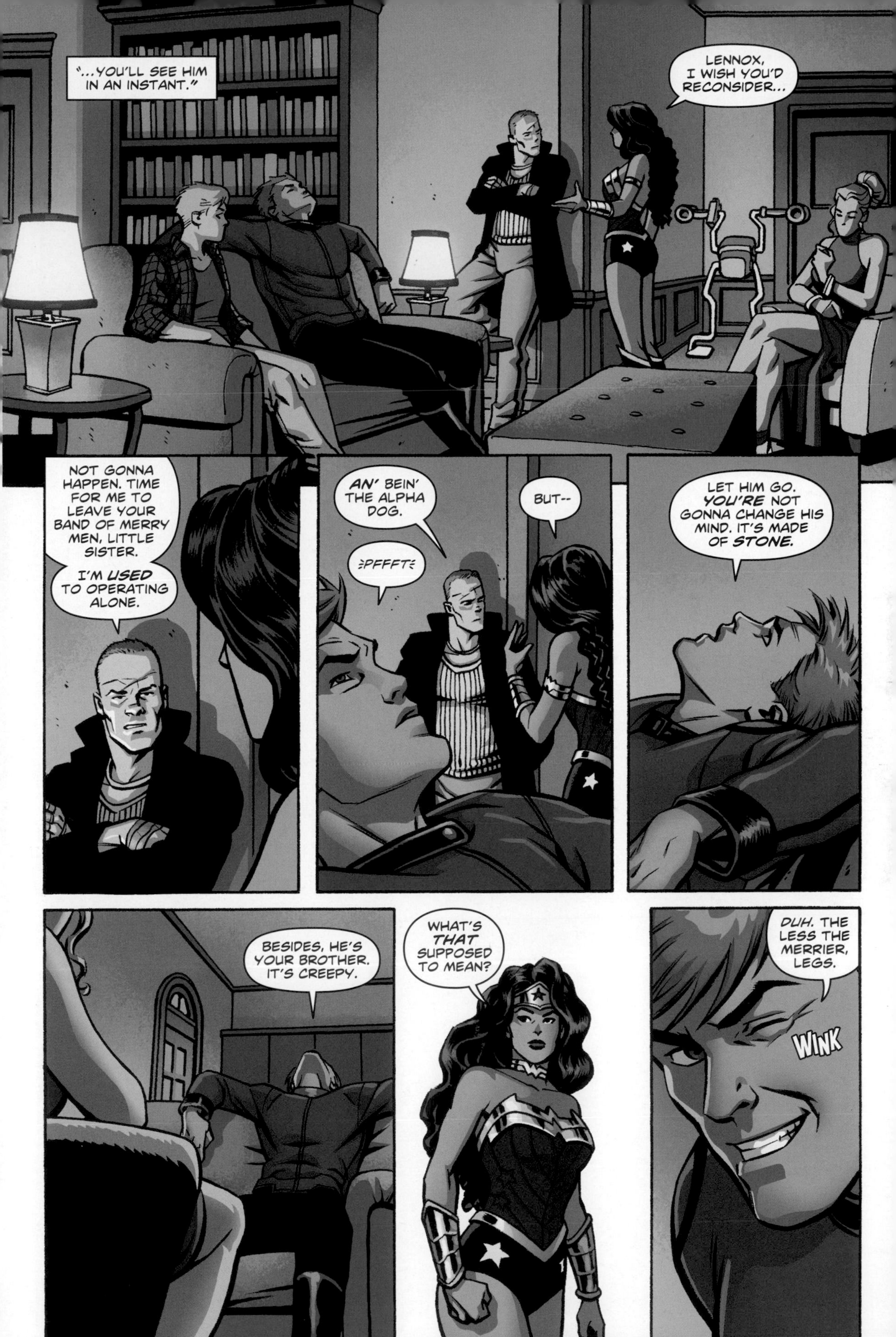
"...YOU'LL SEE HIM IN AN INSTANT."
LENNOX, I WISH YOU'D RECONSIDER...
NOT GONNA HAPPEN. TIME FOR ME TO LEAVE YOUR BAND OF MERRY MEN, LITTLE SISTER.
I'M *USED* TO OPERATING ALONE.
AN' BEIN' THE ALPHA DOG.
PFFFT
BUT--
LET HIM GO. *YOU'RE* NOT GONNA CHANGE HIS MIND. IT'S MADE OF *STONE.*
BESIDES, HE'S YOUR BROTHER. IT'S CREEPY.
WHAT'S *THAT* SUPPOSED TO MEAN?
DUH. THE LESS THE MERRIER, LEGS.
WINK

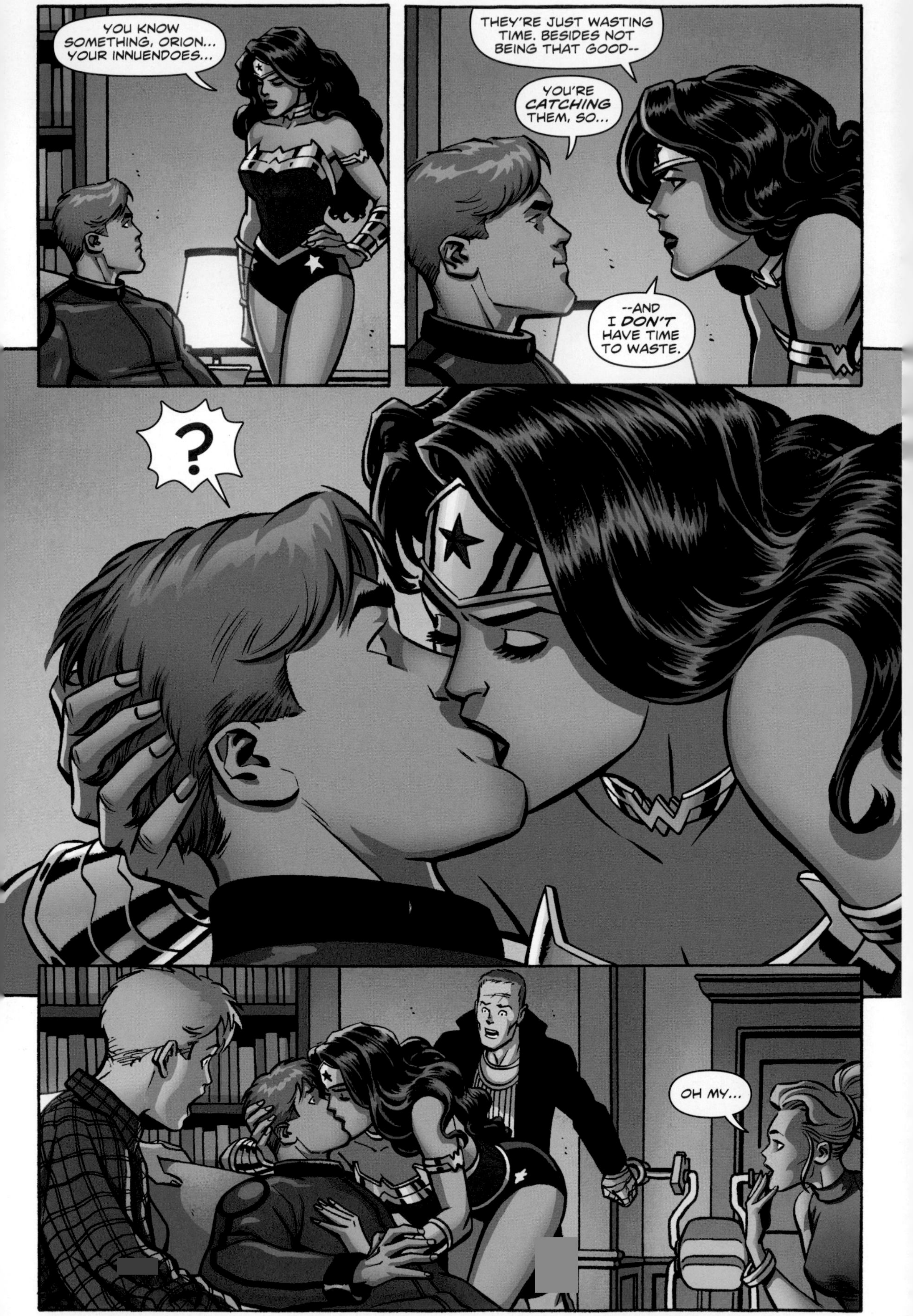
YOU KNOW SOMETHING, ORION... YOUR INNUENDOES...
THEY'RE JUST WASTING TIME. BESIDES NOT BEING THAT GOOD--
YOU'RE *CATCHING* THEM, SO...
--AND I *DON'T* HAVE TIME TO WASTE.
?
OH MY...

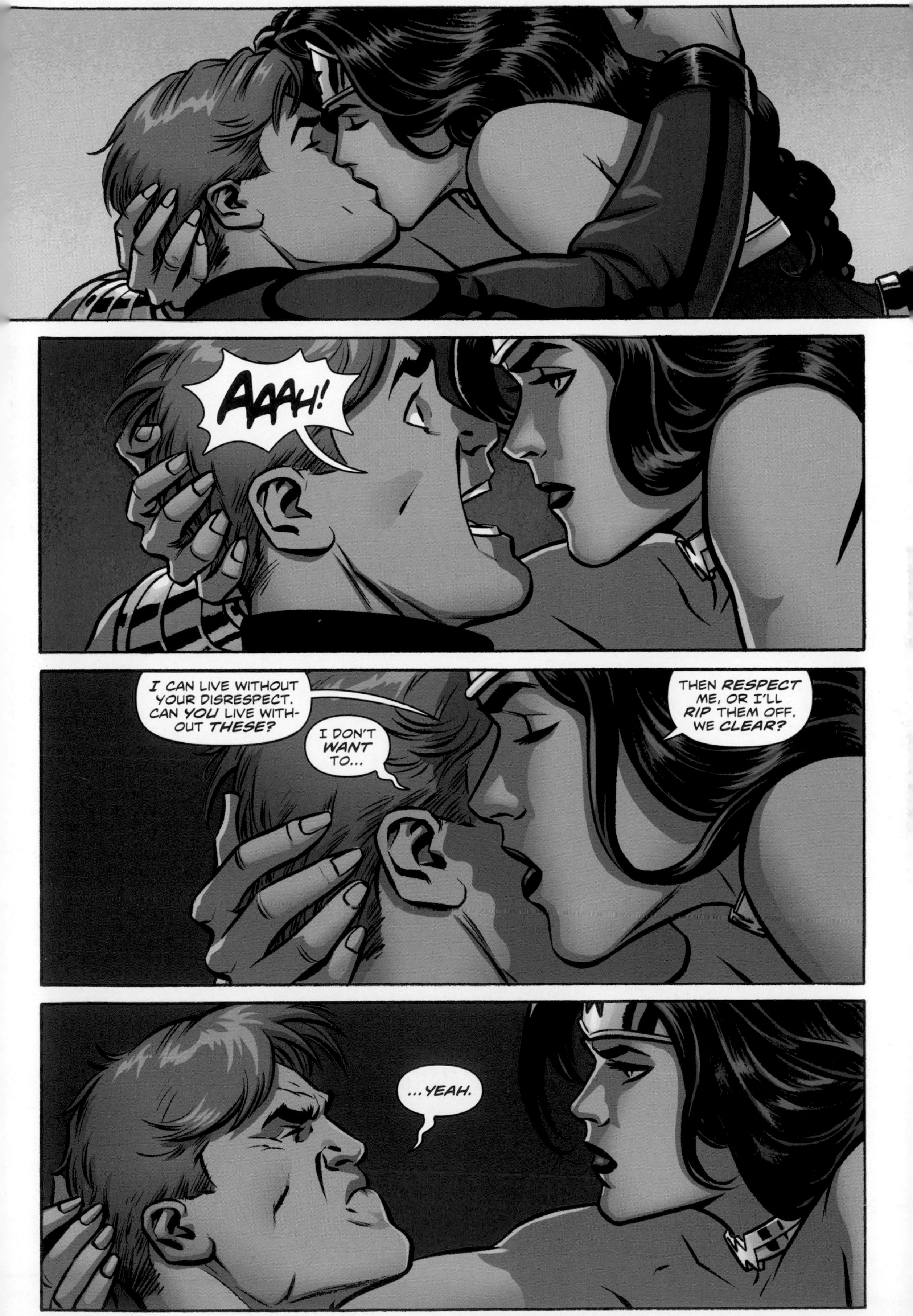
AAAH!
I CAN LIVE WITHOUT YOUR DISRESPECT. CAN YOU LIVE WITHOUT THESE?
I DON'T WANT TO...
THEN RESPECT ME, OR I'LL RIP THEM OFF. WE CLEAR?
...YEAH.

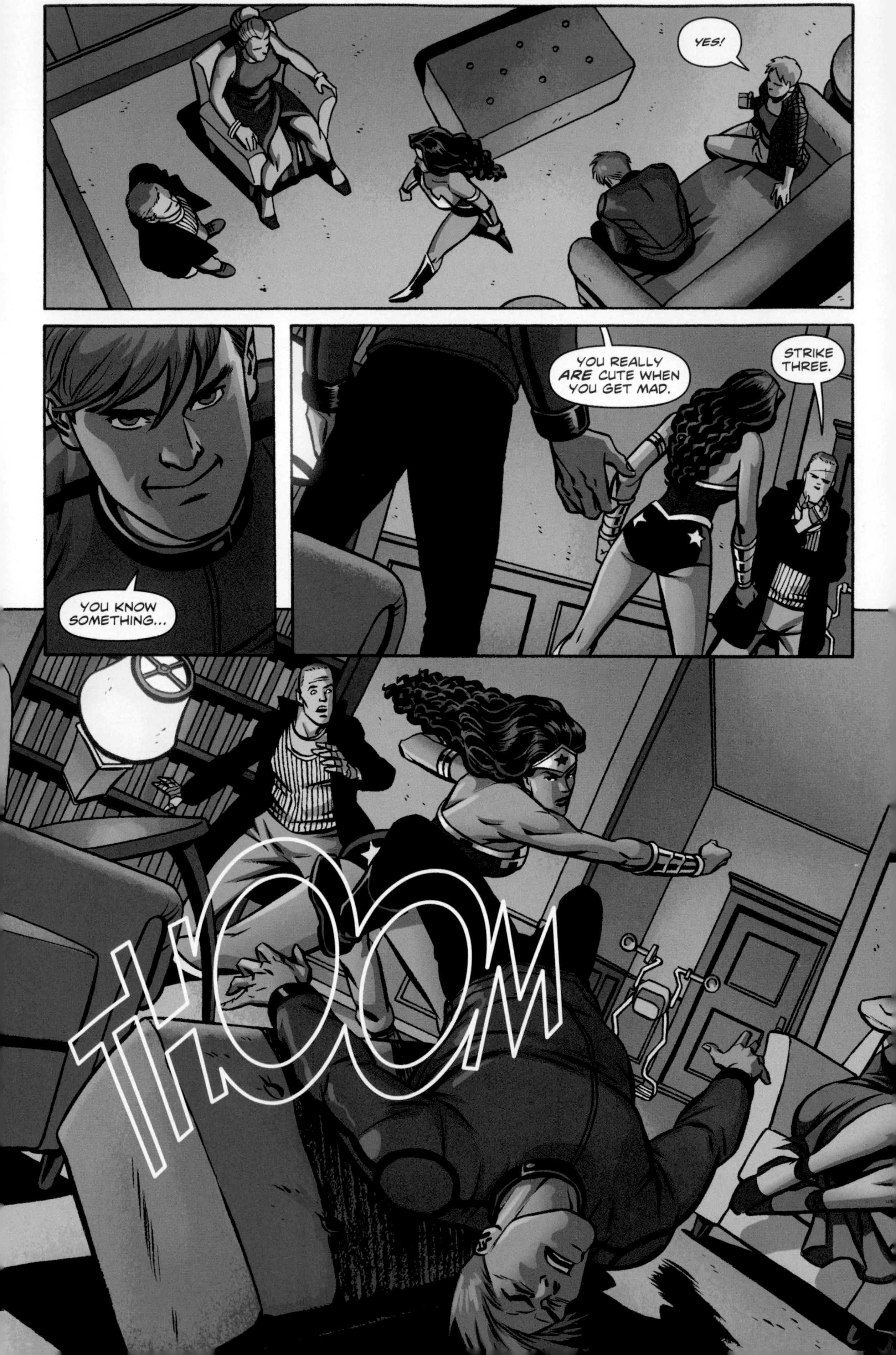
YES!
YOU KNOW SOMETHING...
YOU REALLY ARE CUTE WHEN YOU GET MAD.
STRIKE THREE.
THOOM

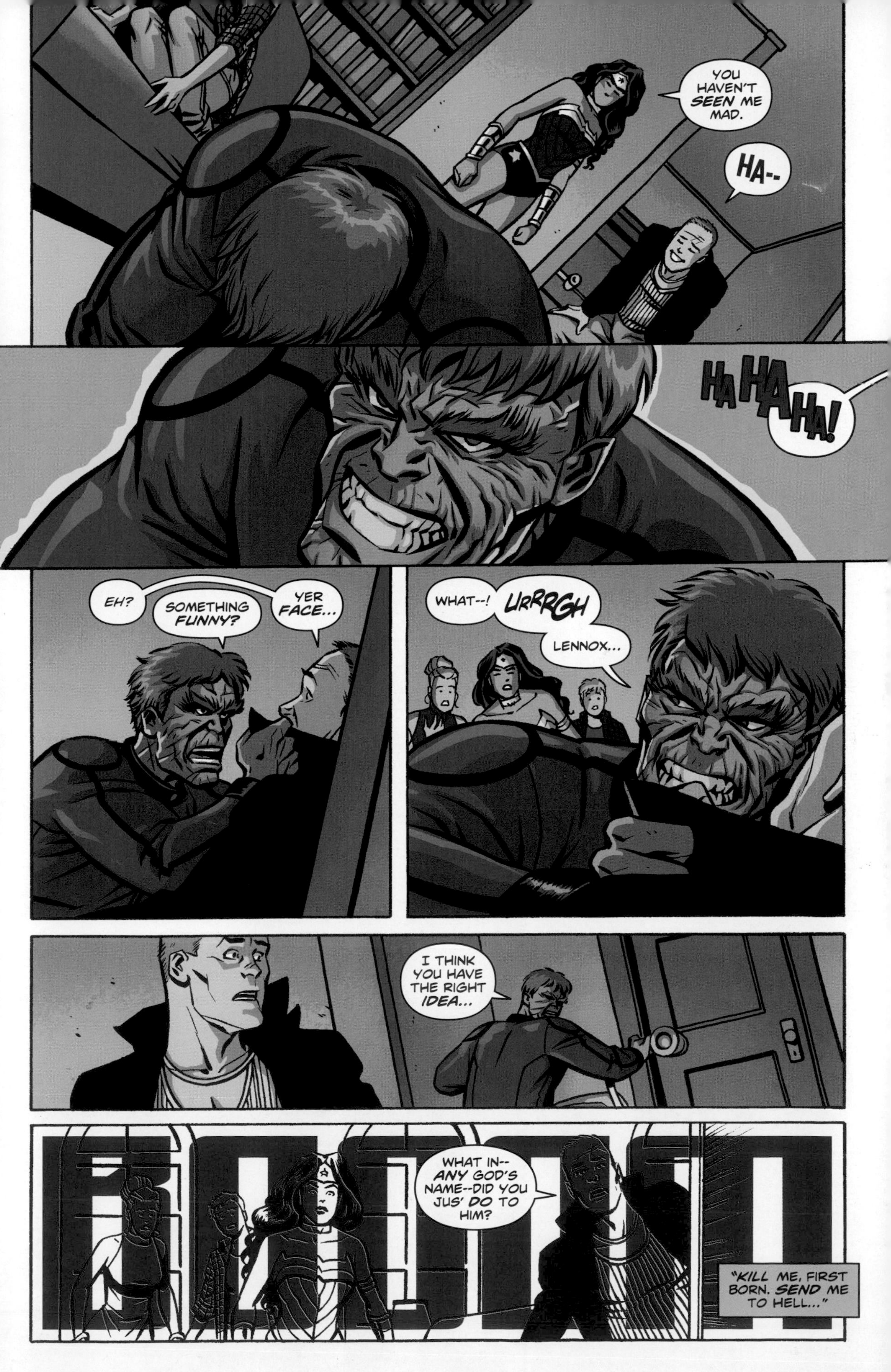
YOU HAVEN'T SEEN ME MAD.
HA--
HAHAHAHA!
EH?
SOMETHING FUNNY?
YER FACE...
WHAT--!
URRRGH
LENNOX...
I THINK YOU HAVE THE RIGHT IDEA...
WHAT IN-- ANY GOD'S NAME--DID YOU JUS' DO TO HIM?
"KILL ME, FIRST BORN. SEND ME TO HELL..."

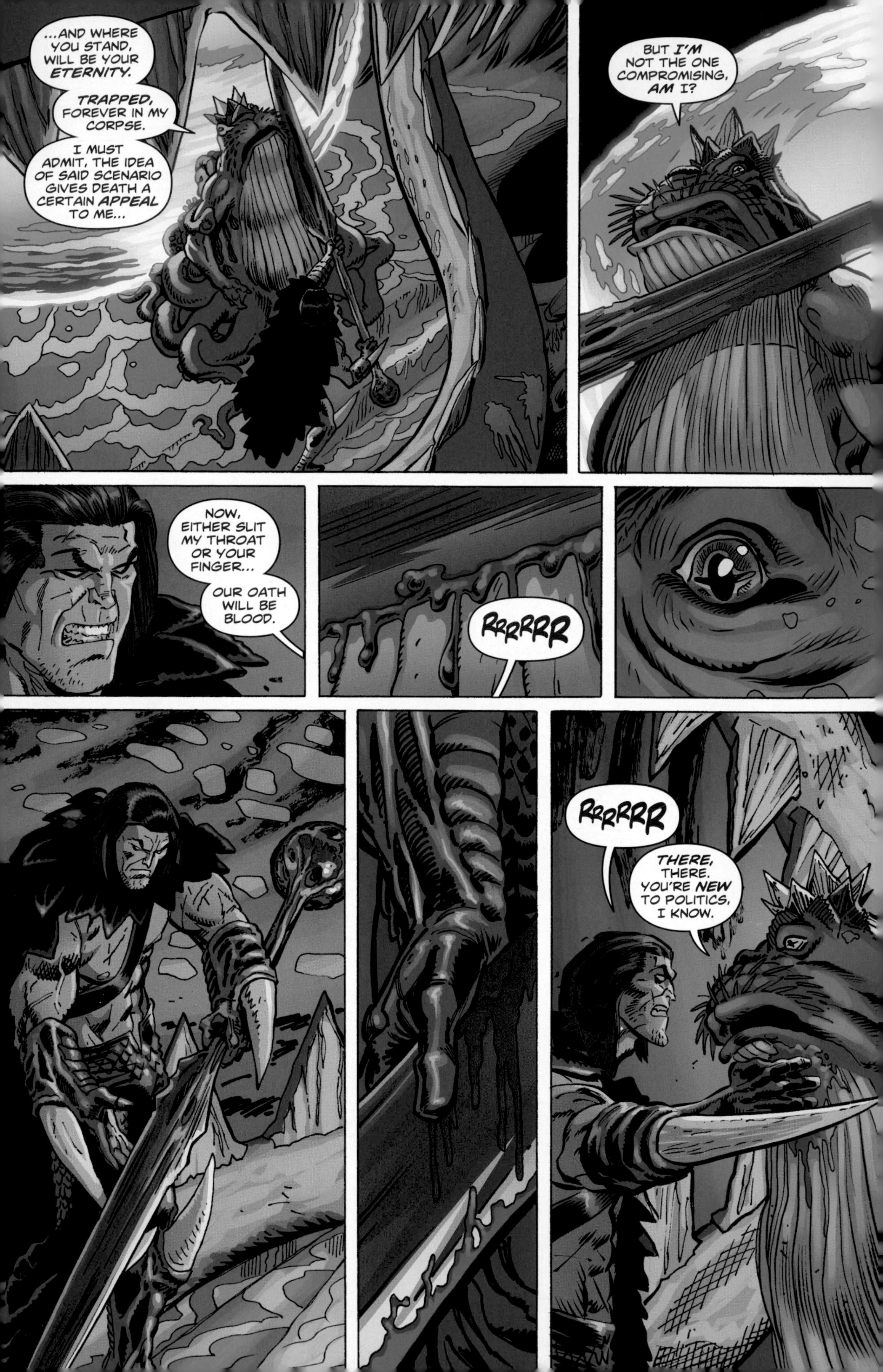
...AND WHERE YOU STAND, WILL BE YOUR ETERNITY.
TRAPPED, FOREVER IN MY CORPSE.
I MUST ADMIT, THE IDEA OF SAID SCENARIO GIVES DEATH A CERTAIN APPEAL TO ME...
BUT I'M NOT THE ONE COMPROMISING, AM I?
NOW, EITHER SLIT MY THROAT OR YOUR FINGER...
OUR OATH WILL BE BLOOD.
RRRRRR
RRRRRR
THERE, THERE. YOU'RE NEW TO POLITICS, I KNOW.

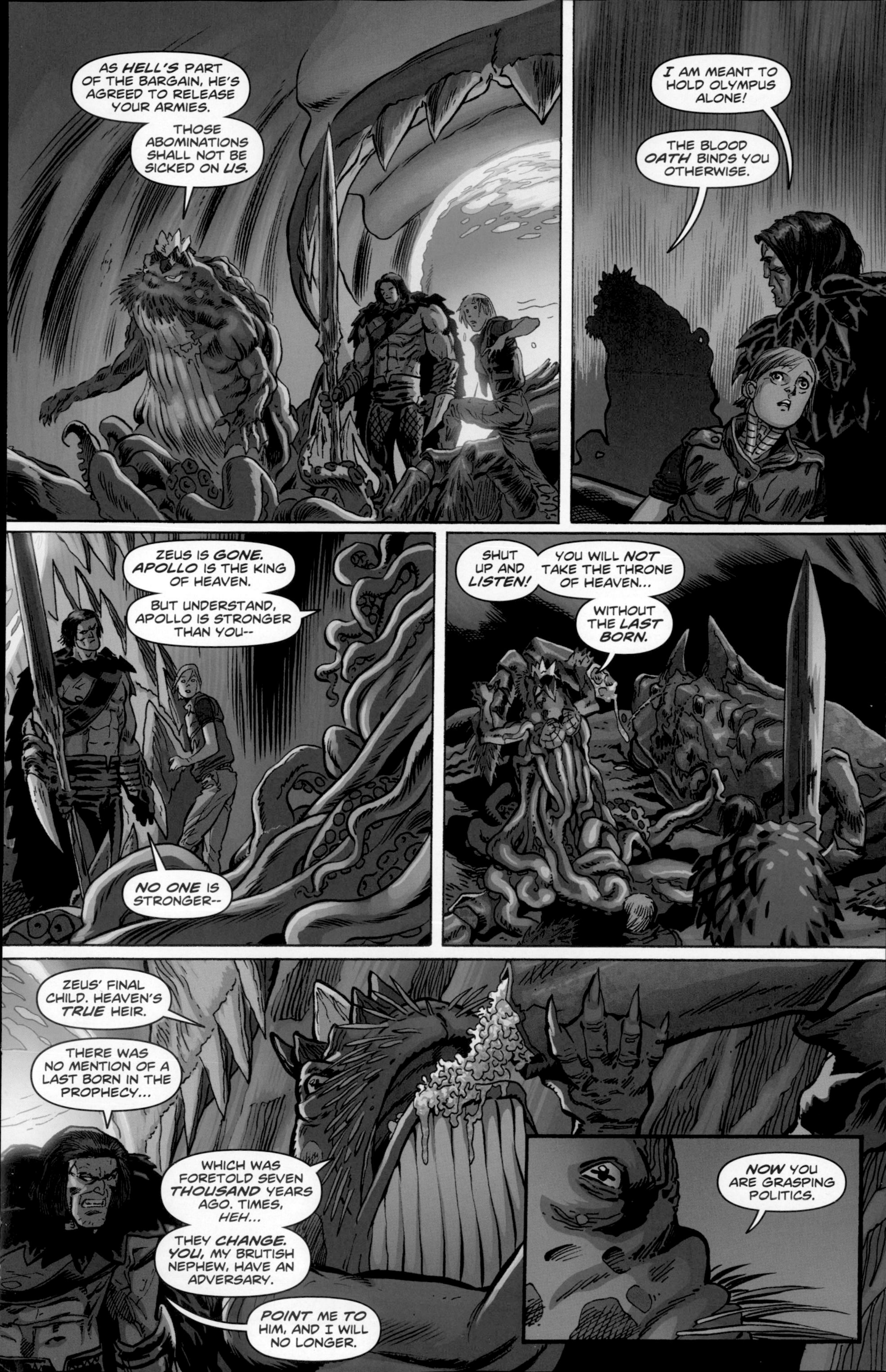
AS HELL'S PART OF THE BARGAIN, HE'S AGREED TO RELEASE YOUR ARMIES.
THOSE ABOMINATIONS SHALL NOT BE SICKED ON US.
I AM MEANT TO HOLD OLYMPUS ALONE!
THE BLOOD OATH BINDS YOU OTHERWISE.
ZEUS IS GONE. APOLLO IS THE KING OF HEAVEN.
BUT UNDERSTAND, APOLLO IS STRONGER THAN YOU--
NO ONE IS STRONGER--
SHUT UP AND LISTEN!
YOU WILL NOT TAKE THE THRONE OF HEAVEN...
WITHOUT THE LAST BORN.
ZEUS' FINAL CHILD. HEAVEN'S TRUE HEIR.
THERE WAS NO MENTION OF A LAST BORN IN THE PROPHECY...
WHICH WAS FORETOLD SEVEN THOUSAND YEARS AGO. TIMES, HEH...
THEY CHANGE. YOU, MY BRUTISH NEPHEW, HAVE AN ADVERSARY.
POINT ME TO HIM, AND I WILL NO LONGER.
NOW YOU ARE GRASPING POLITICS.

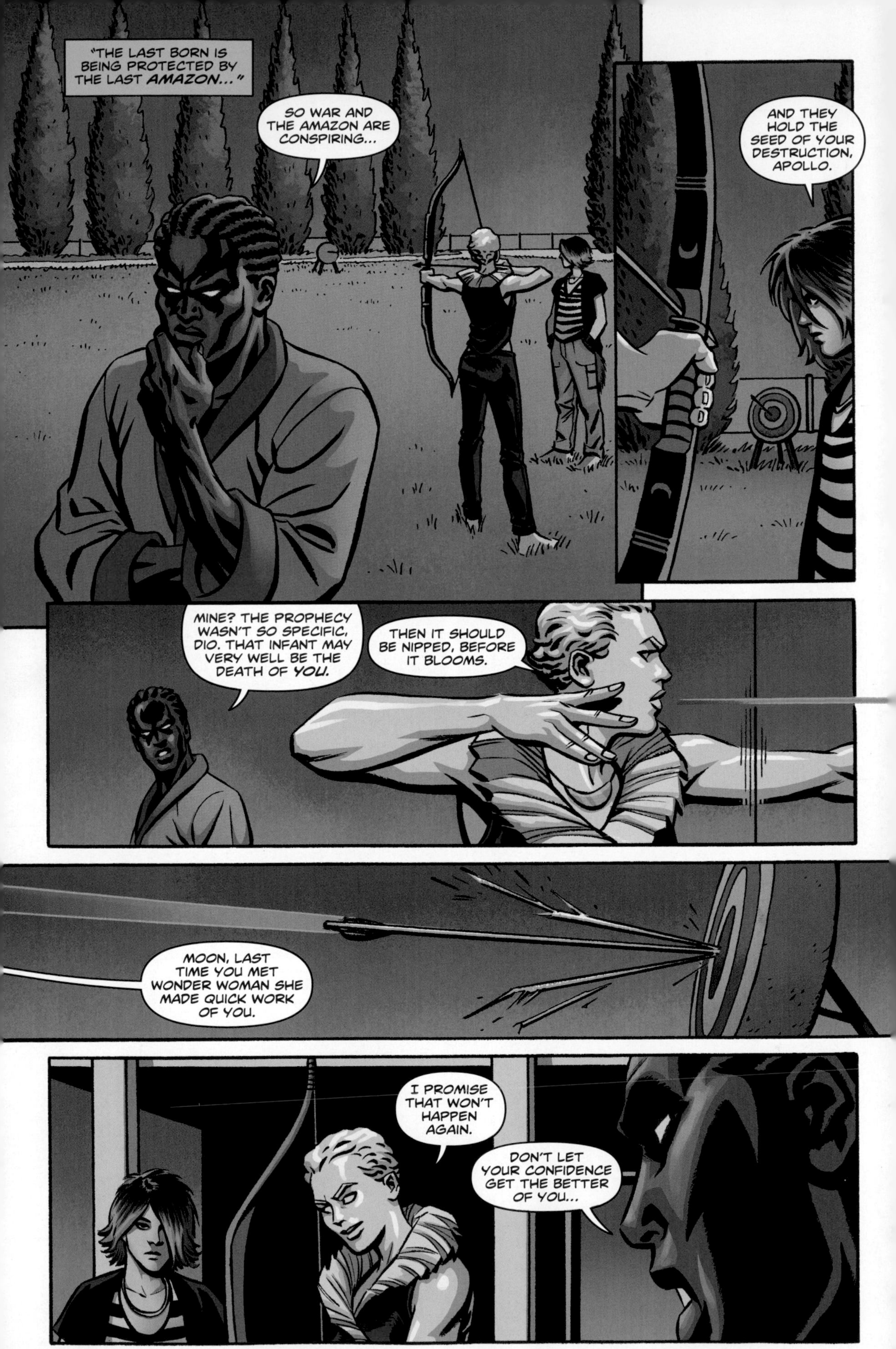
"THE LAST BORN IS BEING PROTECTED BY THE LAST AMAZON..."
SO WAR AND THE AMAZON ARE CONSPIRING...
AND THEY HOLD THE SEED OF YOUR DESTRUCTION, APOLLO.
MINE? THE PROPHECY WASN'T SO SPECIFIC, DIO. THAT INFANT MAY VERY WELL BE THE DEATH OF YOU.
THEN IT SHOULD BE NIPPED, BEFORE IT BLOOMS.
MOON, LAST TIME YOU MET WONDER WOMAN SHE MADE QUICK WORK OF YOU.
I PROMISE THAT WON'T HAPPEN AGAIN.
DON'T LET YOUR CONFIDENCE GET THE BETTER OF YOU...

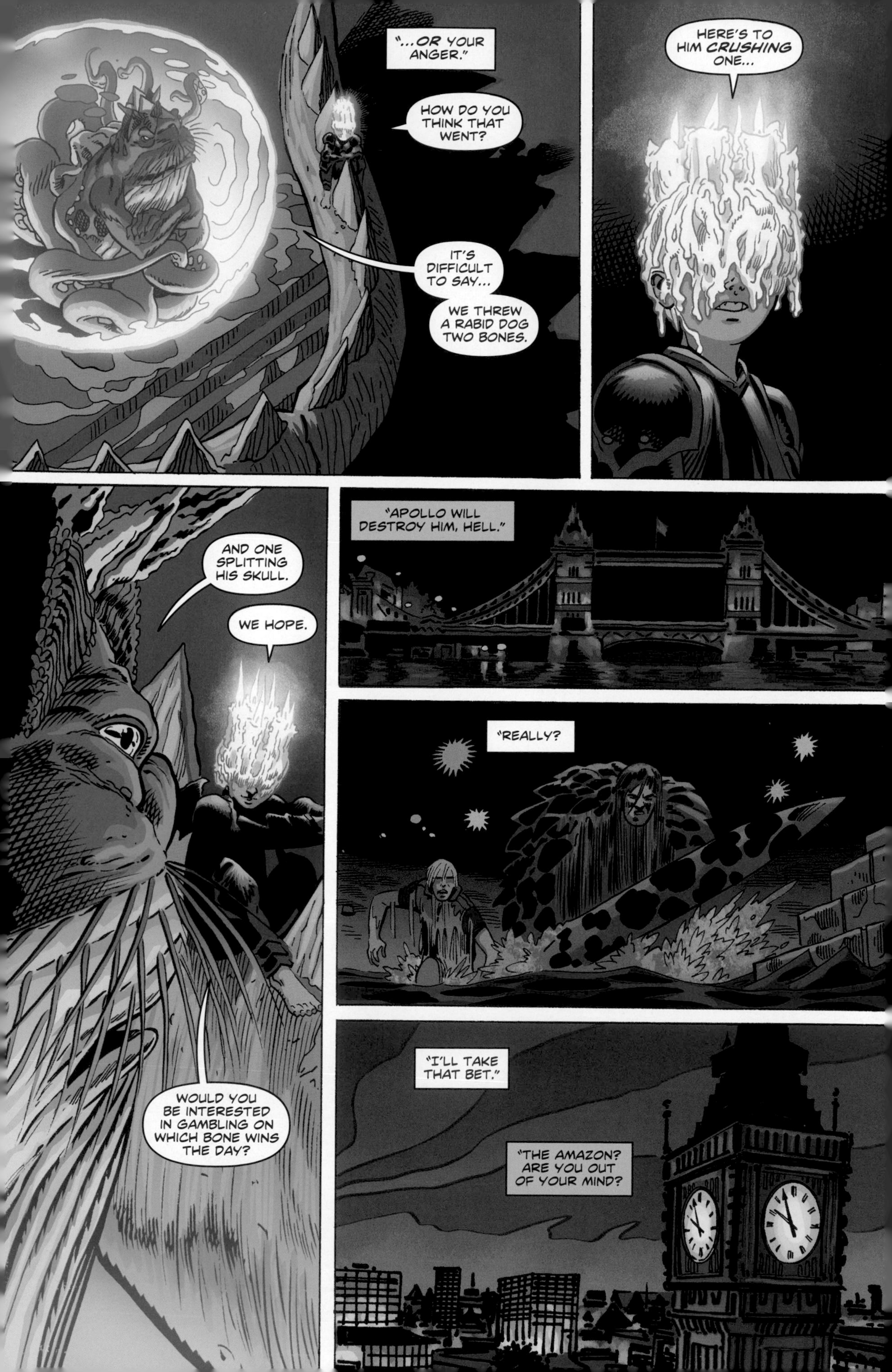
"...OR YOUR ANGER."
HOW DO YOU THINK THAT WENT?
IT'S DIFFICULT TO SAY...
WE THREW A RABID DOG TWO BONES.
HERE'S TO HIM CRUSHING ONE...
AND ONE SPLITTING HIS SKULL.
WE HOPE.
WOULD YOU BE INTERESTED IN GAMBLING ON WHICH BONE WINS THE DAY?
"APOLLO WILL DESTROY HIM, HELL."
"REALLY?
"I'LL TAKE THAT BET."
"THE AMAZON? ARE YOU OUT OF YOUR MIND?

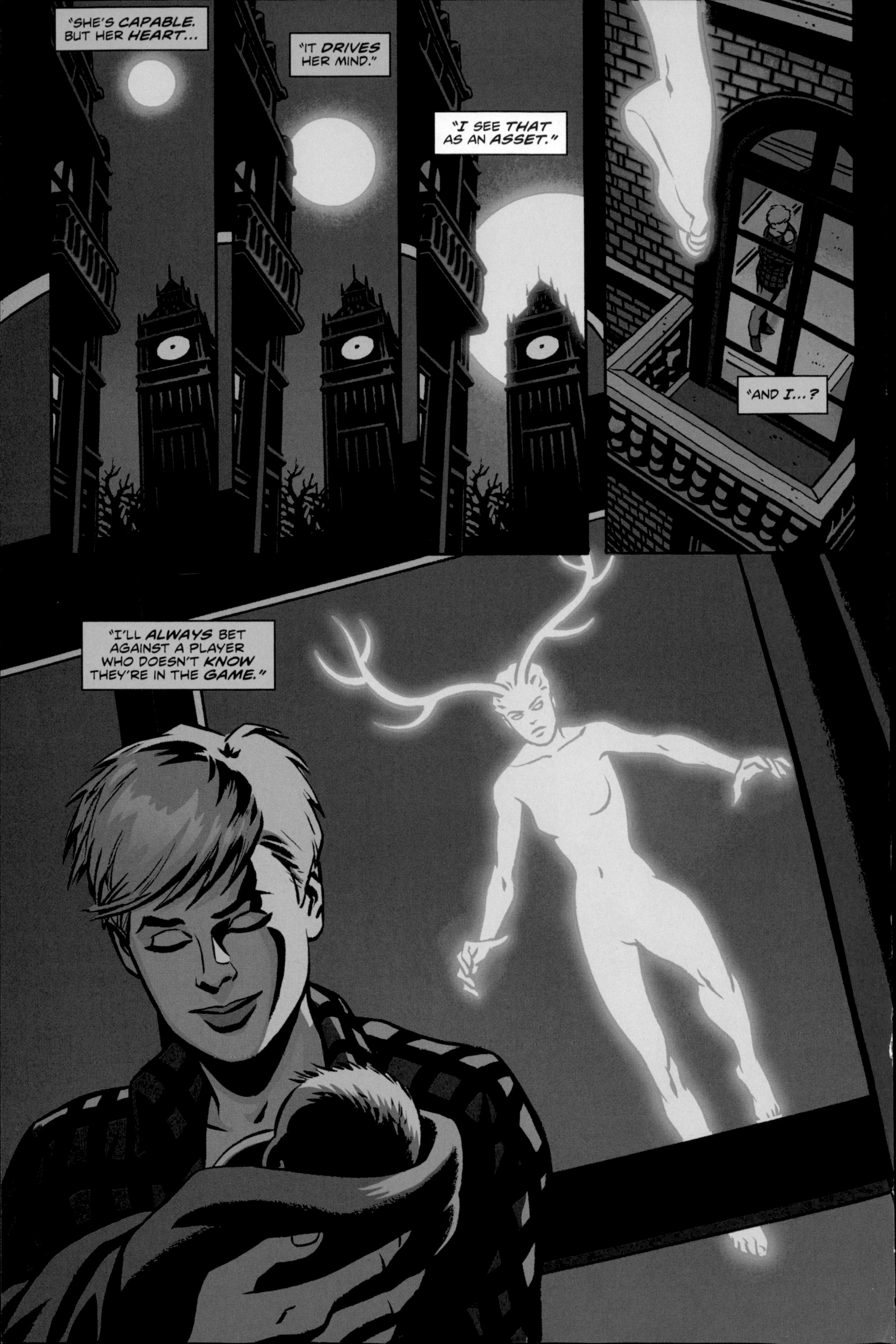
"SHE'S CAPABLE. BUT HER HEART...
"IT DRIVES HER MIND."
"I SEE THAT AS AN ASSET."
"AND I...?
"I'LL ALWAYS BET AGAINST A PLAYER WHO DOESN'T KNOW THEY'RE IN THE GAME."

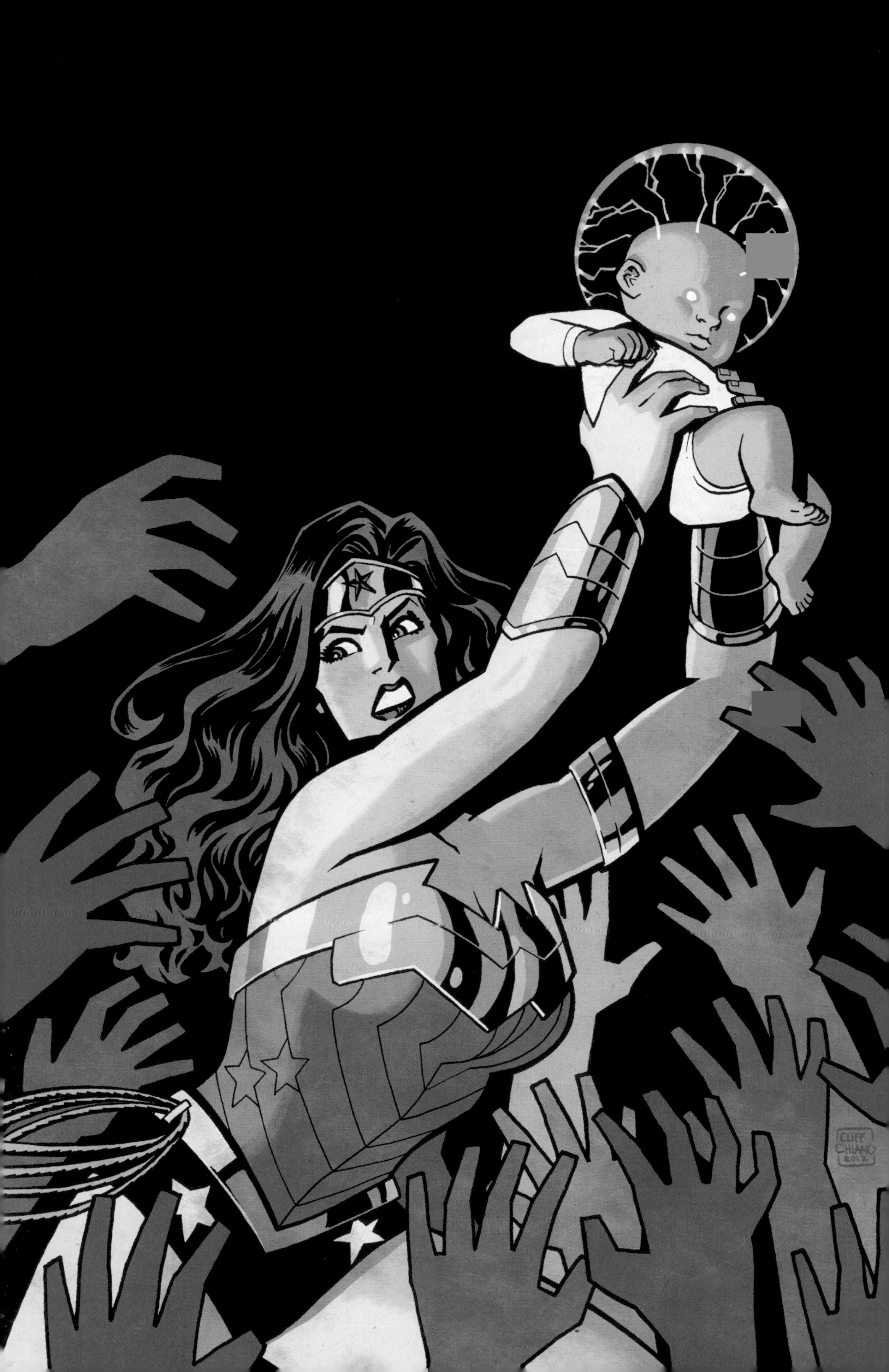
CLIFF
CHIANG
2012

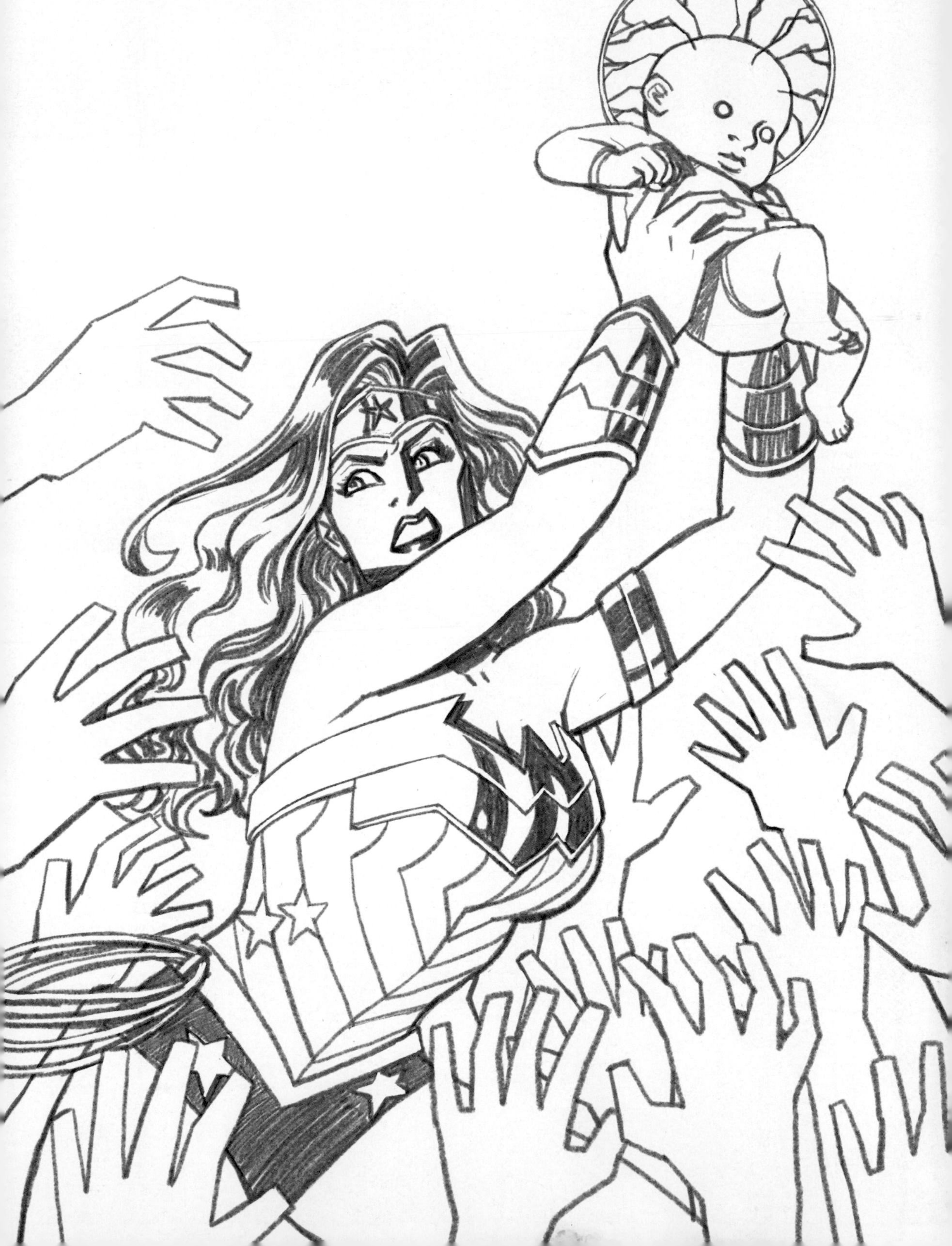

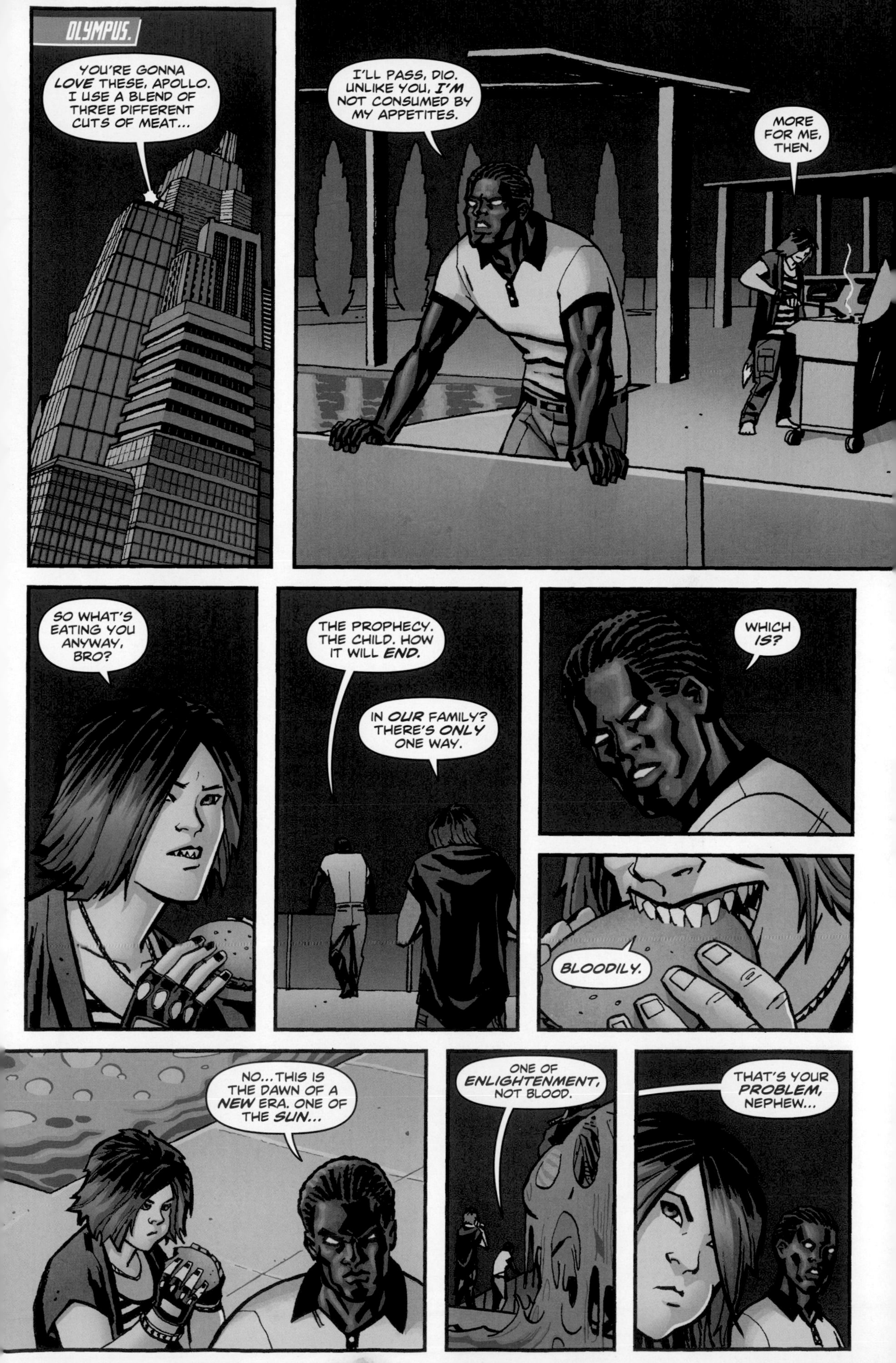
OLYMPUS.
YOU'RE GONNA LOVE THESE, APOLLO. I USE A BLEND OF THREE DIFFERENT CUTS OF MEAT...
I'LL PASS, DIO. UNLIKE YOU, I'M NOT CONSUMED BY MY APPETITES.
MORE FOR ME, THEN.
SO WHAT'S EATING YOU ANYWAY, BRO?
THE PROPHECY. THE CHILD. HOW IT WILL END.
IN OUR FAMILY? THERE'S ONLY ONE WAY.
WHICH IS?
BLOODILY.
NO...THIS IS THE DAWN OF A NEW ERA. ONE OF THE SUN...
ONE OF ENLIGHTENMENT, NOT BLOOD.
THAT'S YOUR PROBLEM, NEPHEW...

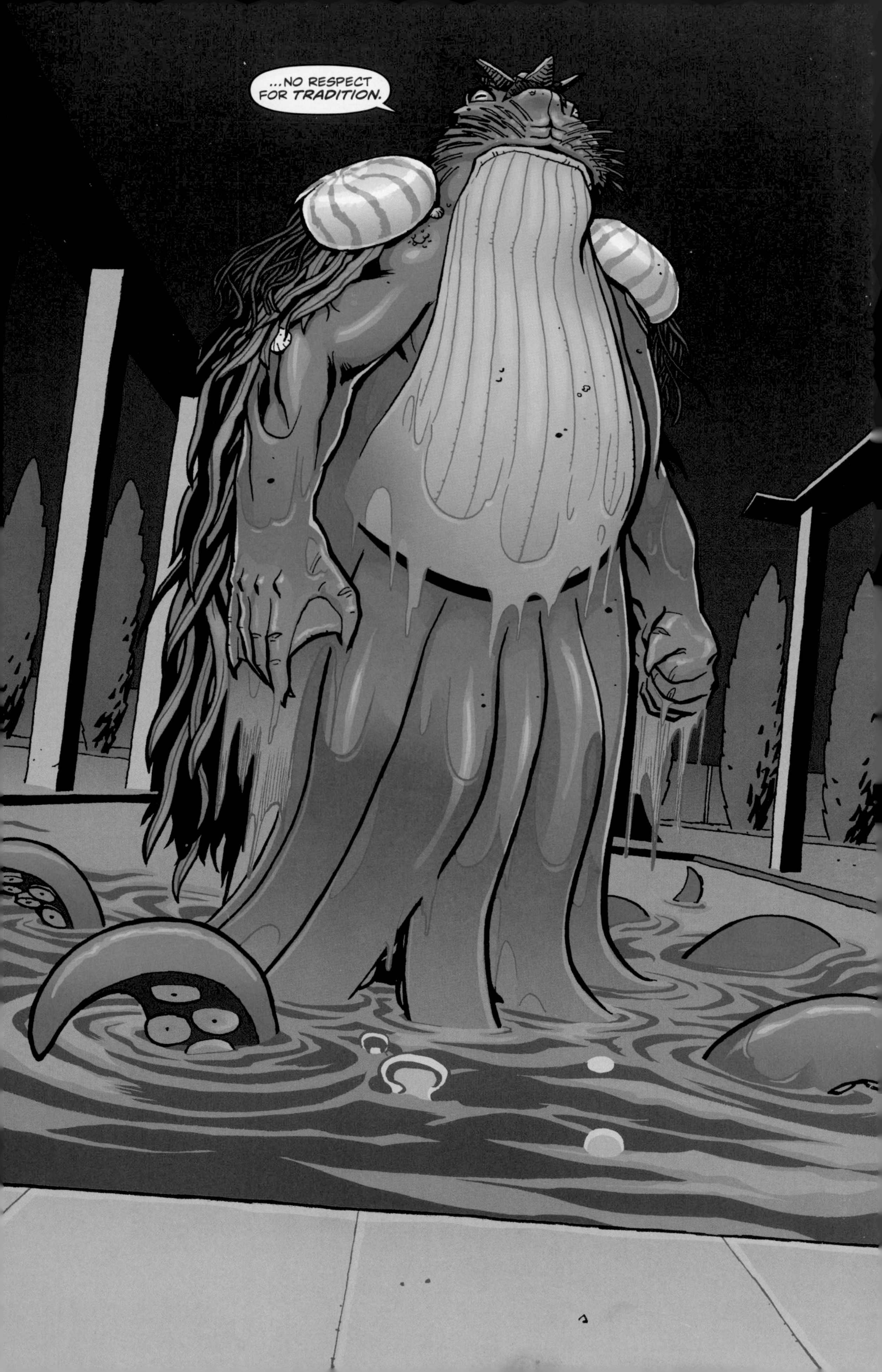
...NO RESPECT FOR TRADITION.

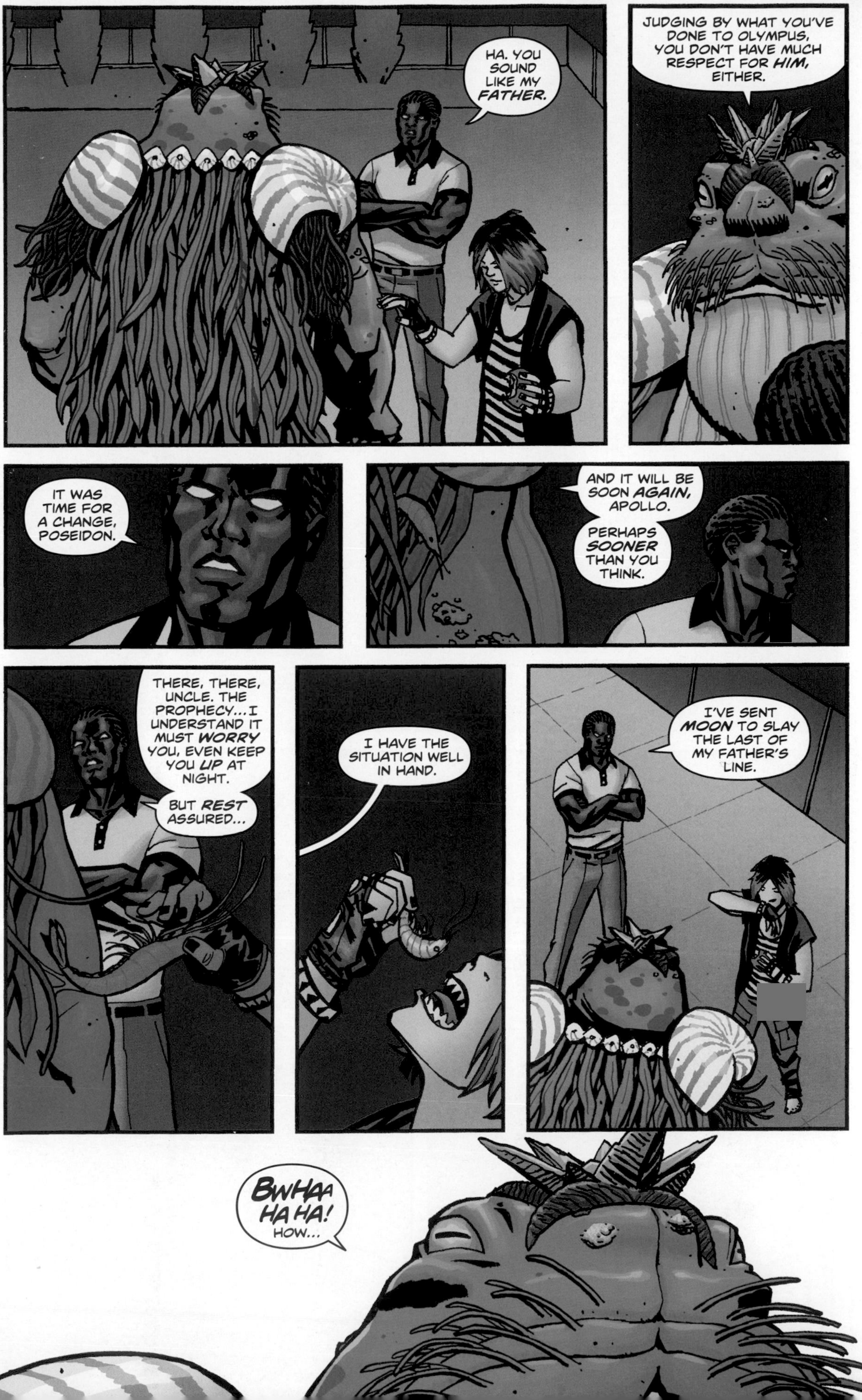
HA. YOU SOUND LIKE MY FATHER.
JUDGING BY WHAT YOU'VE DONE TO OLYMPUS, YOU DON'T HAVE MUCH RESPECT FOR HIM, EITHER.
IT WAS TIME FOR A CHANGE, POSEIDON.
AND IT WILL BE SOON AGAIN, APOLLO.
PERHAPS SOONER THAN YOU THINK.
THERE, THERE, UNCLE. THE PROPHECY...I UNDERSTAND IT MUST WORRY YOU, EVEN KEEP YOU UP AT NIGHT.
BUT REST ASSURED...
I HAVE THE SITUATION WELL IN HAND.
I'VE SENT MOON TO SLAY THE LAST OF MY FATHER'S LINE.
BWHAA HA HA! HOW...

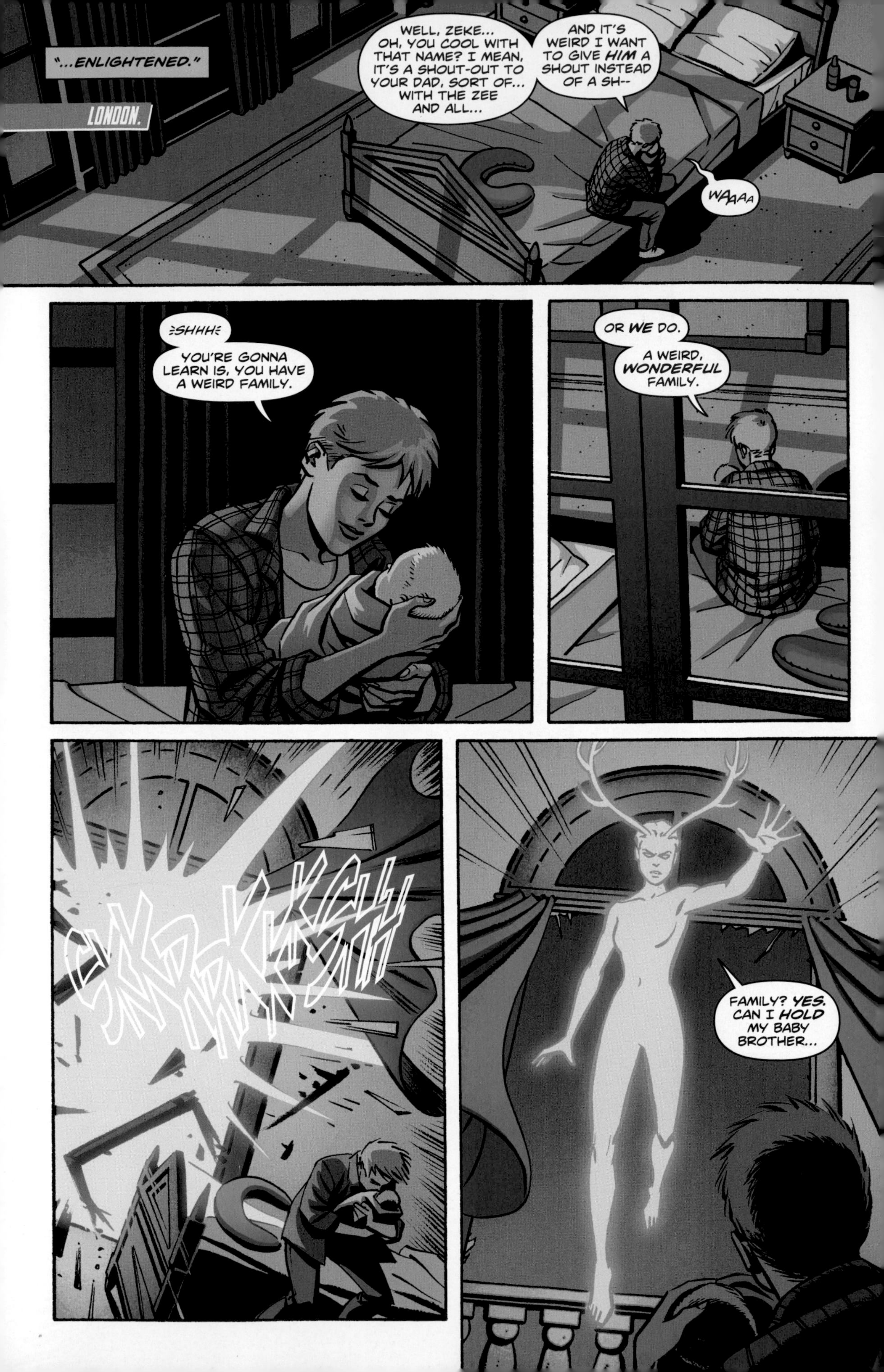
"...ENLIGHTENED."
LONDON.
WELL, ZEKE... OH, YOU COOL WITH THAT NAME? I MEAN, IT'S A SHOUT-OUT TO YOUR DAD, SORT OF... WITH THE ZEE AND ALL...
AND IT'S WEIRD I WANT TO GIVE HIM A SHOUT INSTEAD OF A SH--
WAAAA
SHHH
YOU'RE GONNA LEARN IS, YOU HAVE A WEIRD FAMILY.
OR WE DO.
A WEIRD, WONDERFUL FAMILY.
KRAKASH
FAMILY? YES. CAN I HOLD MY BABY BROTHER...

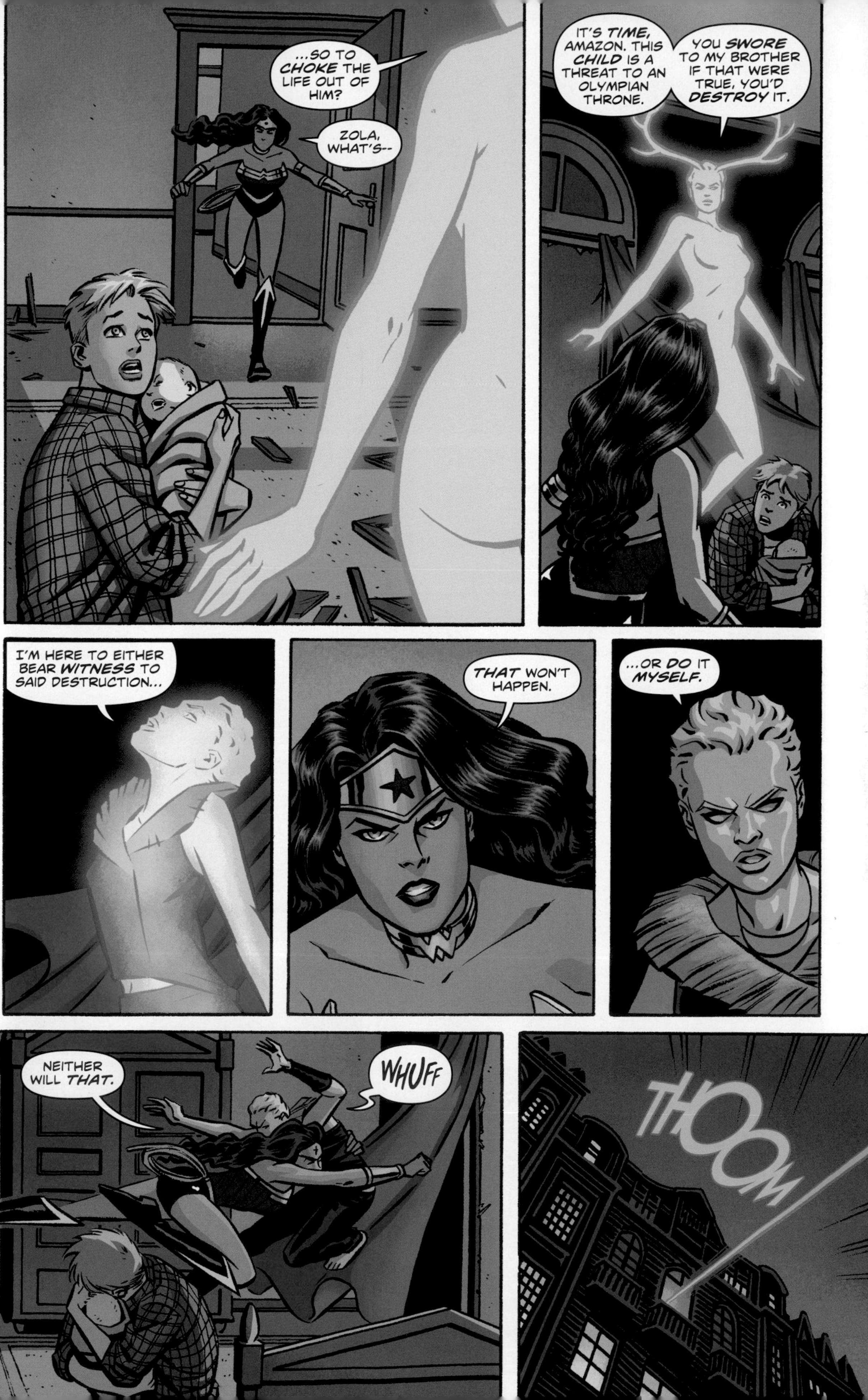
...SO TO CHOKE THE LIFE OUT OF HIM?
ZOLA, WHAT'S--
IT'S TIME, AMAZON. THIS CHILD IS A THREAT TO AN OLYMPIAN THRONE.
YOU SWORE TO MY BROTHER IF THAT WERE TRUE, YOU'D DESTROY IT.
I'M HERE TO EITHER BEAR WITNESS TO SAID DESTRUCTION...
THAT WON'T HAPPEN.
...OR DO IT MYSELF.
NEITHER WILL THAT.
WHUFF
THOOM

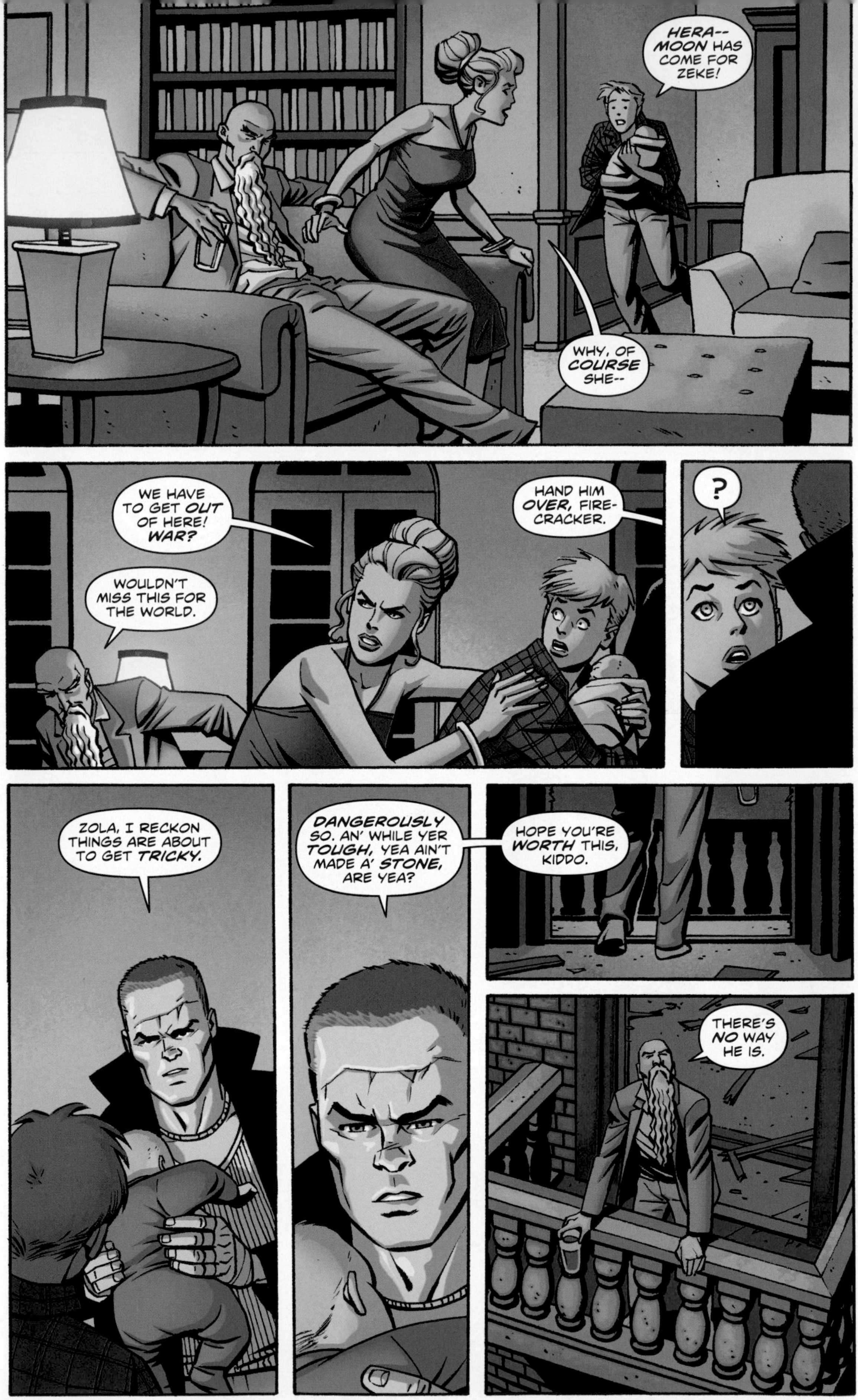
HERA--
MOON HAS COME FOR ZEKE!
WHY, OF COURSE SHE--
WE HAVE TO GET OUT OF HERE! WAR?
WOULDN'T MISS THIS FOR THE WORLD.
HAND HIM OVER, FIRE-CRACKER.
?
ZOLA, I RECKON THINGS ARE ABOUT TO GET TRICKY.
DANGEROUSLY SO. AN' WHILE YER TOUGH, YEA AIN'T MADE A' STONE, ARE YEA?
HOPE YOU'RE WORTH THIS, KIDDO.
THERE'S NO WAY HE IS.

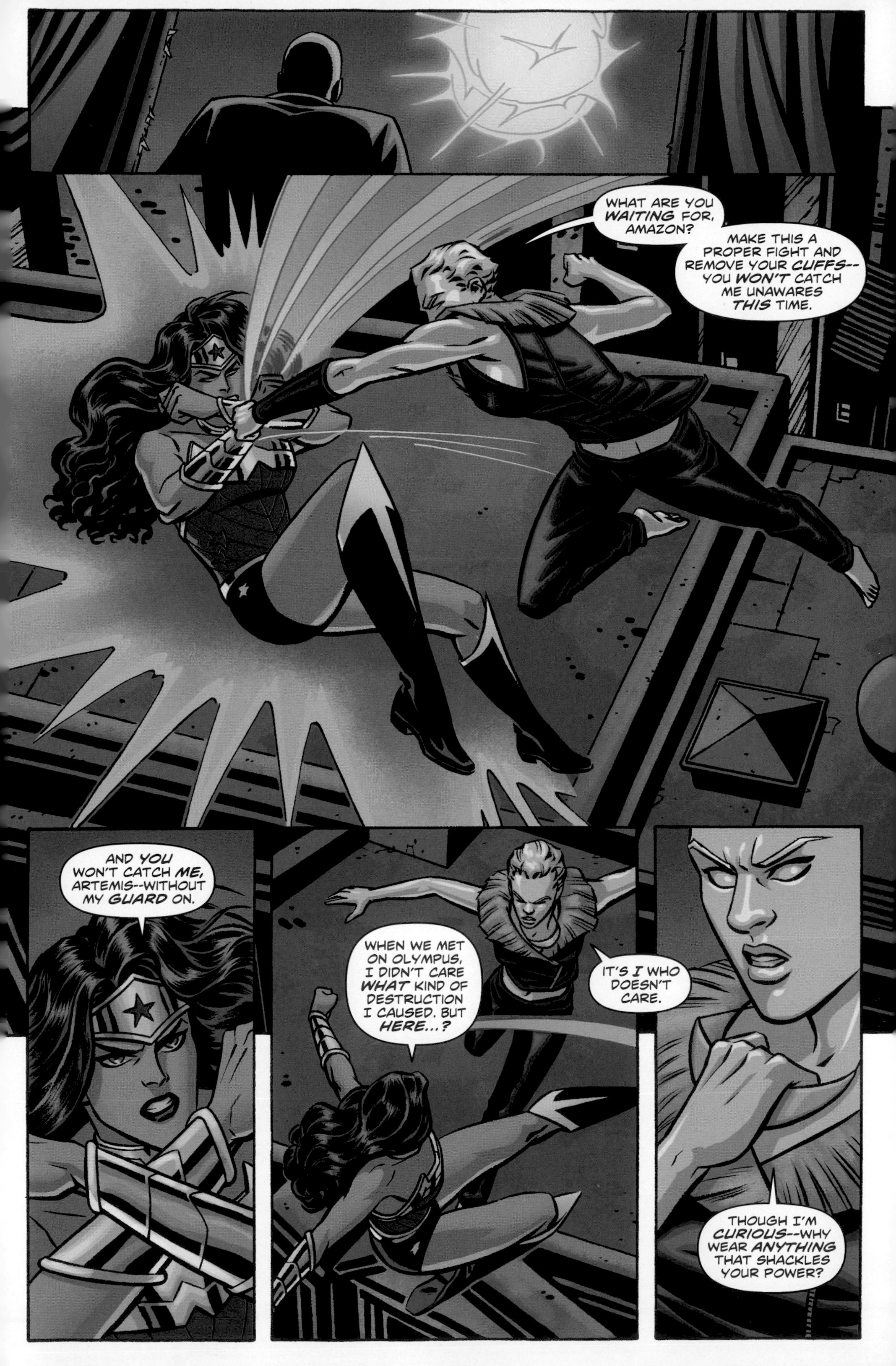
WHAT ARE YOU WAITING FOR, AMAZON?
MAKE THIS A PROPER FIGHT AND REMOVE YOUR CUFFS--YOU WON'T CATCH ME UNAWARES THIS TIME.
AND YOU WON'T CATCH ME, ARTEMIS--WITHOUT MY GUARD ON.
WHEN WE MET ON OLYMPUS, I DIDN'T CARE WHAT KIND OF DESTRUCTION I CAUSED. BUT HERE...?
IT'S I WHO DOESN'T CARE.
THOUGH I'M CURIOUS--WHY WEAR ANYTHING THAT SHACKLES YOUR POWER?

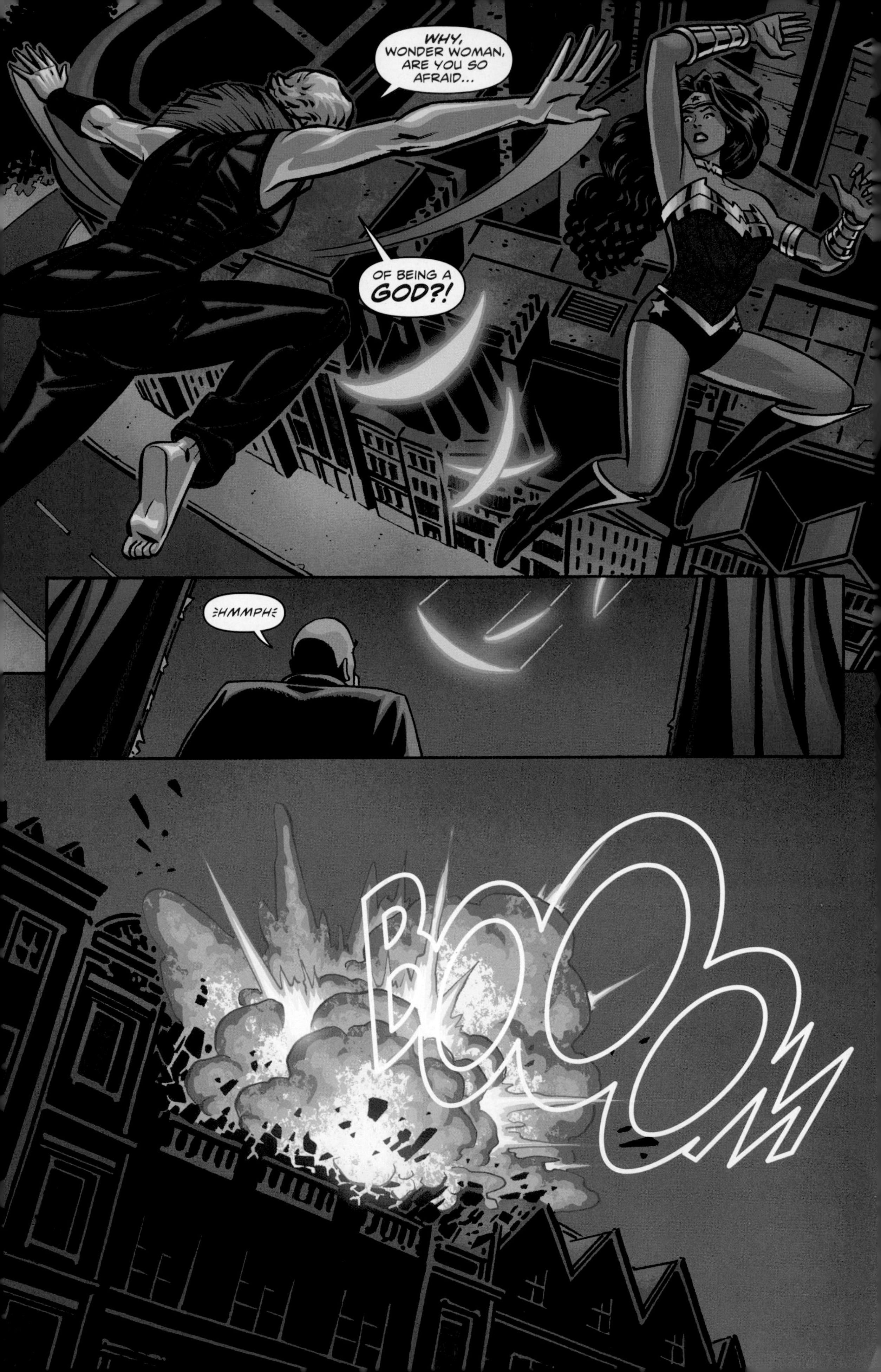
WHY, WONDER WOMAN, ARE YOU SO AFRAID...
OF BEING A GOD?!
HMMPH
BOOOM

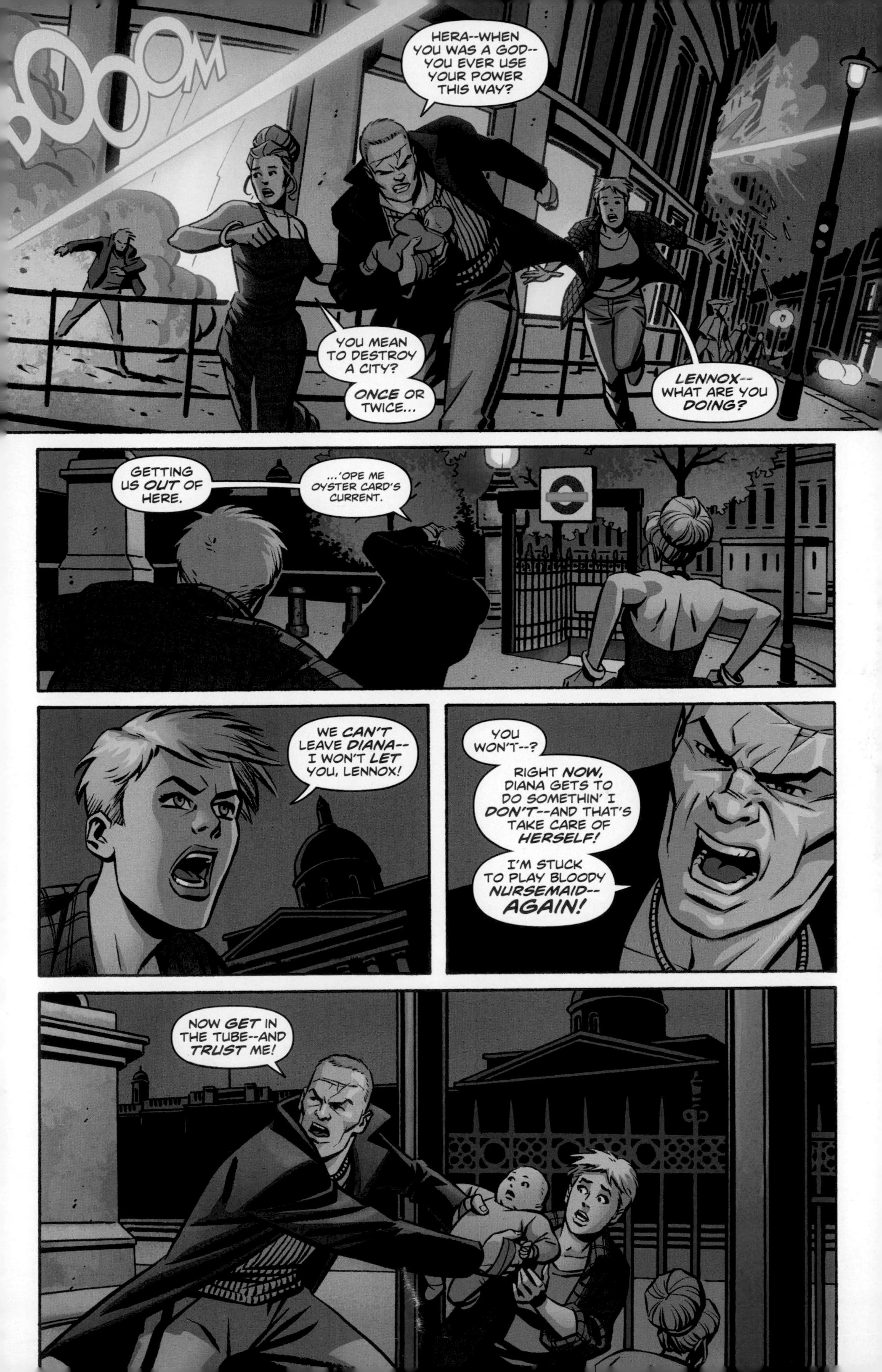
BOOOOM
HERA--WHEN YOU WAS A GOD--YOU EVER USE YOUR POWER THIS WAY?
YOU MEAN TO DESTROY A CITY?
ONCE OR TWICE...
LENNOX--WHAT ARE YOU DOING?
GETTING US OUT OF HERE.
...'OPE ME OYSTER CARD'S CURRENT.
WE CAN'T LEAVE DIANA--I WON'T LET YOU, LENNOX!
YOU WON'T--?
RIGHT NOW, DIANA GETS TO DO SOMETHIN' I DON'T--AND THAT'S TAKE CARE OF HERSELF!
I'M STUCK TO PLAY BLOODY NURSEMAID--AGAIN!
NOW GET IN THE TUBE--AND TRUST ME!

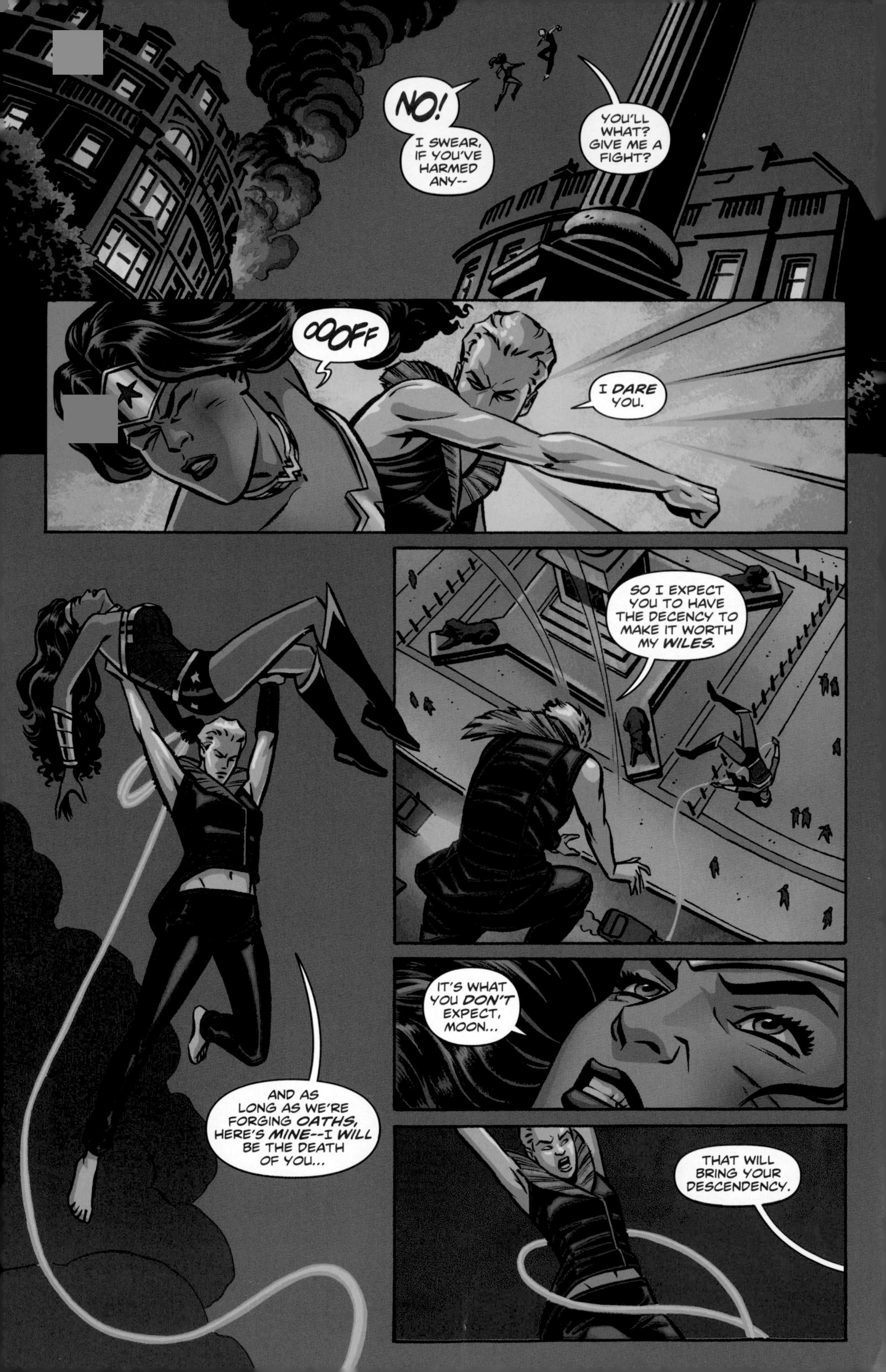
NO!
I SWEAR, IF YOU'VE HARMED ANY--
YOU'LL WHAT? GIVE ME A FIGHT?
OOOFF
I DARE YOU.
SO I EXPECT YOU TO HAVE THE DECENCY TO MAKE IT WORTH MY WILES.
AND AS LONG AS WE'RE FORGING OATHS, HERE'S MINE--I WILL BE THE DEATH OF YOU...
IT'S WHAT YOU DON'T EXPECT, MOON...
THAT WILL BRING YOUR DESCENDENCY.

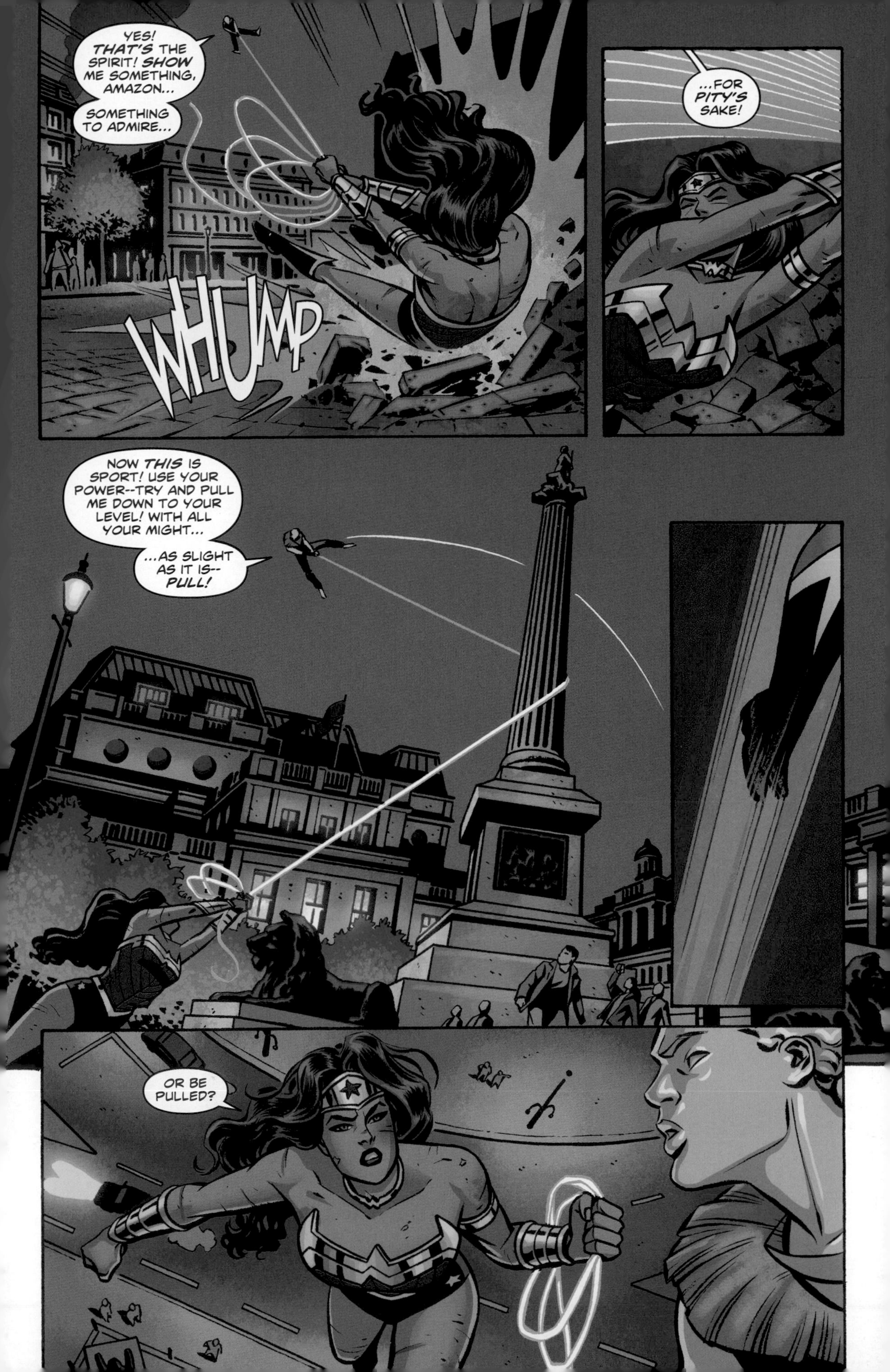
YES! THAT'S THE SPIRIT! SHOW ME SOMETHING, AMAZON...
SOMETHING TO ADMIRE...
WHUMP
...FOR PITY'S SAKE!
NOW THIS IS SPORT! USE YOUR POWER--TRY AND PULL ME DOWN TO YOUR LEVEL! WITH ALL YOUR MIGHT...
...AS SLIGHT AS IT IS--PULL!
OR BE PULLED?

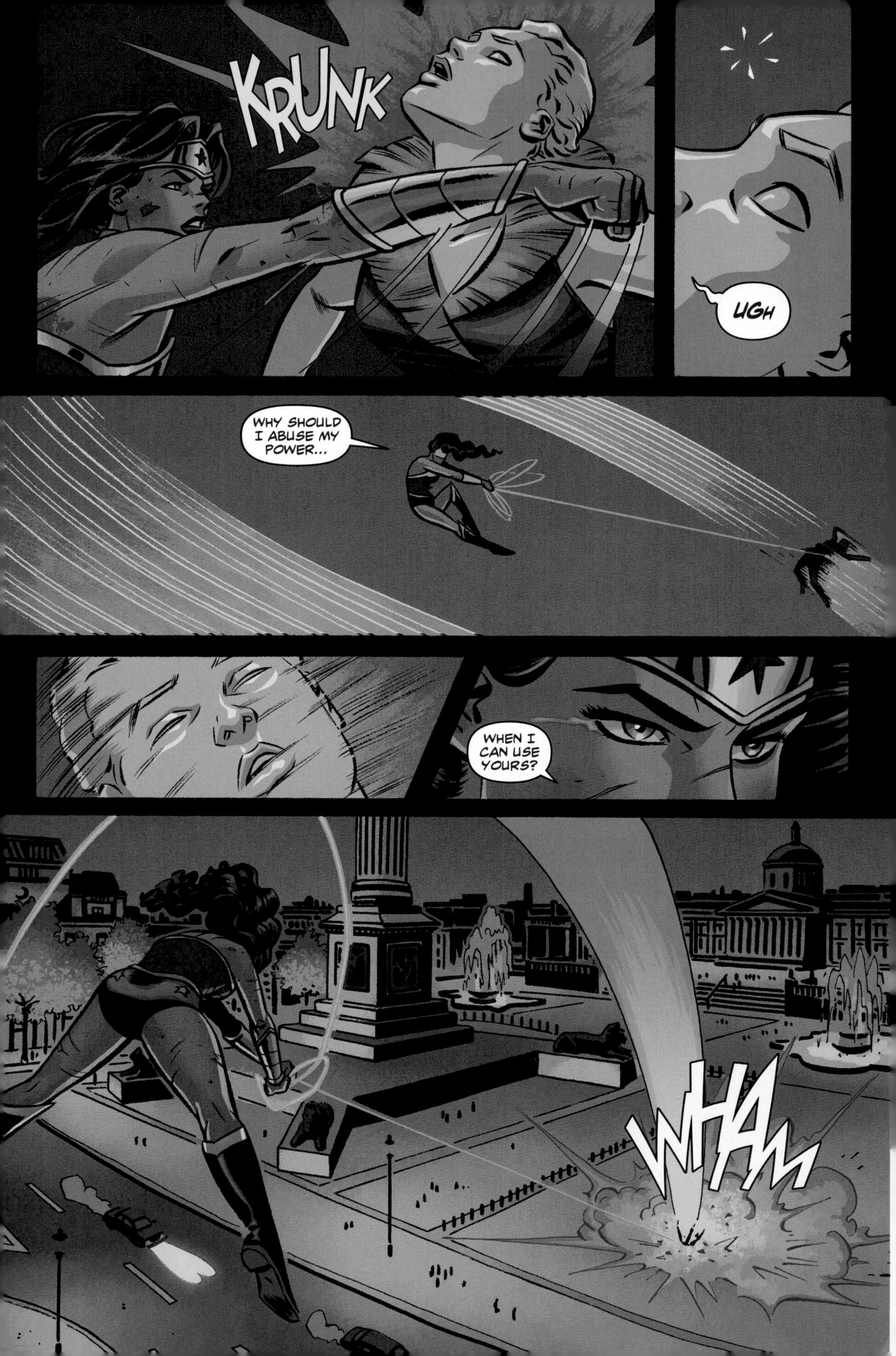
KRUNK
UGH
WHY SHOULD I ABUSE MY POWER...
WHEN I CAN USE YOURS?
WHAM

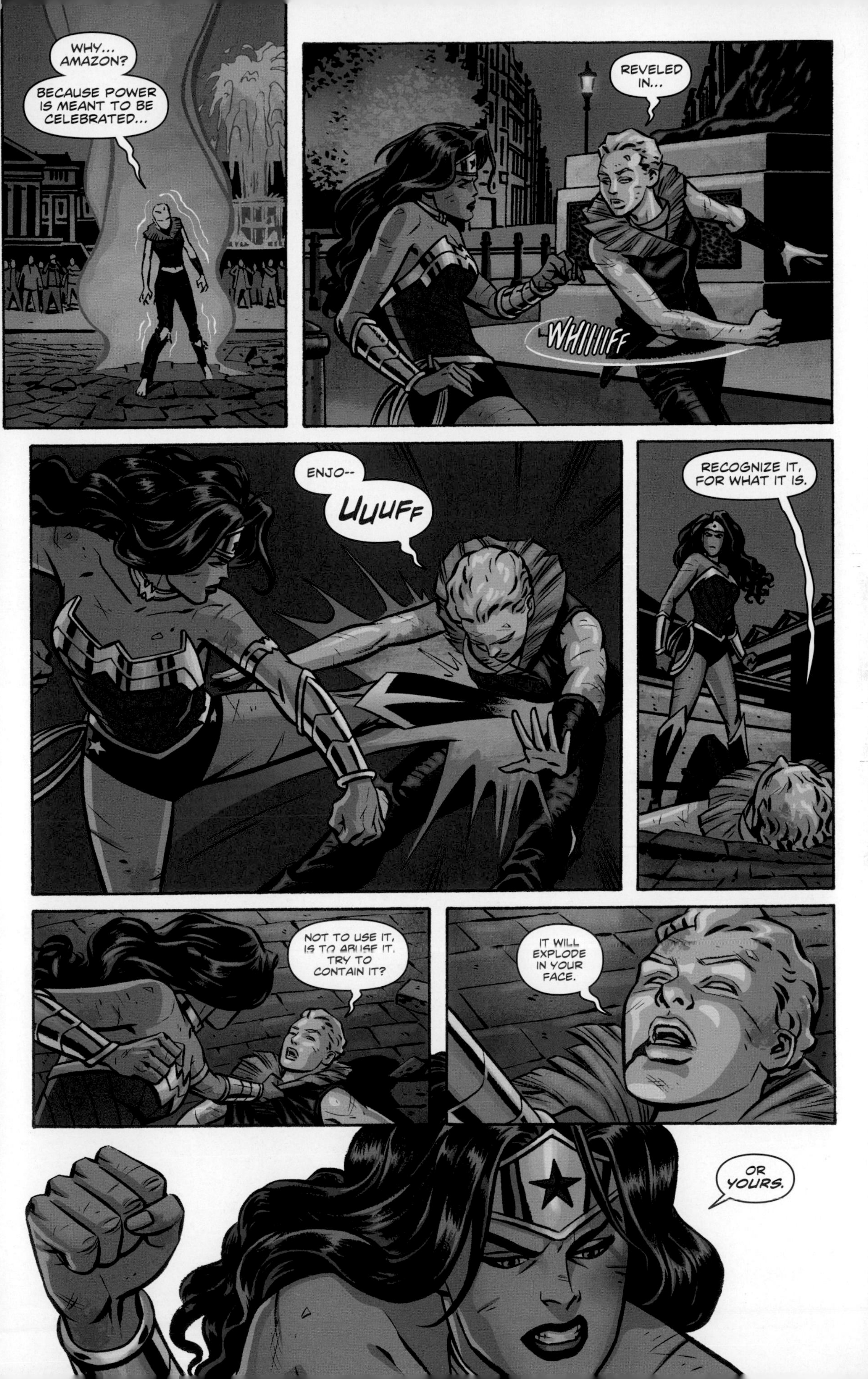
WHY... AMAZON?
BECAUSE POWER IS MEANT TO BE CELEBRATED...
REVELED IN...
WHIIIIFF
ENJO--
UUUFF
RECOGNIZE IT, FOR WHAT IT IS.
NOT TO USE IT, IS TO ABUSE IT. TRY TO CONTAIN IT?
IT WILL EXPLODE IN YOUR FACE.
OR YOURS.

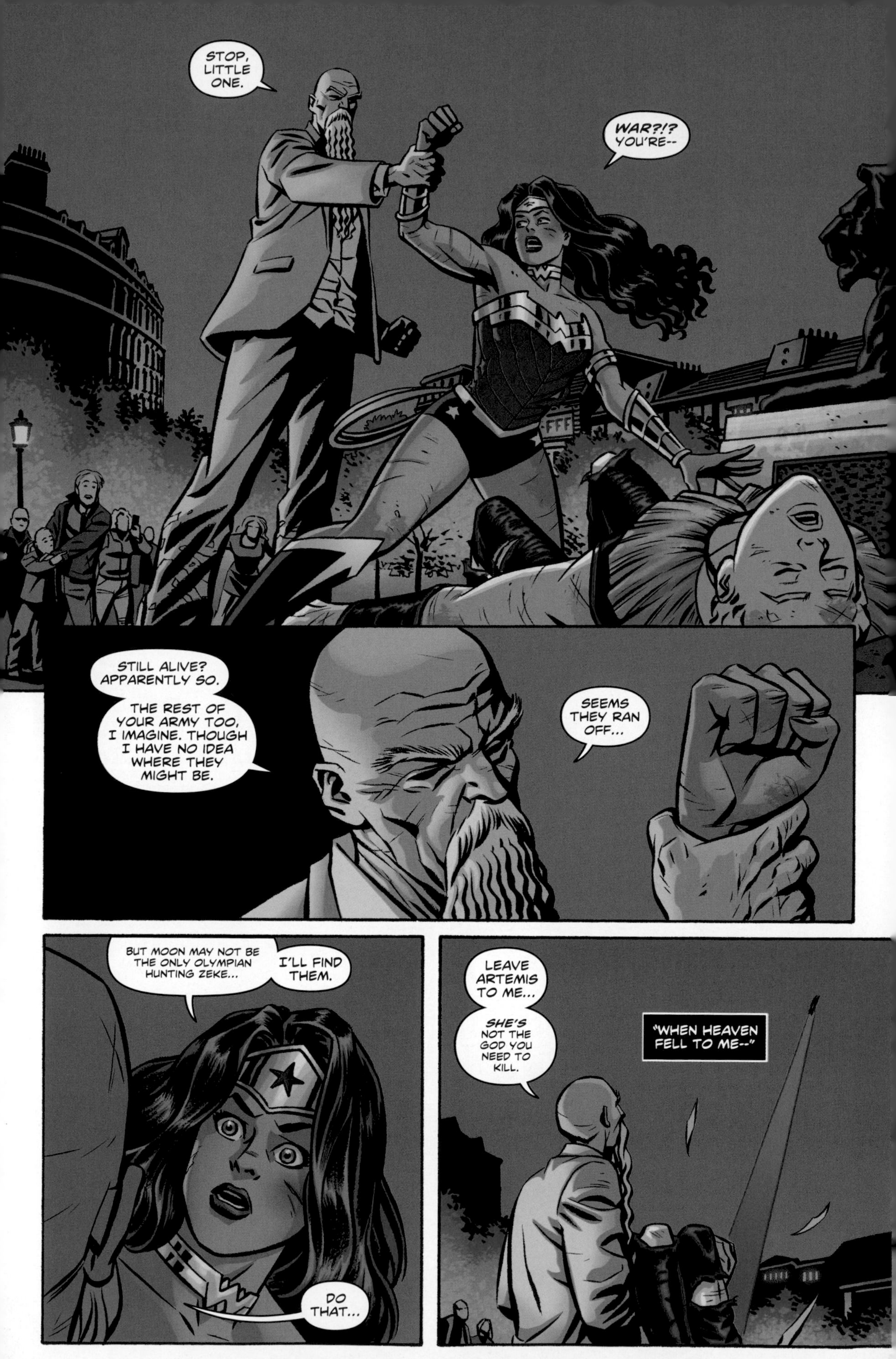
STOP, LITTLE ONE.
WAR?!? YOU'RE--
STILL ALIVE? APPARENTLY SO.
THE REST OF YOUR ARMY TOO, I IMAGINE. THOUGH I HAVE NO IDEA WHERE THEY MIGHT BE.
SEEMS THEY RAN OFF...
BUT MOON MAY NOT BE THE ONLY OLYMPIAN HUNTING ZEKE...
I'LL FIND THEM.
DO THAT...
LEAVE ARTEMIS TO ME...
SHE'S NOT THE GOD YOU NEED TO KILL.
"WHEN HEAVEN FELL TO ME--"

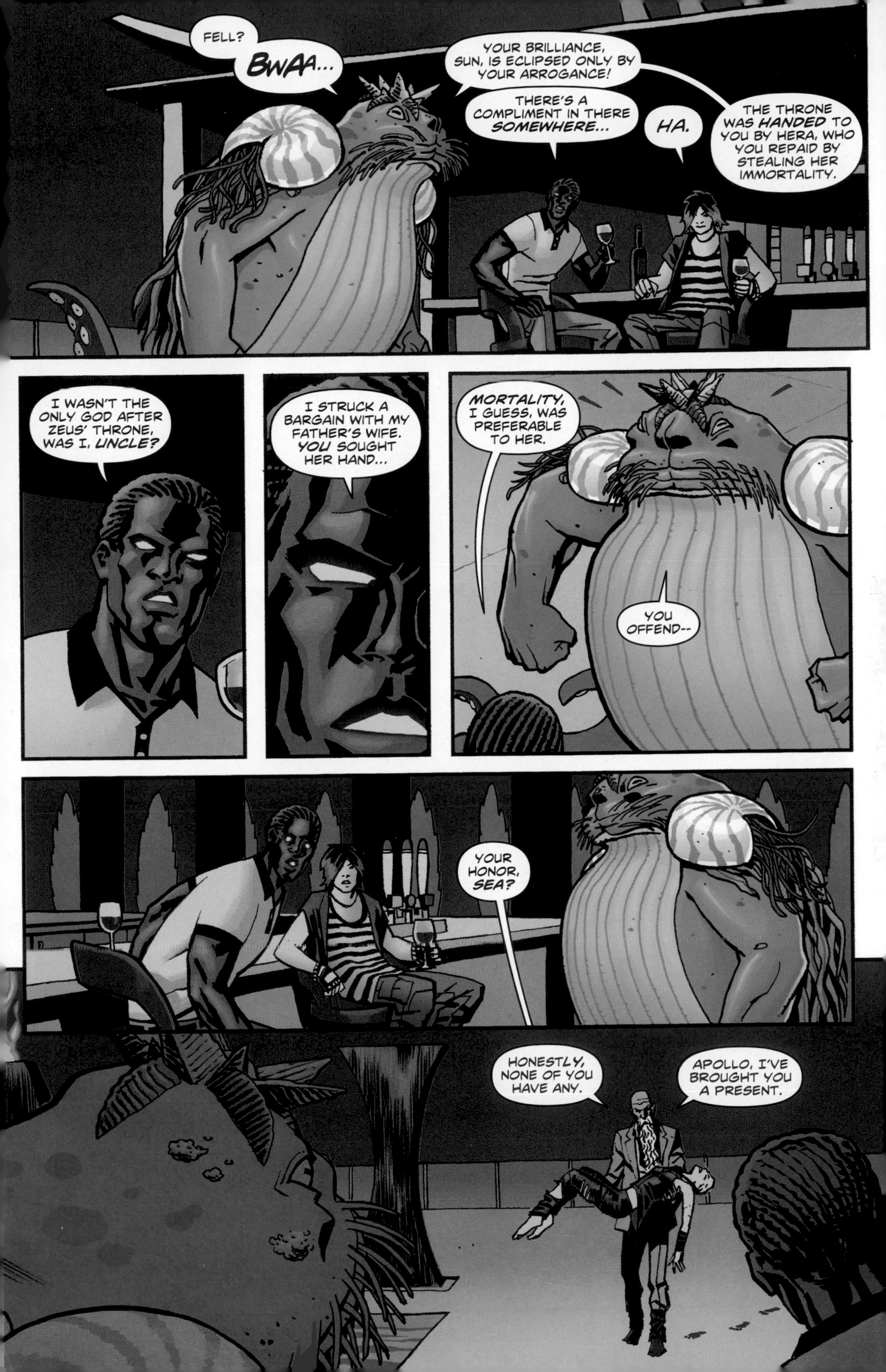
FELL?
BWAA...
YOUR BRILLIANCE, SUN, IS ECLIPSED ONLY BY YOUR ARROGANCE!
THERE'S A COMPLIMENT IN THERE SOMEWHERE...
HA.
THE THRONE WAS HANDED TO YOU BY HERA, WHO YOU REPAID BY STEALING HER IMMORTALITY.
I WASN'T THE ONLY GOD AFTER ZEUS' THRONE, WAS I, UNCLE?
I STRUCK A BARGAIN WITH MY FATHER'S WIFE. YOU SOUGHT HER HAND...
MORTALITY, I GUESS, WAS PREFERABLE TO HER.
YOU OFFEND--
YOUR HONOR, SEA?
HONESTLY, NONE OF YOU HAVE ANY.
APOLLO, I'VE BROUGHT YOU A PRESENT.

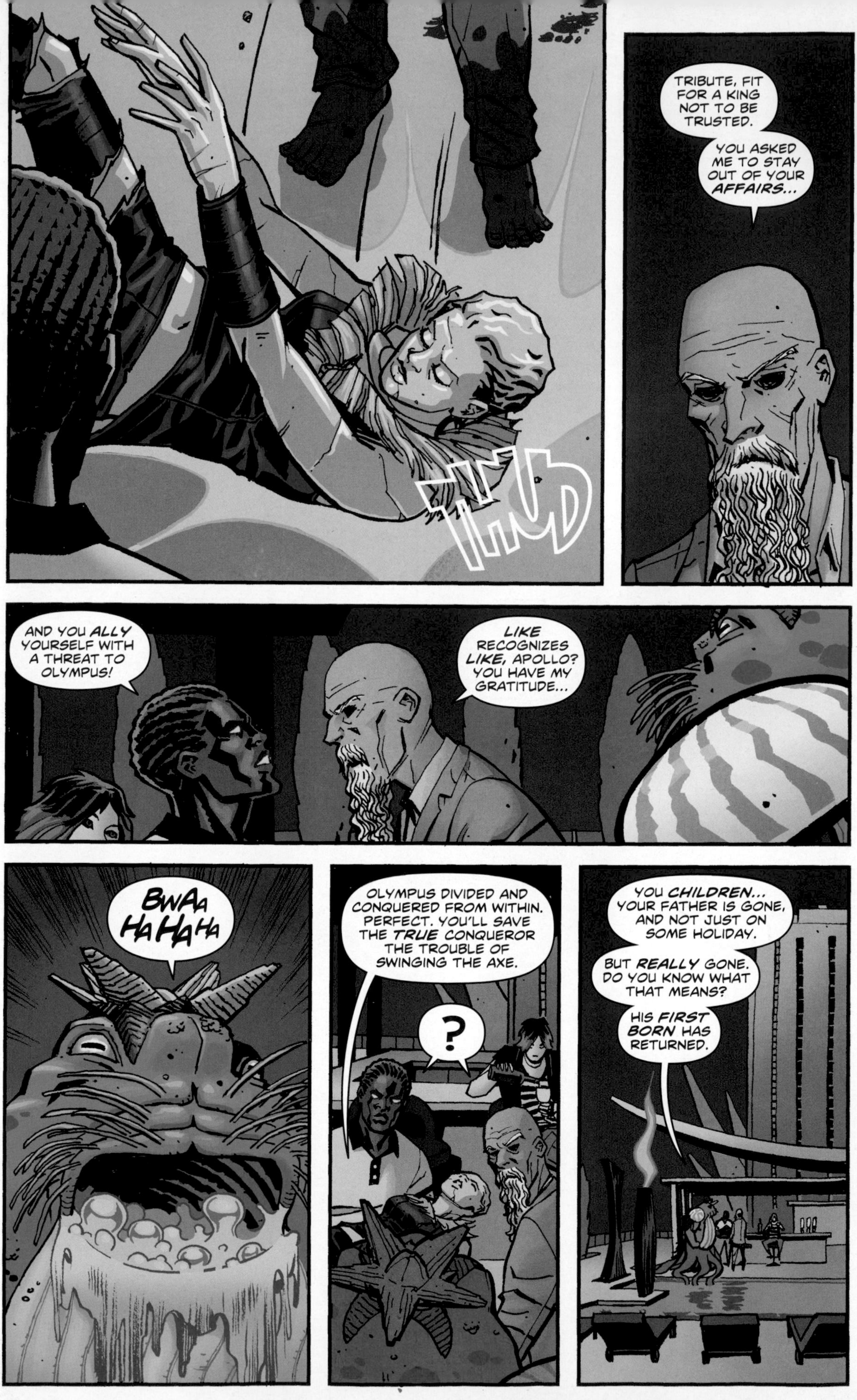
THUD
TRIBUTE, FIT FOR A KING NOT TO BE TRUSTED.
YOU ASKED ME TO STAY OUT OF YOUR AFFAIRS...
AND YOU ALLY YOURSELF WITH A THREAT TO OLYMPUS!
LIKE RECOGNIZES LIKE, APOLLO? YOU HAVE MY GRATITUDE...
BWAA HA HA HA
OLYMPUS DIVIDED AND CONQUERED FROM WITHIN. PERFECT. YOU'LL SAVE THE TRUE CONQUEROR THE TROUBLE OF SWINGING THE AXE.
?
YOU CHILDREN... YOUR FATHER IS GONE, AND NOT JUST ON SOME HOLIDAY.
BUT REALLY GONE. DO YOU KNOW WHAT THAT MEANS?
HIS FIRST BORN HAS RETURNED.

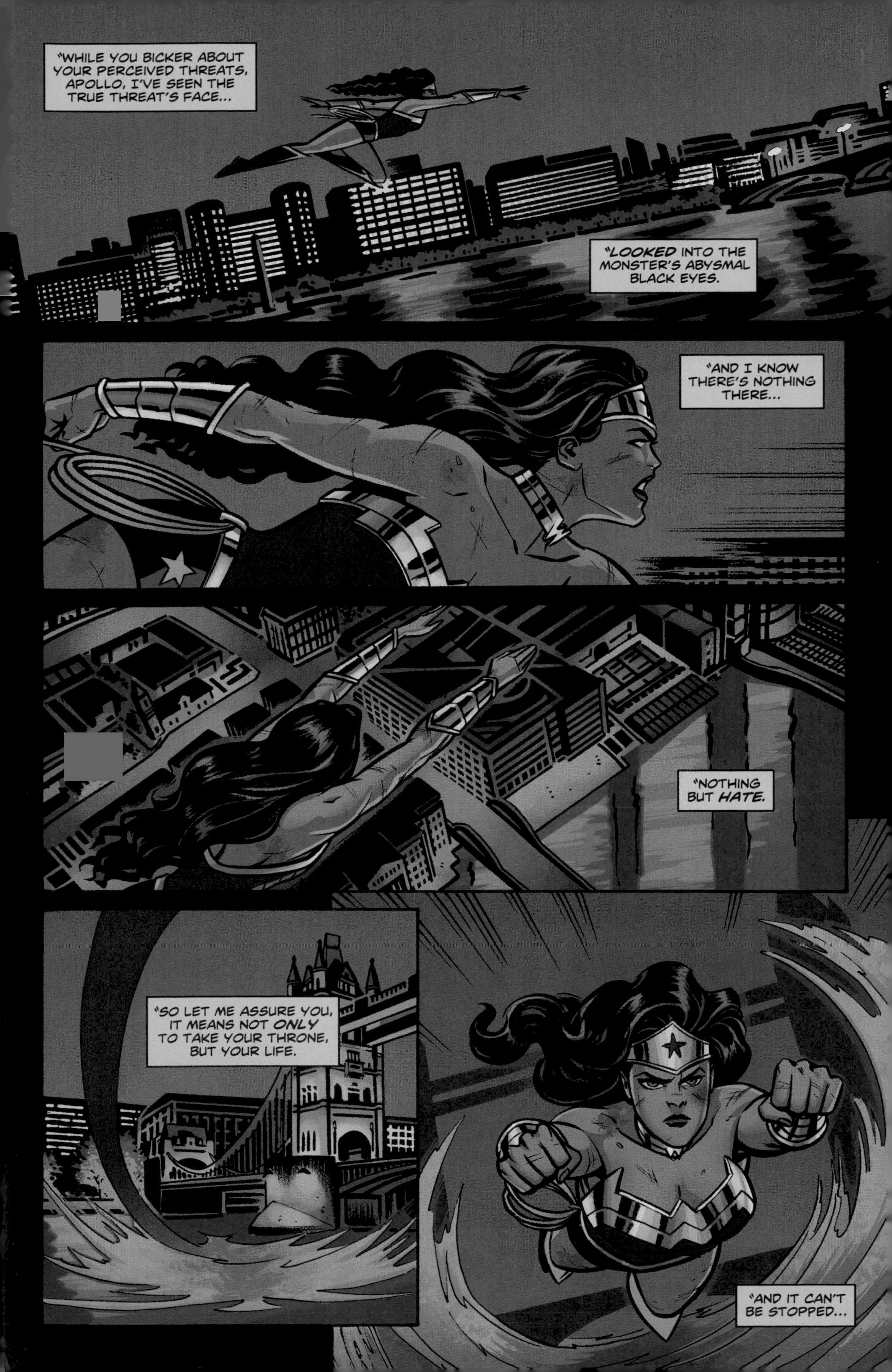
"WHILE YOU BICKER ABOUT YOUR PERCEIVED THREATS, APOLLO, I'VE SEEN THE TRUE THREAT'S FACE...
"LOOKED INTO THE MONSTER'S ABYSMAL BLACK EYES.
"AND I KNOW THERE'S NOTHING THERE...
"NOTHING BUT HATE.
"SO LET ME ASSURE YOU, IT MEANS NOT ONLY TO TAKE YOUR THRONE, BUT YOUR LIFE.
"AND IT CAN'T BE STOPPED...

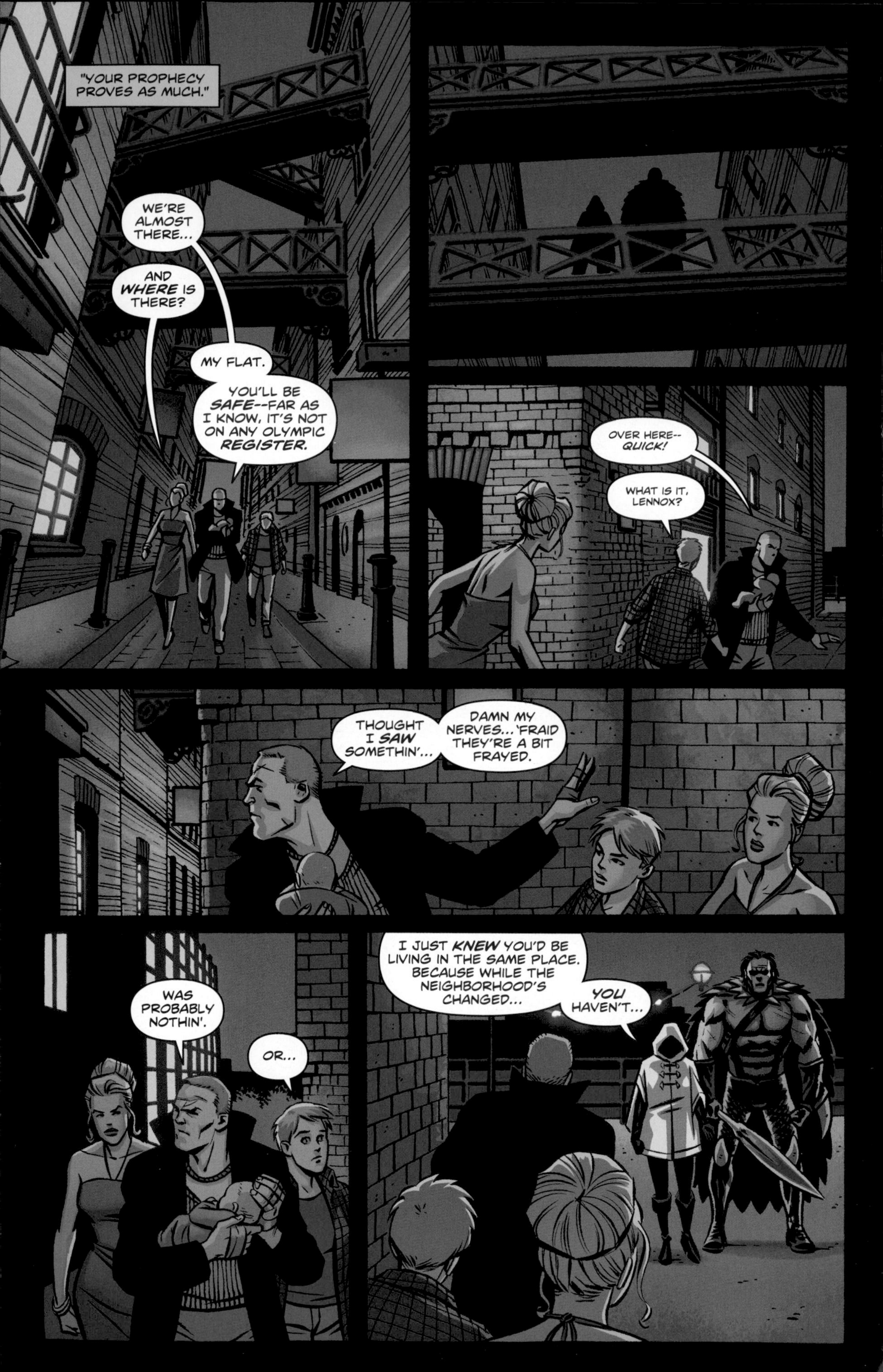
"YOUR PROPHECY PROVES AS MUCH."
WE'RE ALMOST THERE...
AND WHERE IS THERE?
MY FLAT.
YOU'LL BE SAFE--FAR AS I KNOW, IT'S NOT ON ANY OLYMPIC REGISTER.
OVER HERE-- QUICK!
WHAT IS IT, LENNOX?
THOUGHT I SAW SOMETHIN'...
DAMN MY NERVES...'FRAID THEY'RE A BIT FRAYED.
WAS PROBABLY NOTHIN'.
OR...
I JUST KNEW YOU'D BE LIVING IN THE SAME PLACE. BECAUSE WHILE THE NEIGHBORHOOD'S CHANGED...
YOU HAVEN'T...

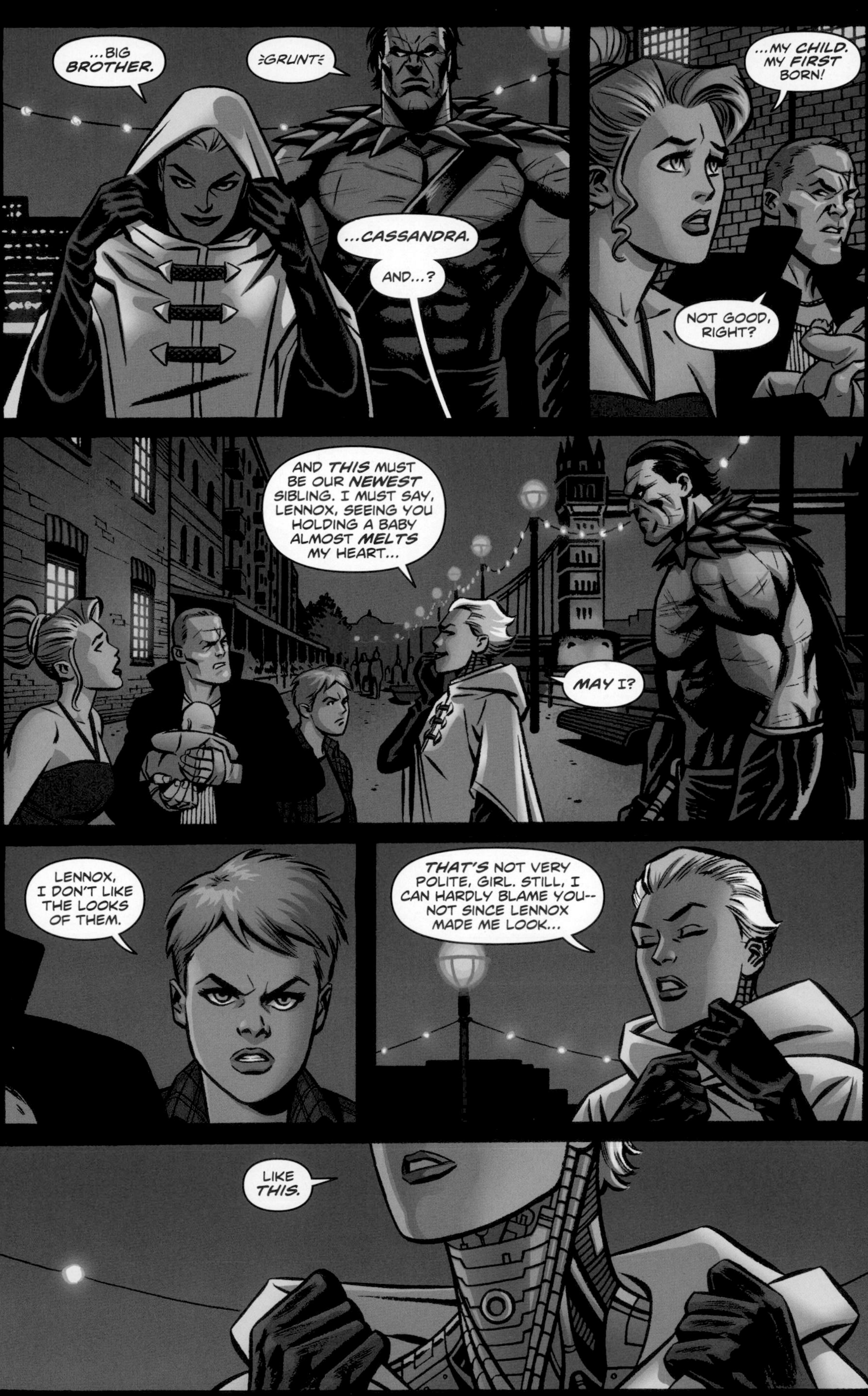

...BIG BROTHER.
GRUNT
...CASSANDRA.
AND...?
...MY CHILD. MY FIRST BORN!
NOT GOOD, RIGHT?
AND THIS MUST BE OUR NEWEST SIBLING. I MUST SAY, LENNOX, SEEING YOU HOLDING A BABY ALMOST MELTS MY HEART...
MAY I?
LENNOX, I DON'T LIKE THE LOOKS OF THEM.
THAT'S NOT VERY POLITE, GIRL. STILL, I CAN HARDLY BLAME YOU-- NOT SINCE LENNOX MADE ME LOOK...
LIKE THIS.

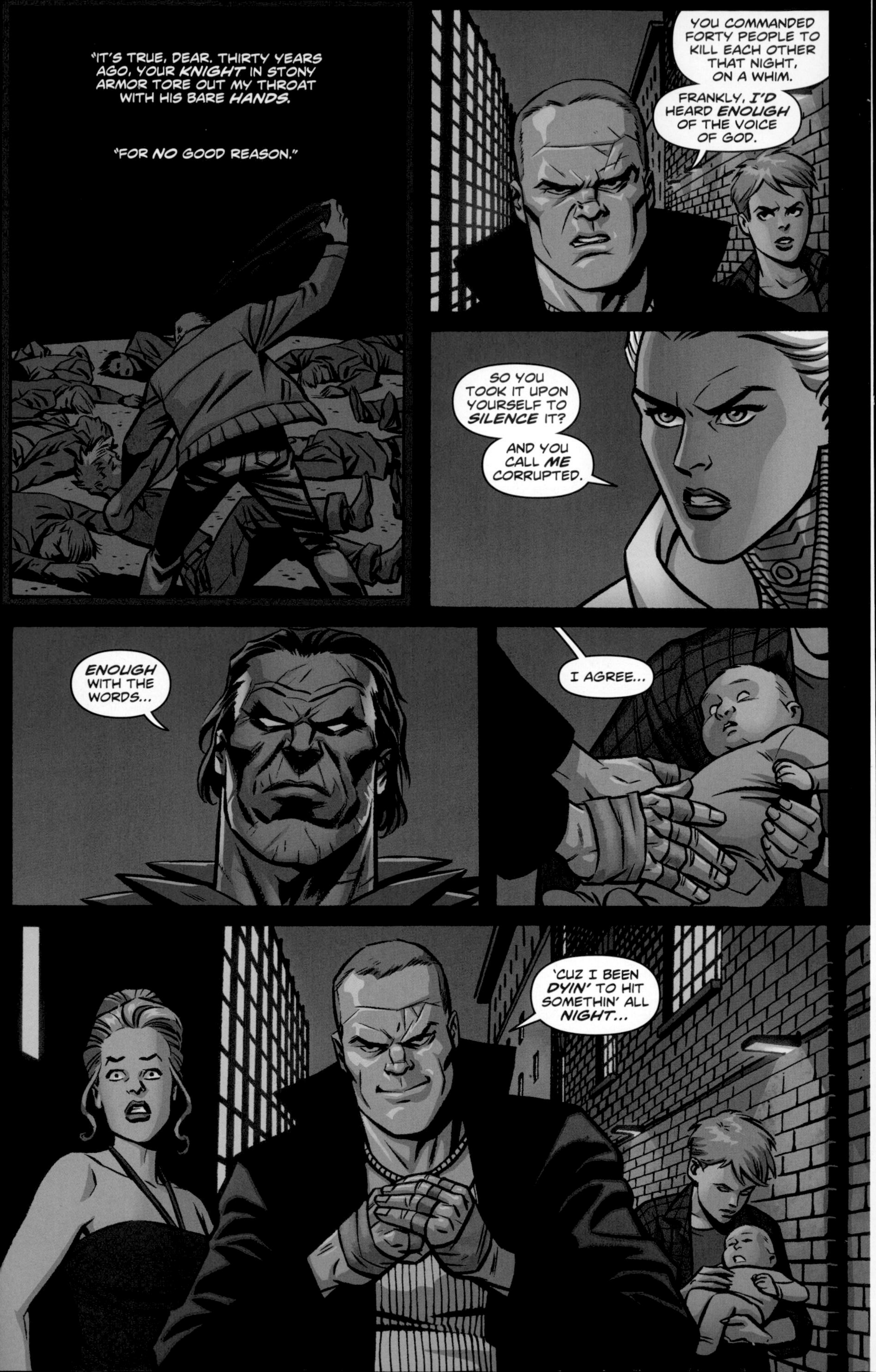
"IT'S TRUE, DEAR. THIRTY YEARS AGO, YOUR KNIGHT IN STONY ARMOR TORE OUT MY THROAT WITH HIS BARE HANDS.
"FOR NO GOOD REASON."
YOU COMMANDED FORTY PEOPLE TO KILL EACH OTHER THAT NIGHT, ON A WHIM.
FRANKLY, I'D HEARD ENOUGH OF THE VOICE OF GOD.
SO YOU TOOK IT UPON YOURSELF TO SILENCE IT?
AND YOU CALL ME CORRUPTED.
ENOUGH WITH THE WORDS...
I AGREE...
'CUZ I BEEN DYIN' TO HIT SOMETHIN' ALL NIGHT...

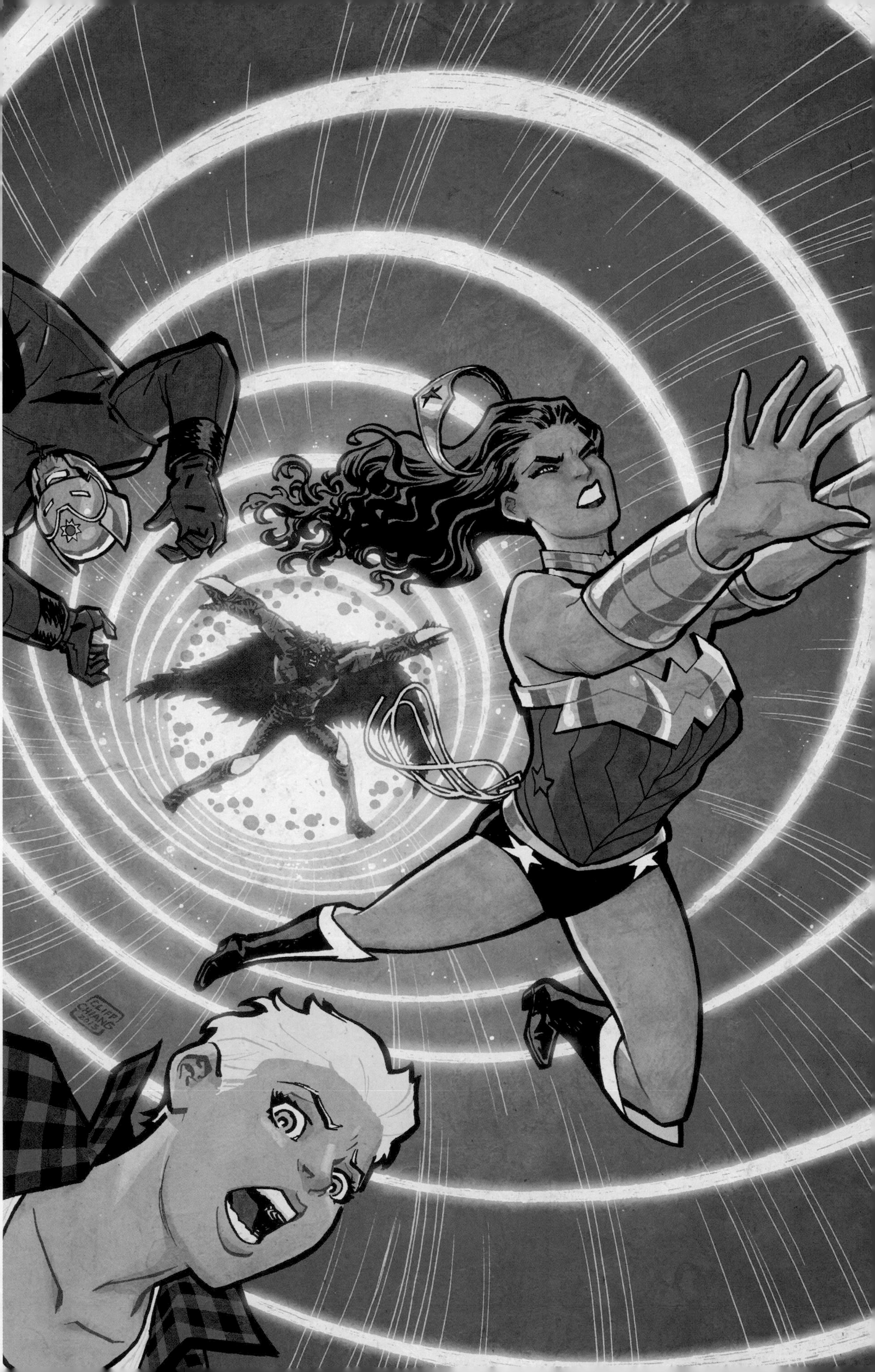
CLIFF
CHIANG
2015

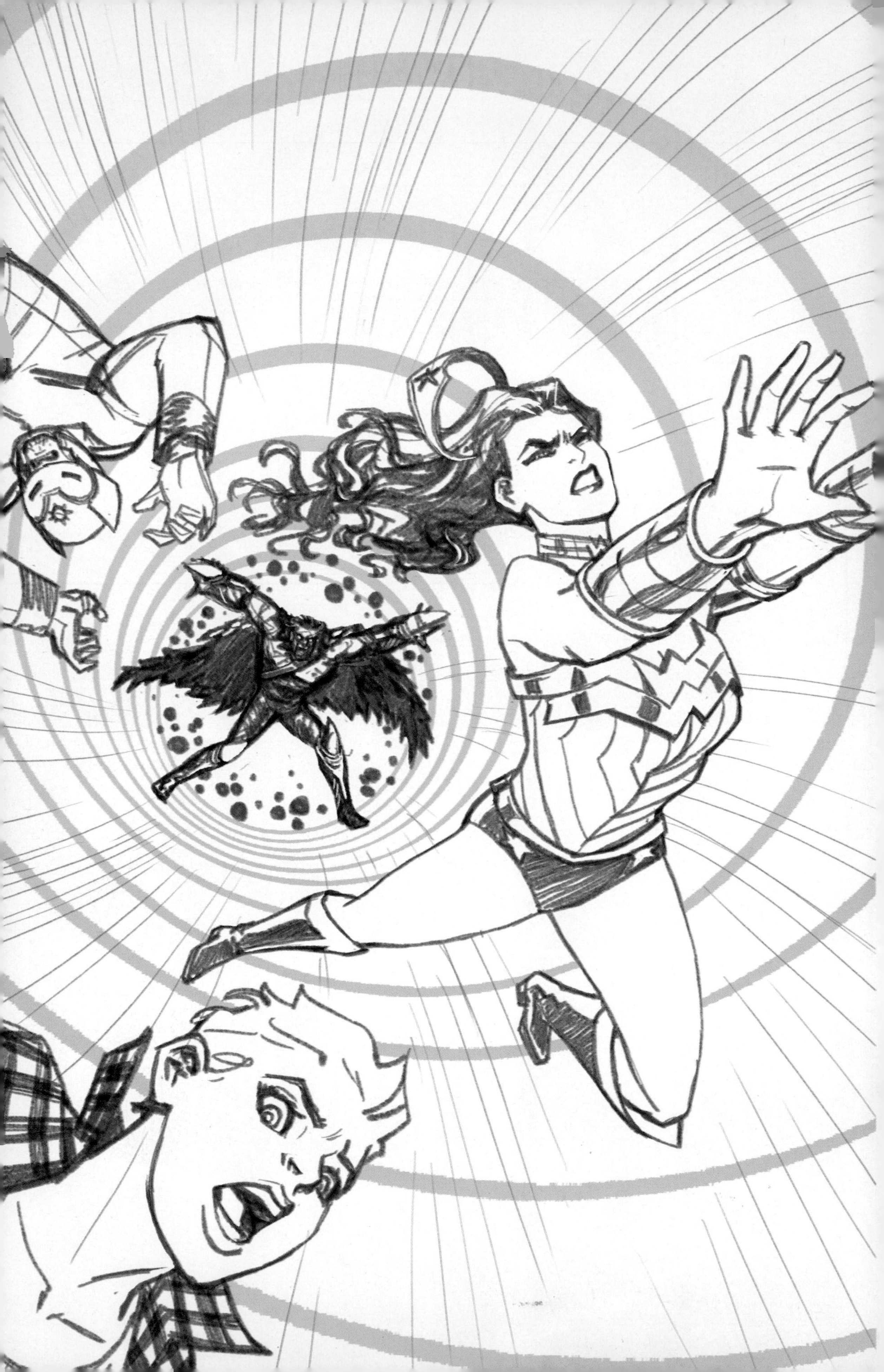

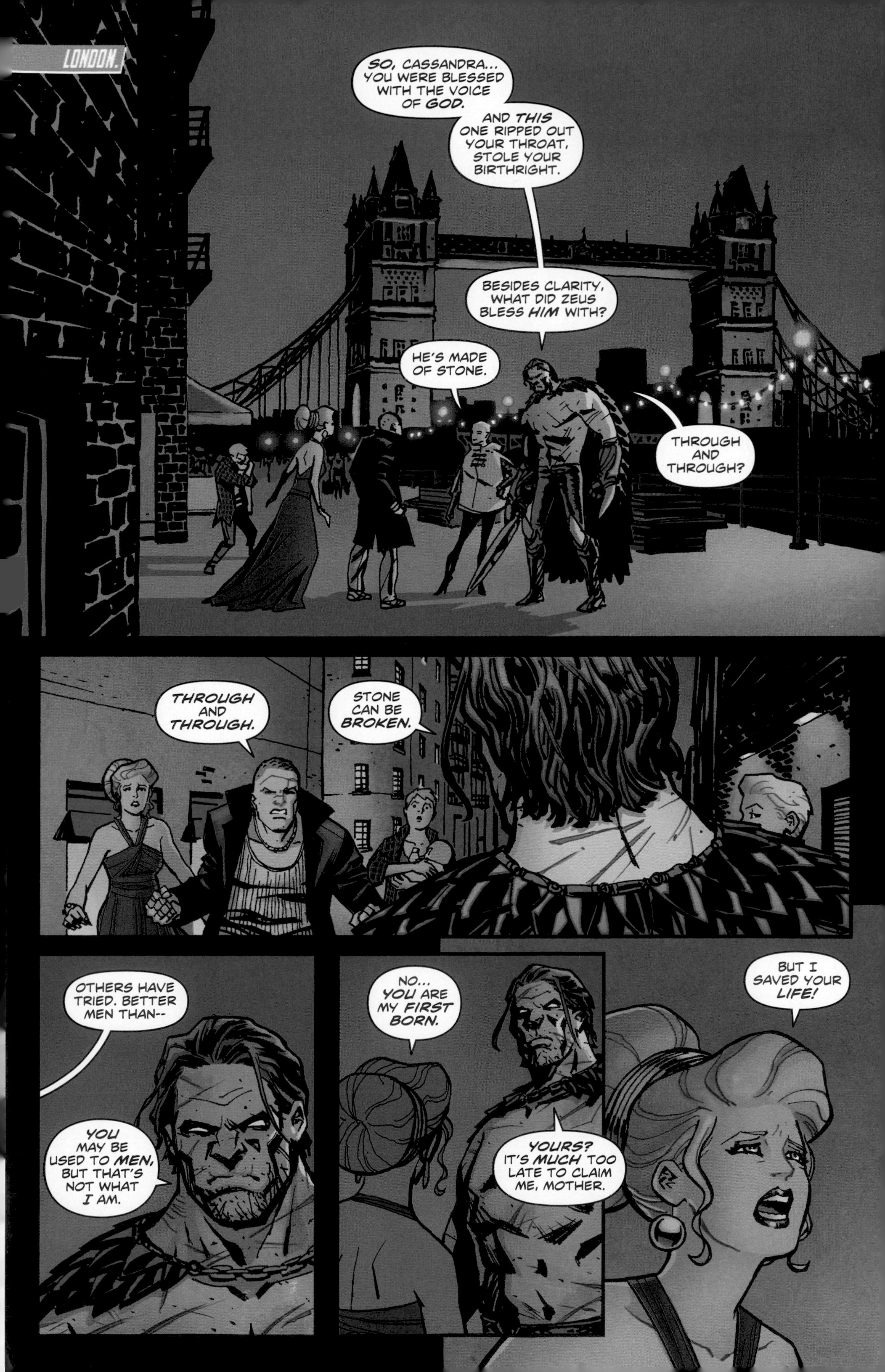
LONDON.
SO, CASSANDRA... YOU WERE BLESSED WITH THE VOICE OF GOD.
AND THIS ONE RIPPED OUT YOUR THROAT, STOLE YOUR BIRTHRIGHT.
BESIDES CLARITY, WHAT DID ZEUS BLESS HIM WITH?
HE'S MADE OF STONE.
THROUGH AND THROUGH?
THROUGH AND THROUGH.
STONE CAN BE BROKEN.
OTHERS HAVE TRIED. BETTER MEN THAN--
YOU MAY BE USED TO MEN, BUT THAT'S NOT WHAT I AM.
NO... YOU ARE MY FIRST BORN.
YOURS? IT'S MUCH TOO LATE TO CLAIM ME, MOTHER.
BUT I SAVED YOUR LIFE!

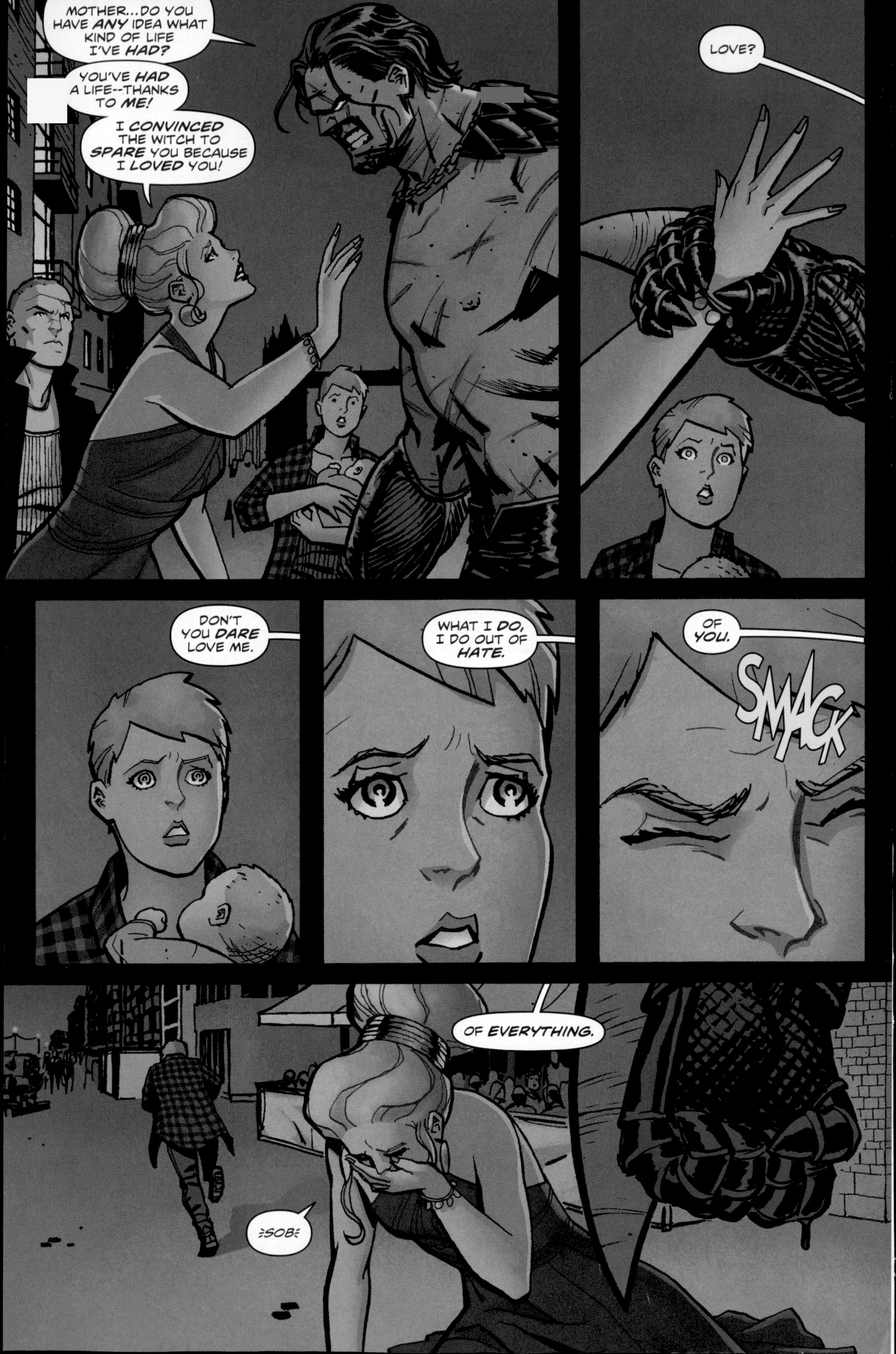
MOTHER...DO YOU HAVE ANY IDEA WHAT KIND OF LIFE I'VE HAD?
YOU'VE HAD A LIFE--THANKS TO ME!
I CONVINCED THE WITCH TO SPARE YOU BECAUSE I LOVED YOU!
LOVE?
DON'T YOU DARE LOVE ME.
WHAT I DO, I DO OUT OF HATE.
OF YOU.
SMACK
OF EVERYTHING.
SOB

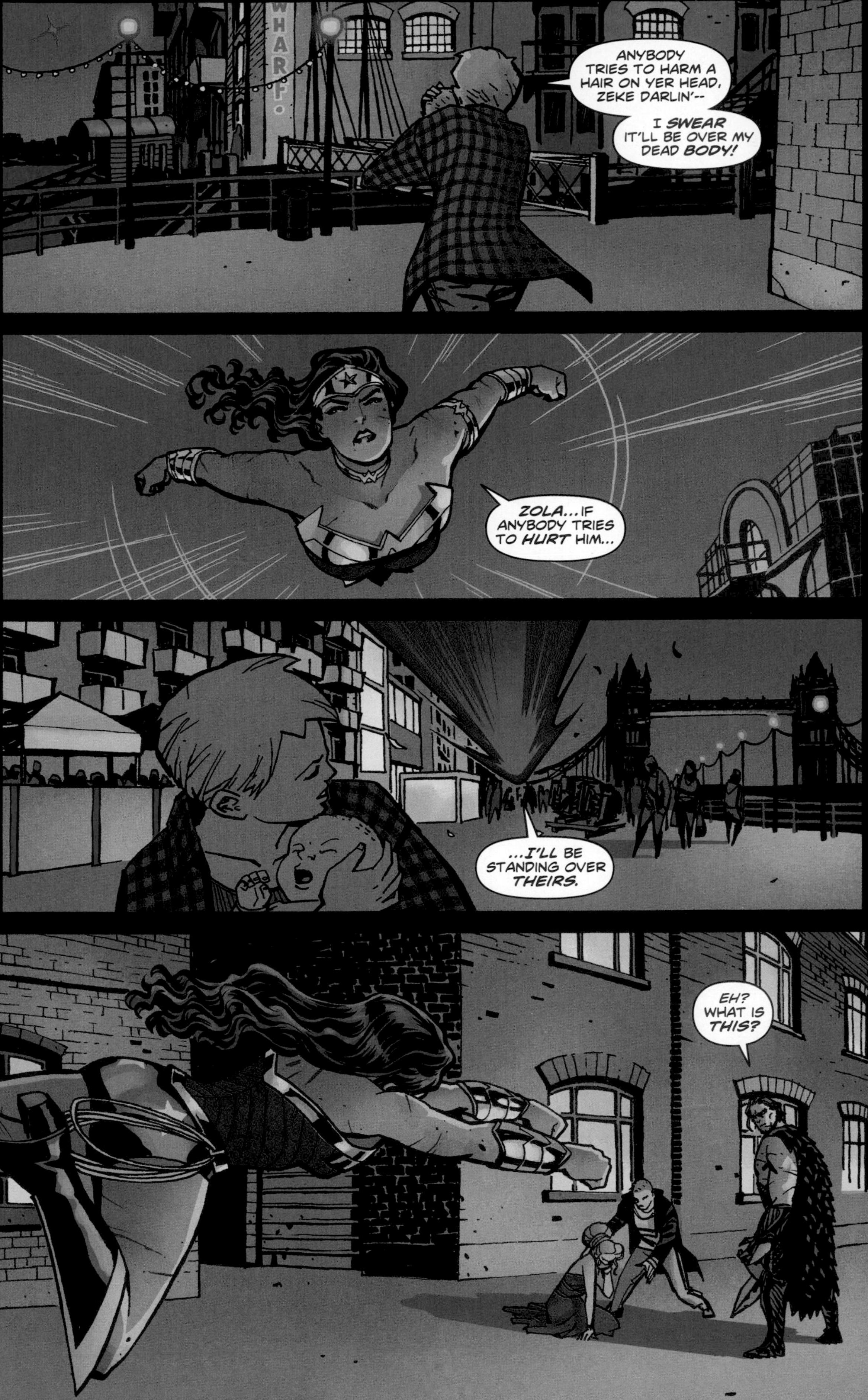

WHARF
ANYBODY TRIES TO HARM A HAIR ON YER HEAD, ZEKE DARLIN'--
I SWEAR IT'LL BE OVER MY DEAD BODY!
ZOLA... IF ANYBODY TRIES TO HURT HIM...
...I'LL BE STANDING OVER THEIRS.
EH? WHAT IS THIS?

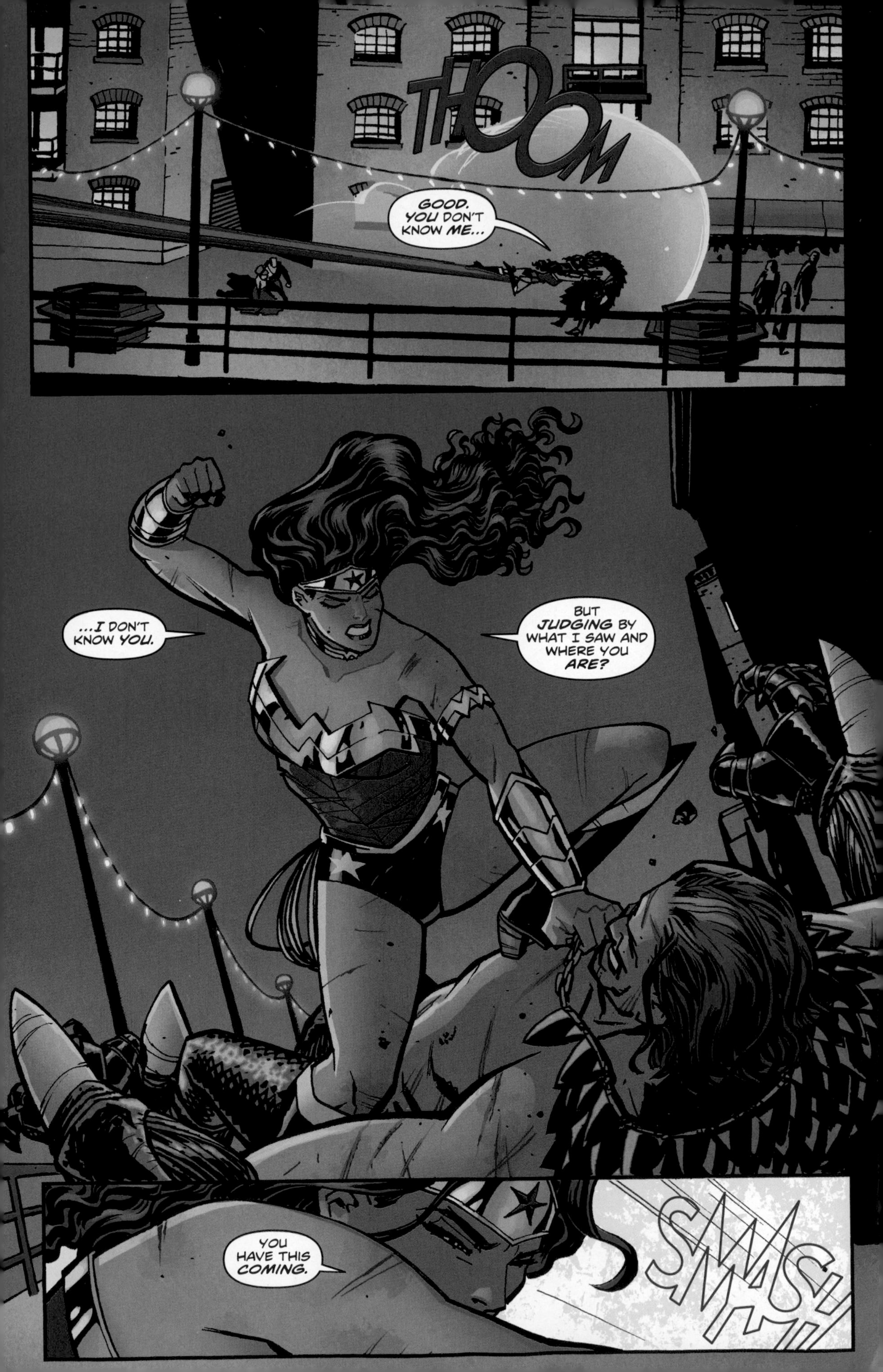
THOOM
GOOD. YOU DON'T KNOW ME...
...I DON'T KNOW YOU.
BUT JUDGING BY WHAT I SAW AND WHERE YOU ARE?
YOU HAVE THIS COMING.
SMASH

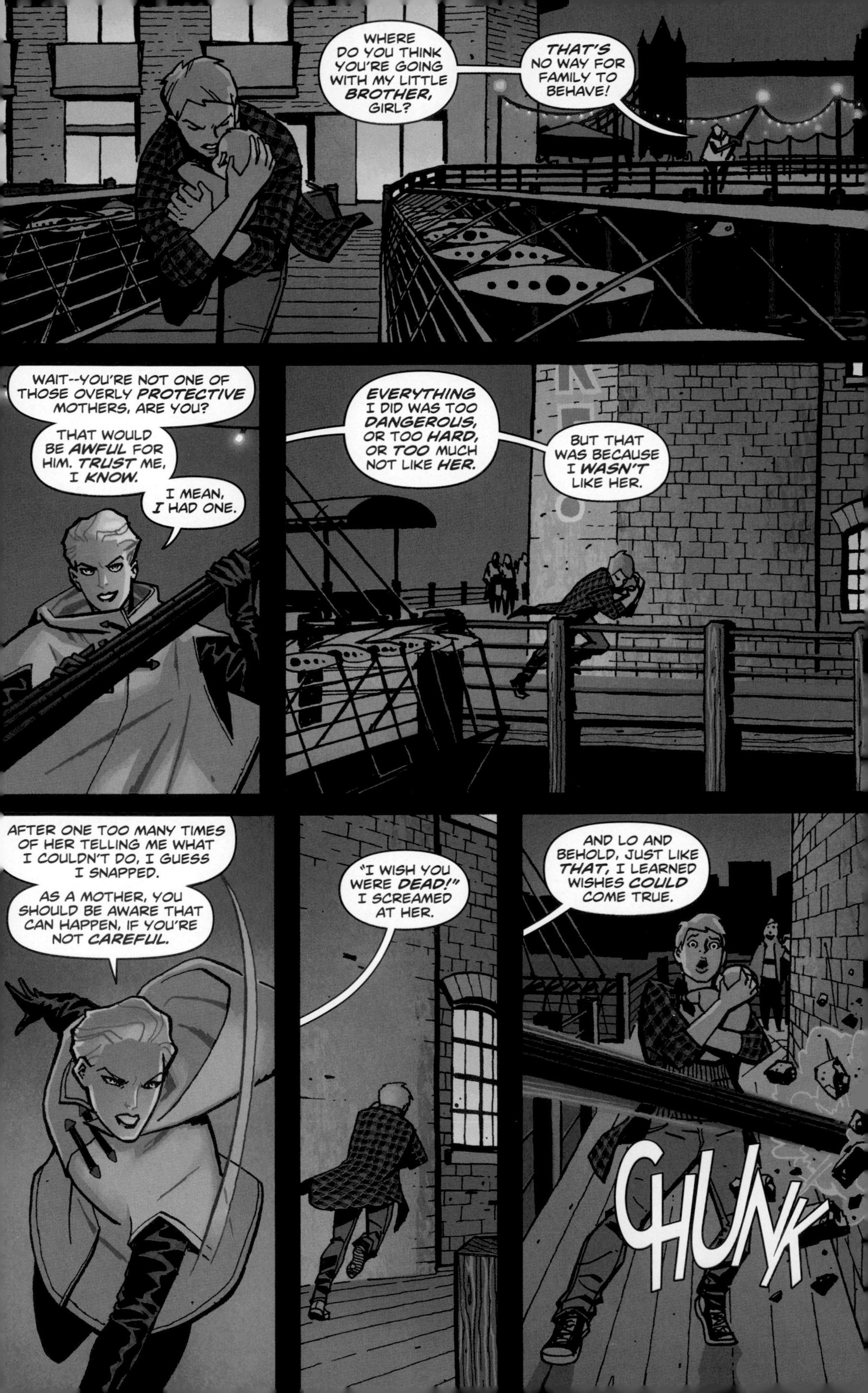
WHERE DO YOU THINK YOU'RE GOING WITH MY LITTLE BROTHER, GIRL?
THAT'S NO WAY FOR FAMILY TO BEHAVE!
WAIT--YOU'RE NOT ONE OF THOSE OVERLY PROTECTIVE MOTHERS, ARE YOU?
THAT WOULD BE AWFUL FOR HIM. TRUST ME, I KNOW.
I MEAN, I HAD ONE.
EVERYTHING I DID WAS TOO DANGEROUS, OR TOO HARD, OR TOO MUCH NOT LIKE HER.
BUT THAT WAS BECAUSE I WASN'T LIKE HER.
AFTER ONE TOO MANY TIMES OF HER TELLING ME WHAT I COULDN'T DO, I GUESS I SNAPPED.
AS A MOTHER, YOU SHOULD BE AWARE THAT CAN HAPPEN, IF YOU'RE NOT CAREFUL.
"I WISH YOU WERE DEAD!" I SCREAMED AT HER.
AND LO AND BEHOLD, JUST LIKE THAT, I LEARNED WISHES COULD COME TRUE.
CHUNK

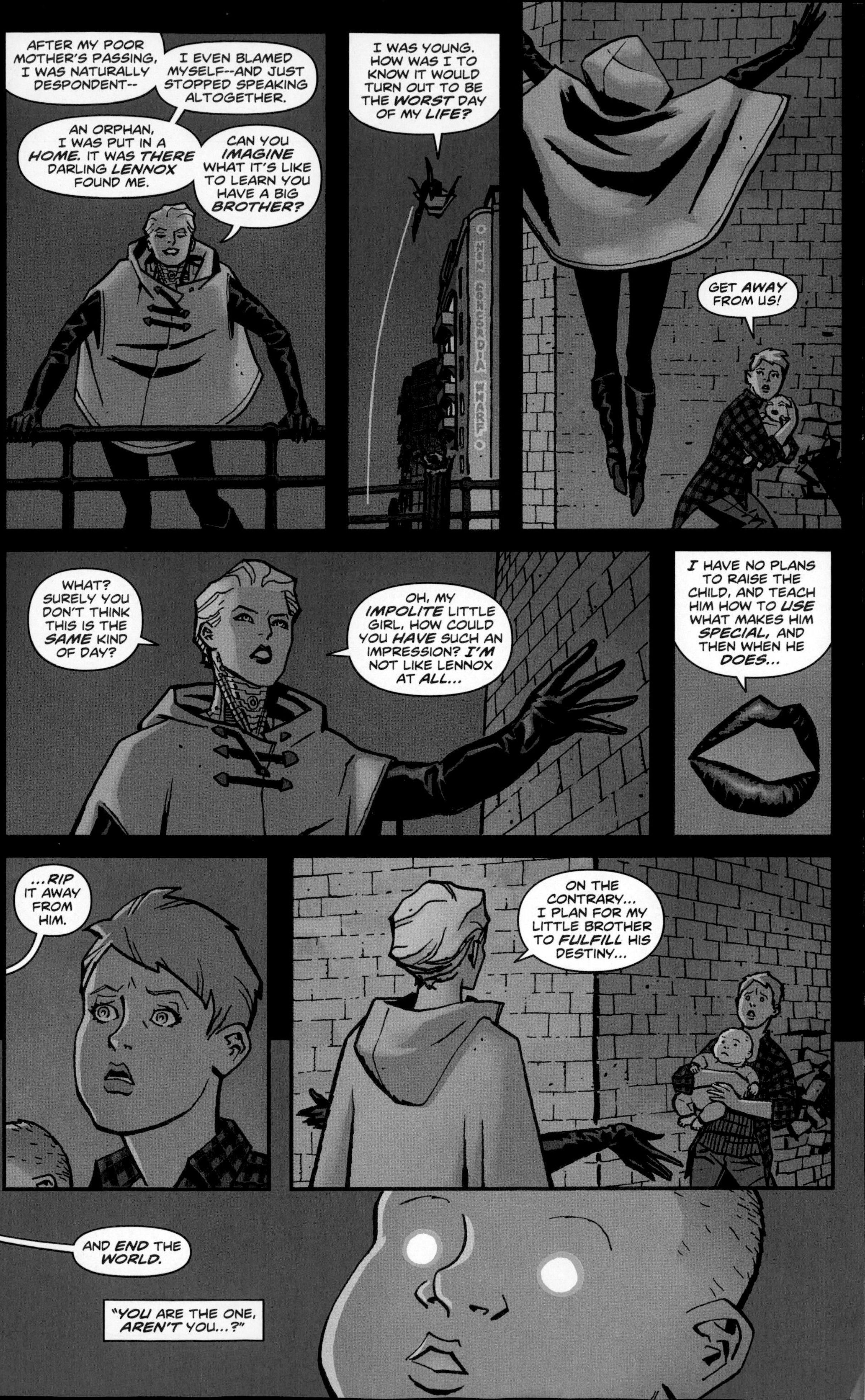
AFTER MY POOR MOTHER'S PASSING, I WAS NATURALLY DESPONDENT--
I EVEN BLAMED MYSELF--AND JUST STOPPED SPEAKING ALTOGETHER.
AN ORPHAN, I WAS PUT IN A HOME. IT WAS THERE DARLING LENNOX FOUND ME.
CAN YOU IMAGINE WHAT IT'S LIKE TO LEARN YOU HAVE A BIG BROTHER?
I WAS YOUNG. HOW WAS I TO KNOW IT WOULD TURN OUT TO BE THE WORST DAY OF MY LIFE?
NEW CONCORDIA WHARF
GET AWAY FROM US!
WHAT? SURELY YOU DON'T THINK THIS IS THE SAME KIND OF DAY?
OH, MY IMPOLITE LITTLE GIRL, HOW COULD YOU HAVE SUCH AN IMPRESSION? I'M NOT LIKE LENNOX AT ALL...
I HAVE NO PLANS TO RAISE THE CHILD, AND TEACH HIM HOW TO USE WHAT MAKES HIM SPECIAL, AND THEN WHEN HE DOES...
...RIP IT AWAY FROM HIM.
ON THE CONTRARY... I PLAN FOR MY LITTLE BROTHER TO FULFILL HIS DESTINY...
AND END THE WORLD.
"YOU ARE THE ONE, AREN'T YOU...?"

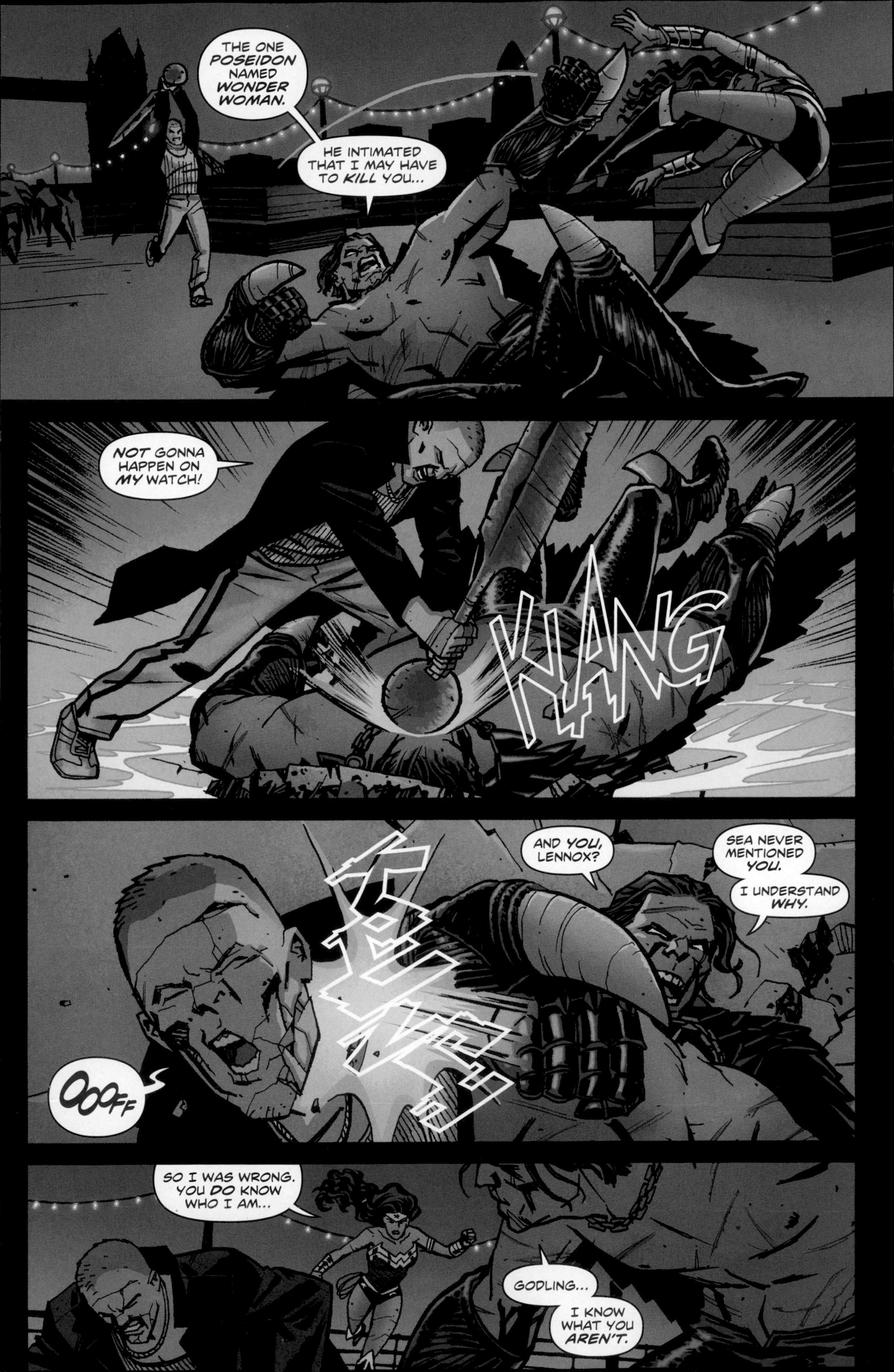
THE ONE POSEIDON NAMED WONDER WOMAN.
HE INTIMATED THAT I MAY HAVE TO KILL YOU...
NOT GONNA HAPPEN ON MY WATCH!
KLANG
AND YOU, LENNOX?
SEA NEVER MENTIONED YOU.
I UNDERSTAND WHY.
OOOFF
SO I WAS WRONG. YOU DO KNOW WHO I AM...
GODLING...
I KNOW WHAT YOU AREN'T.

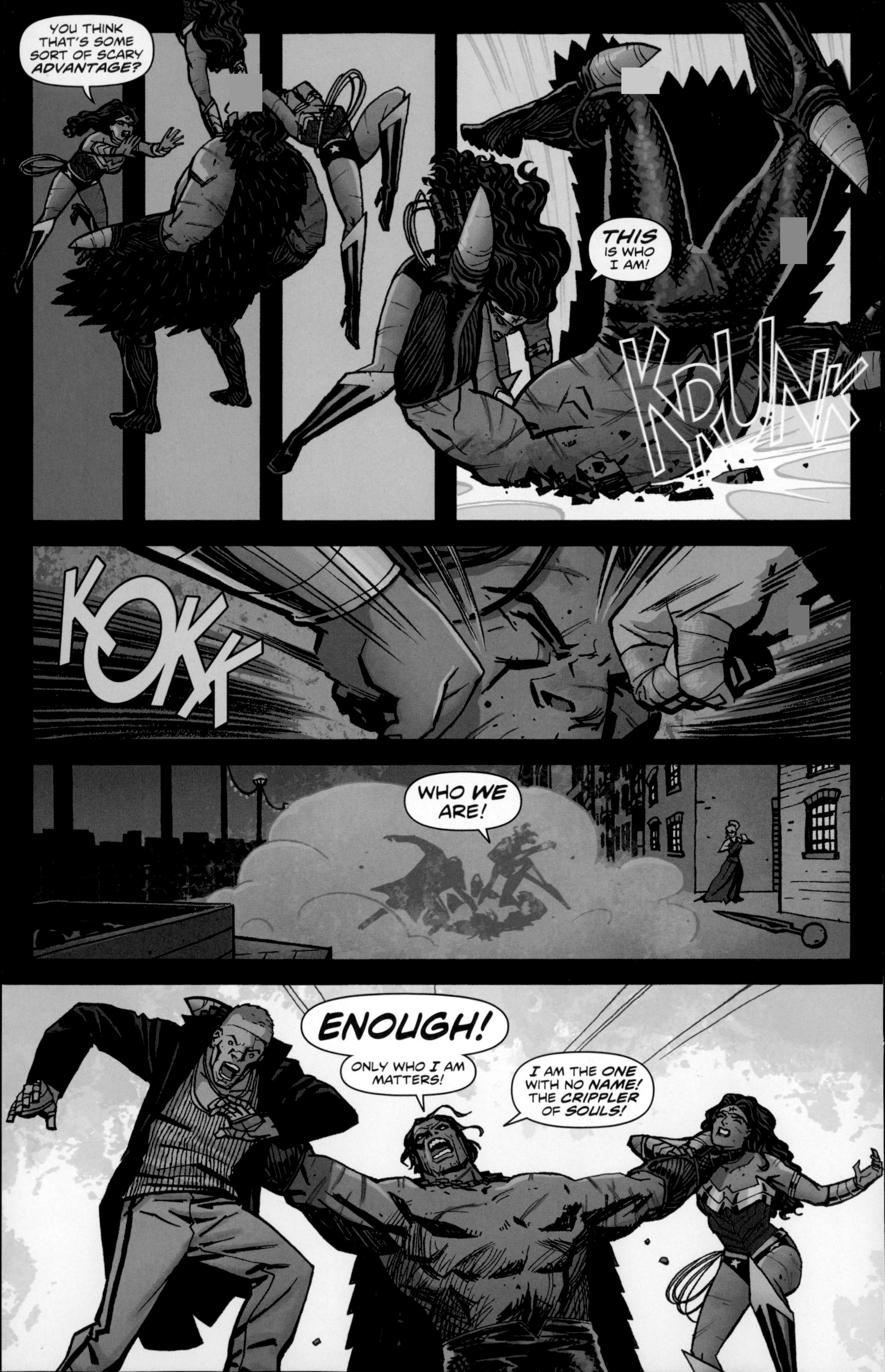
YOU THINK THAT'S SOME SORT OF SCARY ADVANTAGE?
THIS IS WHO I AM!
KRUNK
KOKK
WHO WE ARE!
ENOUGH!
ONLY WHO I AM MATTERS!
I AM THE ONE WITH NO NAME! THE CRIPPLER OF SOULS!

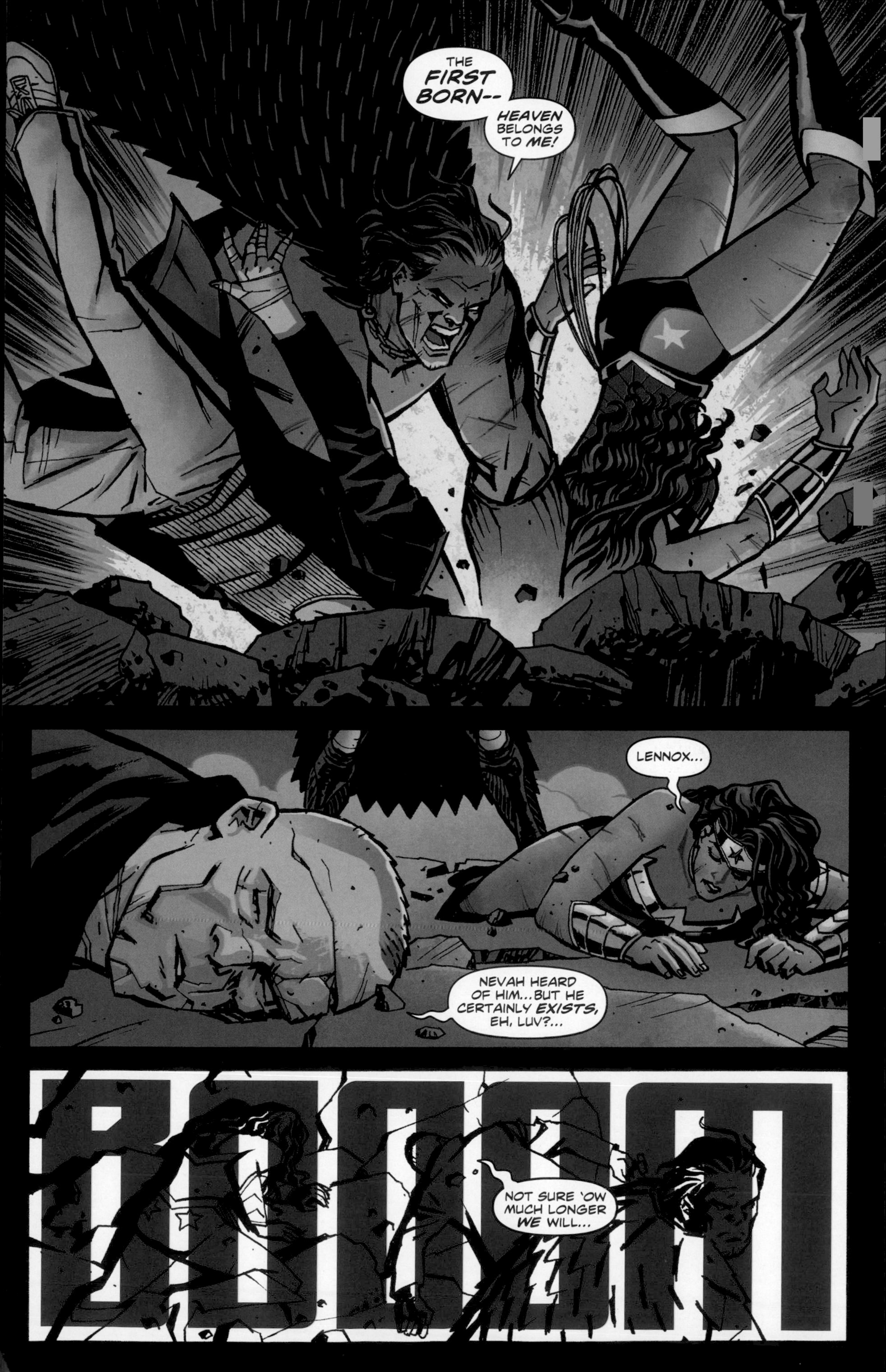
THE FIRST BORN--
HEAVEN BELONGS TO ME!
LENNOX...
NEVAH HEARD OF HIM...BUT HE CERTAINLY EXISTS, EH, LUV?...
NOT SURE 'OW MUCH LONGER WE WILL...

YOU'VE MADE A *HUGE* MISTAKE...

CRACK

BABY!

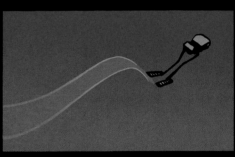

...I THOUGHT... I TOLD YOU TO *RESPECT* ME, ORION...

NOT *NOW*, LEGS...

I GOT *ASS* TO KICK!

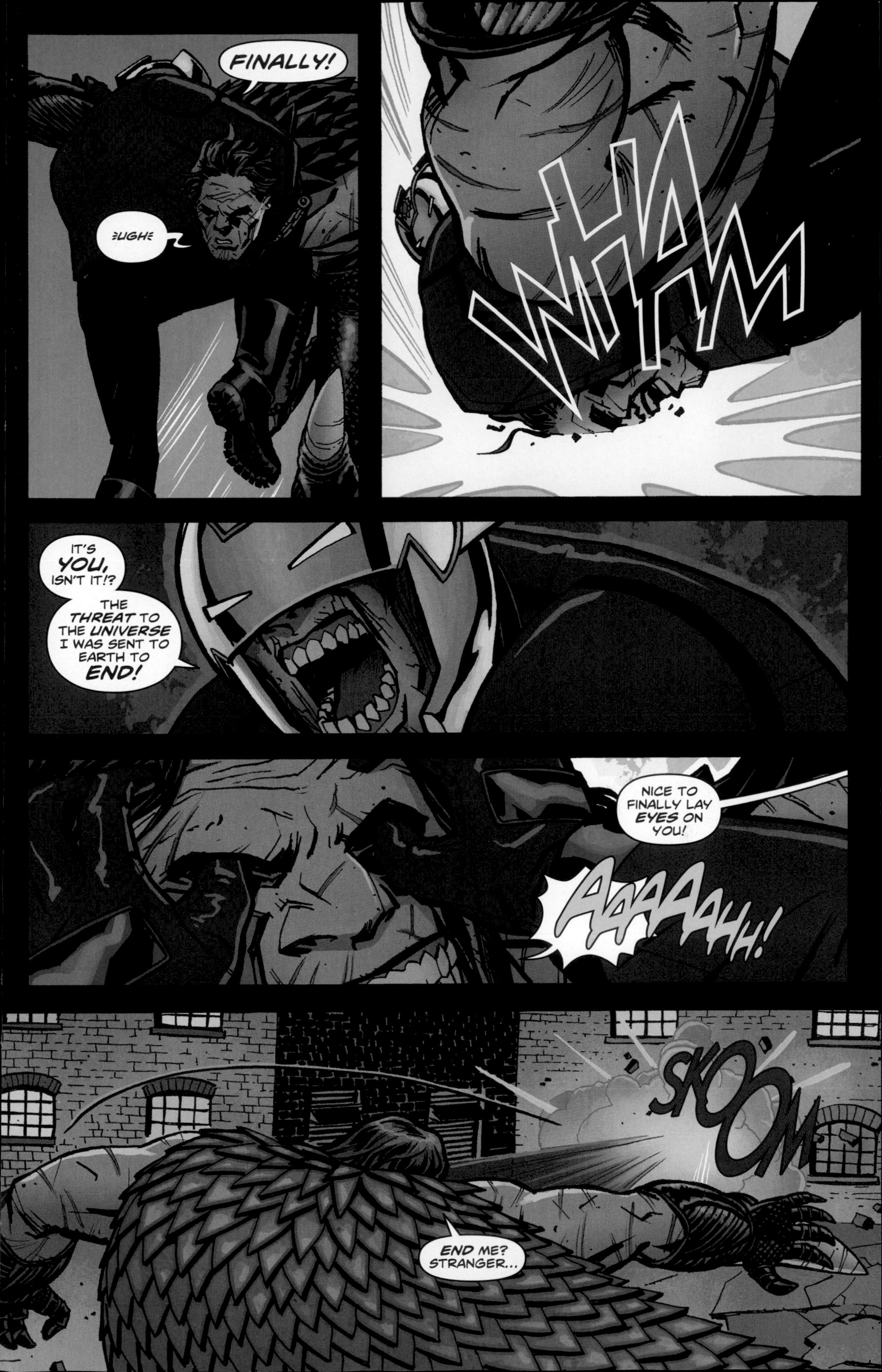
FINALLY!
UGH
WHAM
IT'S YOU, ISN'T IT!?
THE THREAT TO THE UNIVERSE I WAS SENT TO EARTH TO END!
NICE TO FINALLY LAY EYES ON YOU!
AAAAAHH!
SKOOM
END ME? STRANGER...

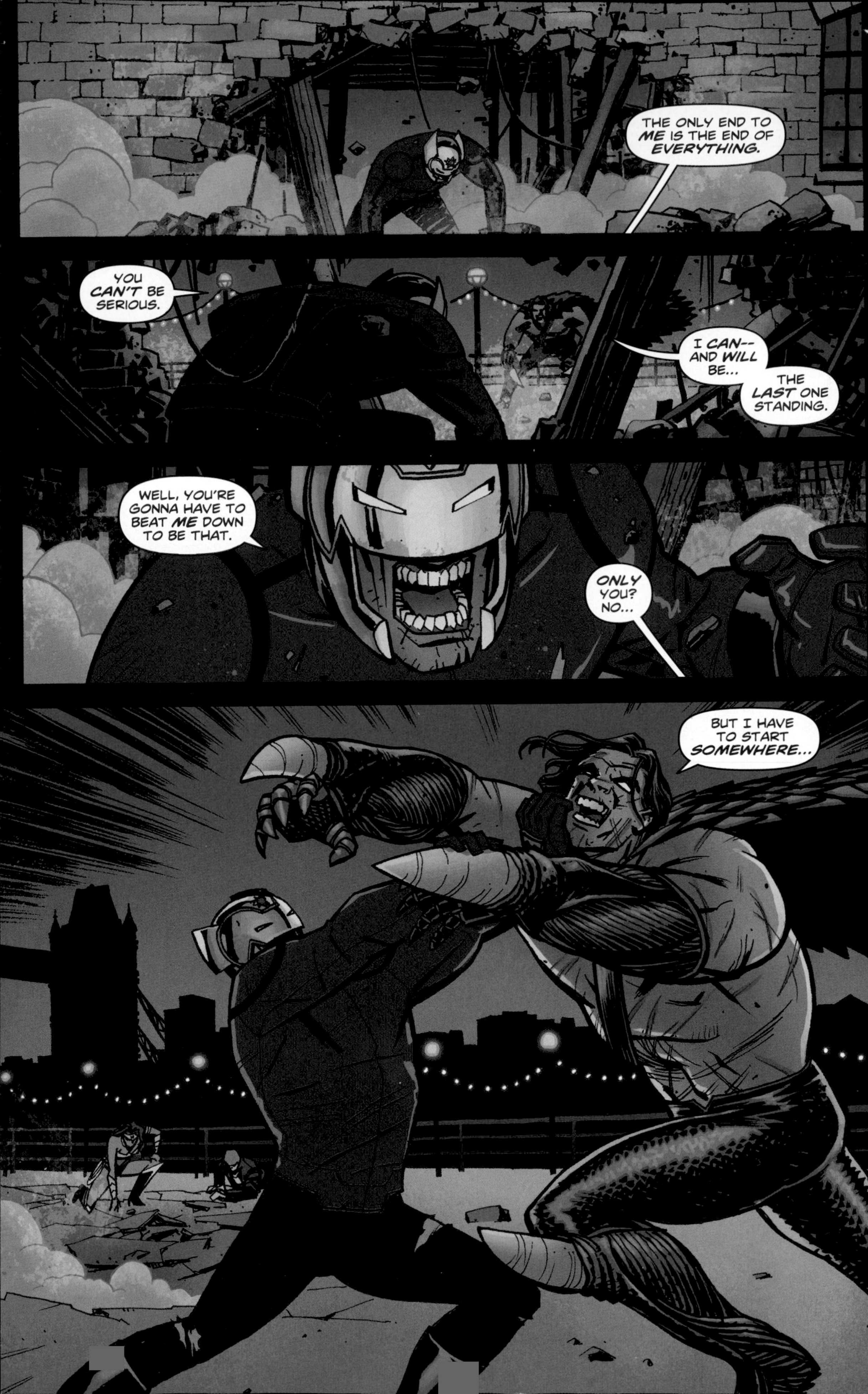
THE ONLY END TO ME IS THE END OF EVERYTHING.
YOU CAN'T BE SERIOUS.
I CAN-- AND WILL BE...
THE LAST ONE STANDING.
WELL, YOU'RE GONNA HAVE TO BEAT ME DOWN TO BE THAT.
ONLY YOU? NO...
BUT I HAVE TO START SOMEWHERE...

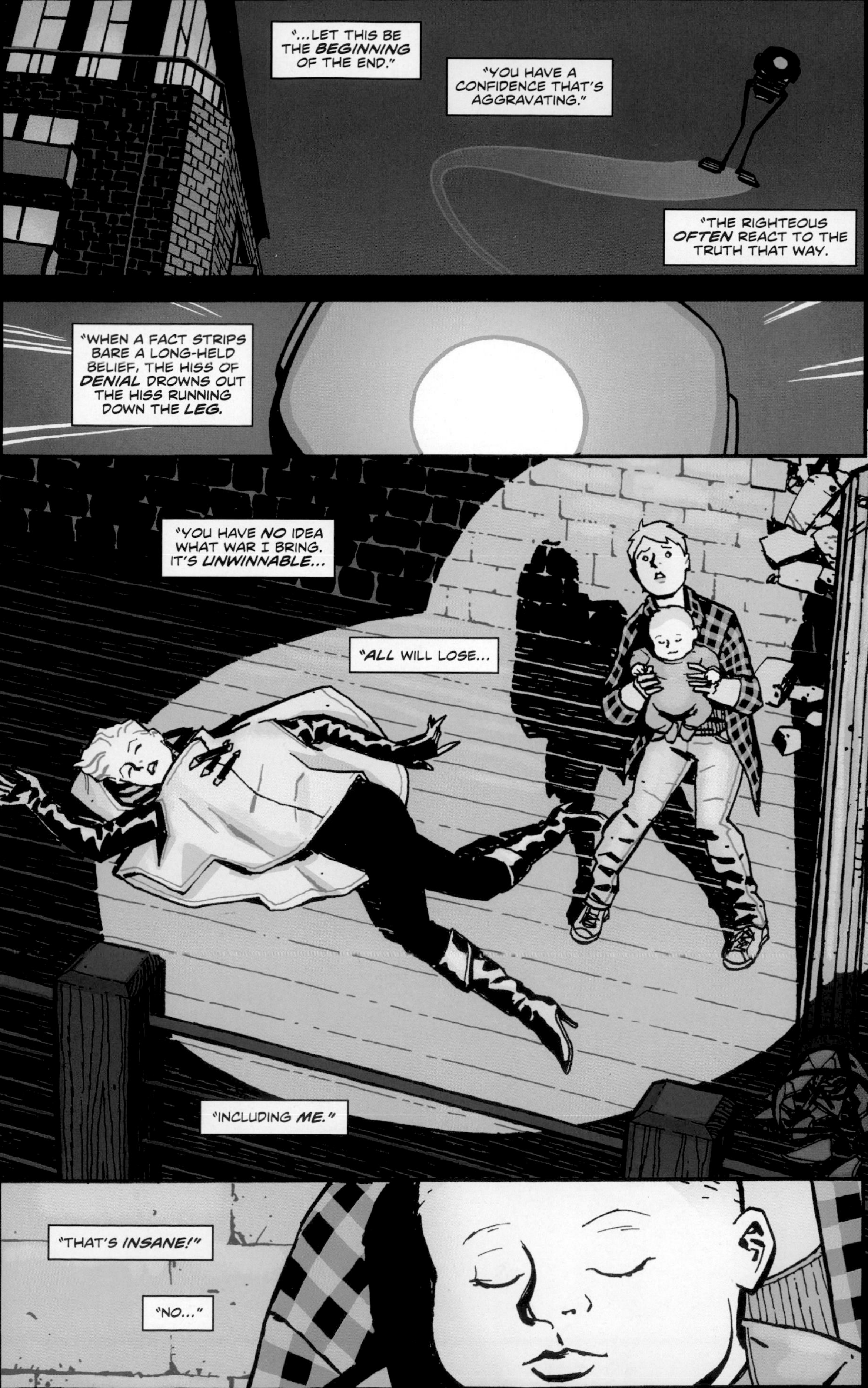
"...LET THIS BE THE BEGINNING OF THE END."
"YOU HAVE A CONFIDENCE THAT'S AGGRAVATING."
"THE RIGHTEOUS OFTEN REACT TO THE TRUTH THAT WAY.
"WHEN A FACT STRIPS BARE A LONG-HELD BELIEF, THE HISS OF DENIAL DROWNS OUT THE HISS RUNNING DOWN THE LEG.
"YOU HAVE NO IDEA WHAT WAR I BRING. IT'S UNWINNABLE...
"ALL WILL LOSE...
"INCLUDING ME."
"THAT'S INSANE!"
"NO..."

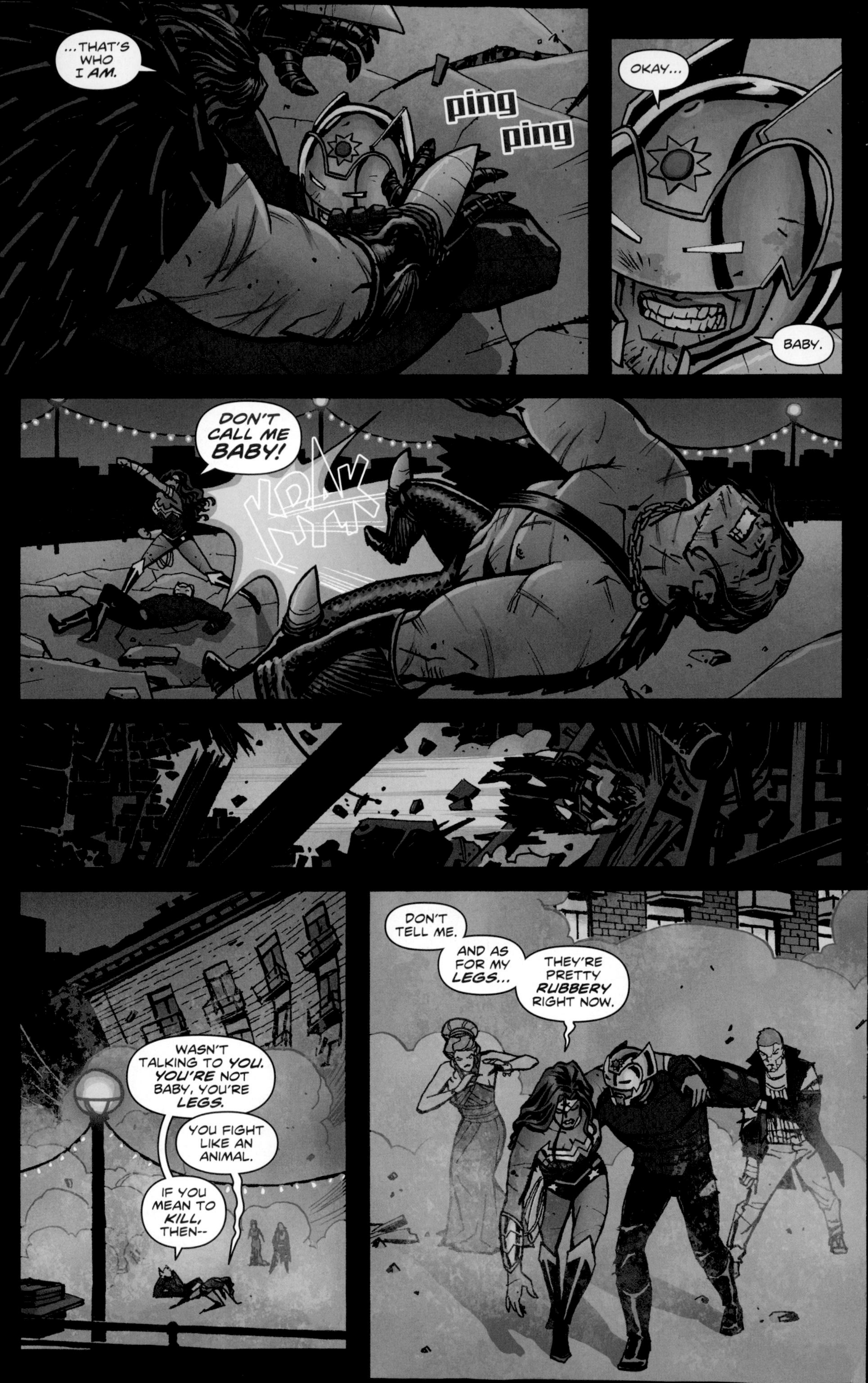
...THAT'S WHO I AM.
ping ping
OKAY...
BABY.
DON'T CALL ME BABY!
KRAKK
WASN'T TALKING TO YOU. YOU'RE NOT BABY, YOU'RE LEGS.
YOU FIGHT LIKE AN ANIMAL.
IF YOU MEAN TO KILL, THEN--
DON'T TELL ME.
AND AS FOR MY LEGS...
THEY'RE PRETTY RUBBERY RIGHT NOW.

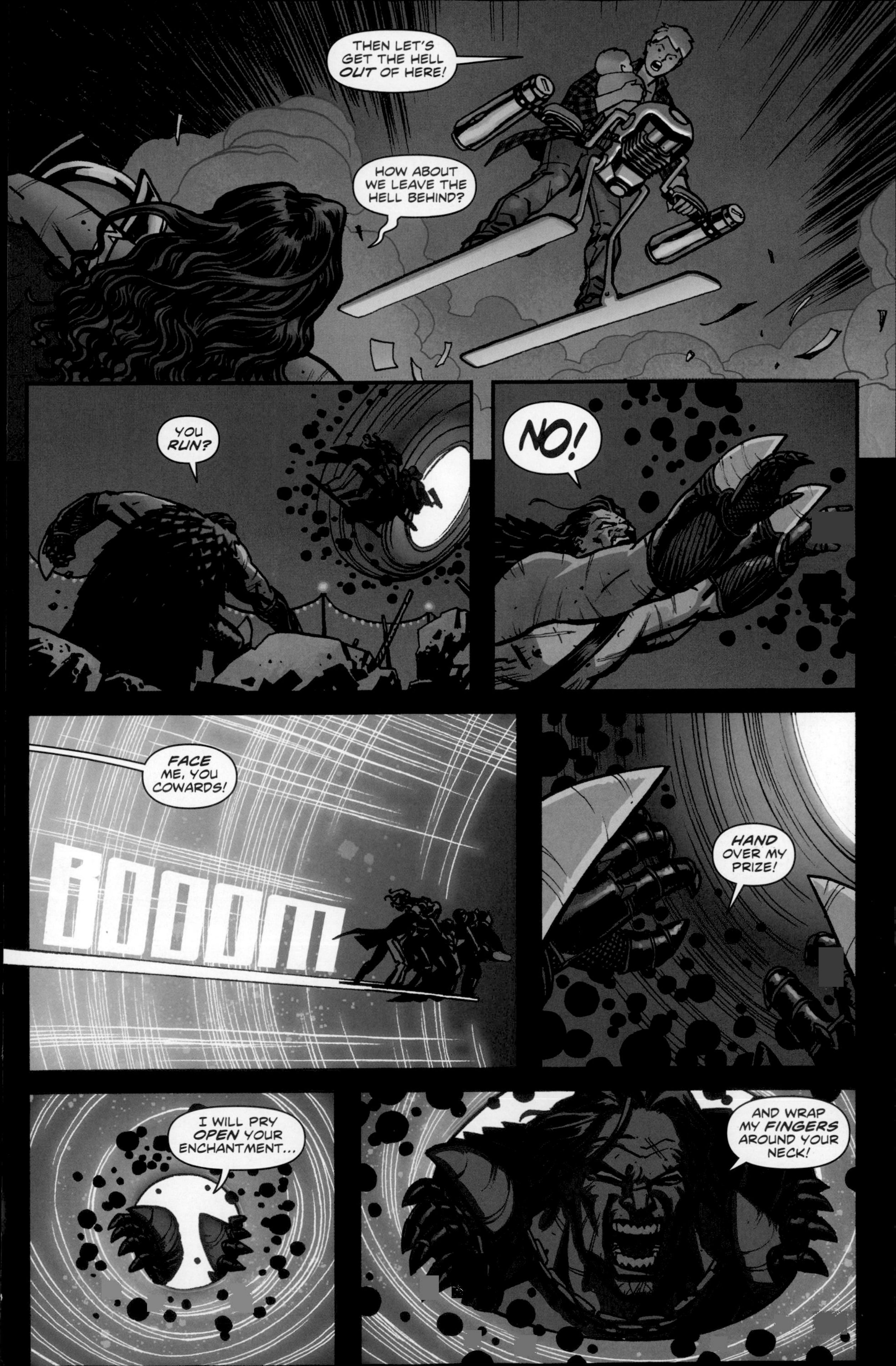
THEN LET'S GET THE HELL OUT OF HERE!
HOW ABOUT WE LEAVE THE HELL BEHIND?
YOU RUN?
NO!
FACE ME, YOU COWARDS!
BOOOM
HAND OVER MY PRIZE!
I WILL PRY OPEN YOUR ENCHANTMENT...
AND WRAP MY FINGERS AROUND YOUR NECK!

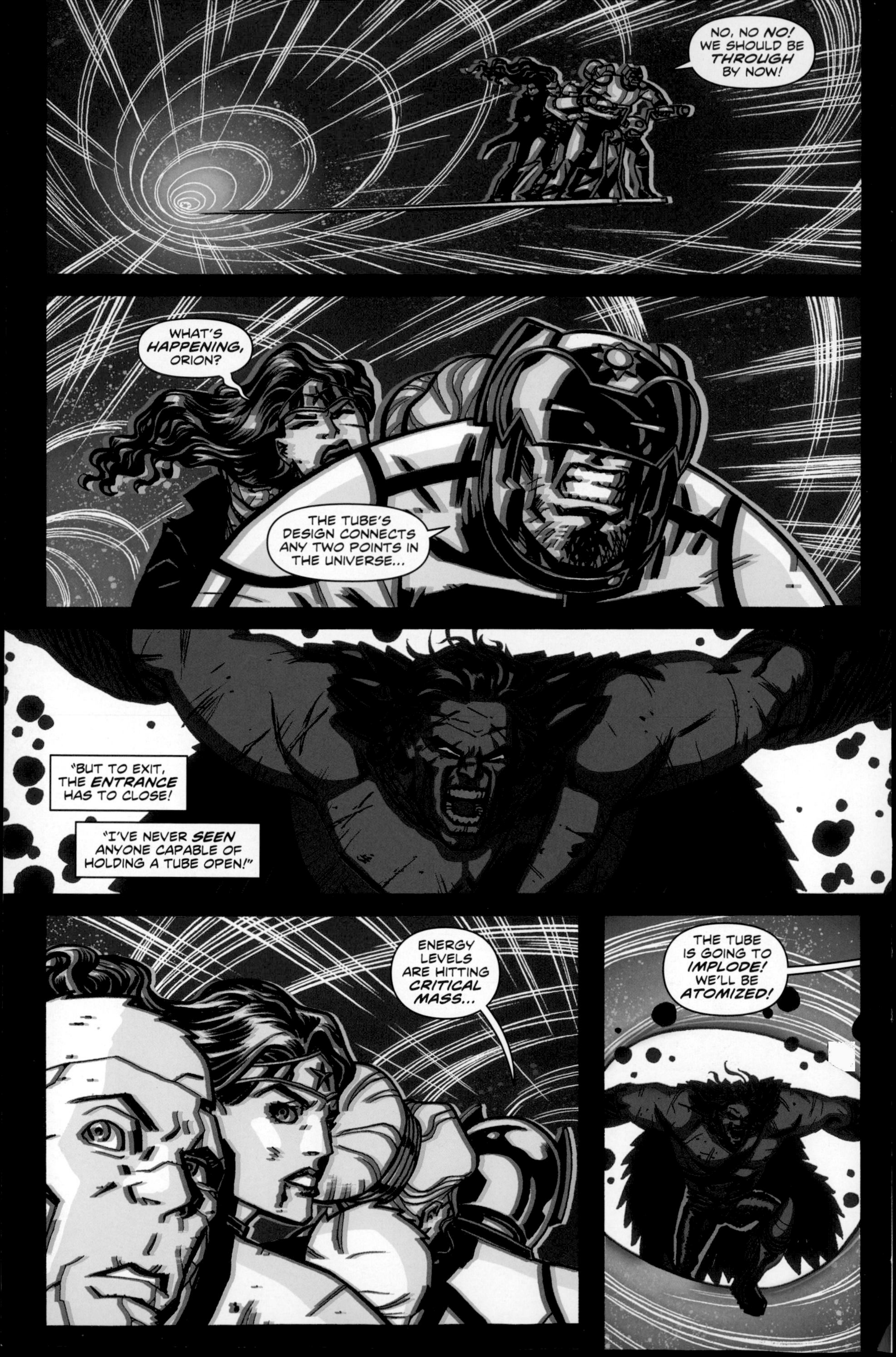
NO, NO NO! WE SHOULD BE THROUGH BY NOW!
WHAT'S HAPPENING, ORION?
THE TUBE'S DESIGN CONNECTS ANY TWO POINTS IN THE UNIVERSE...
"BUT TO EXIT, THE ENTRANCE HAS TO CLOSE!
"I'VE NEVER SEEN ANYONE CAPABLE OF HOLDING A TUBE OPEN!"
ENERGY LEVELS ARE HITTING CRITICAL MASS...
THE TUBE IS GOING TO IMPLODE! WE'LL BE ATOMIZED!

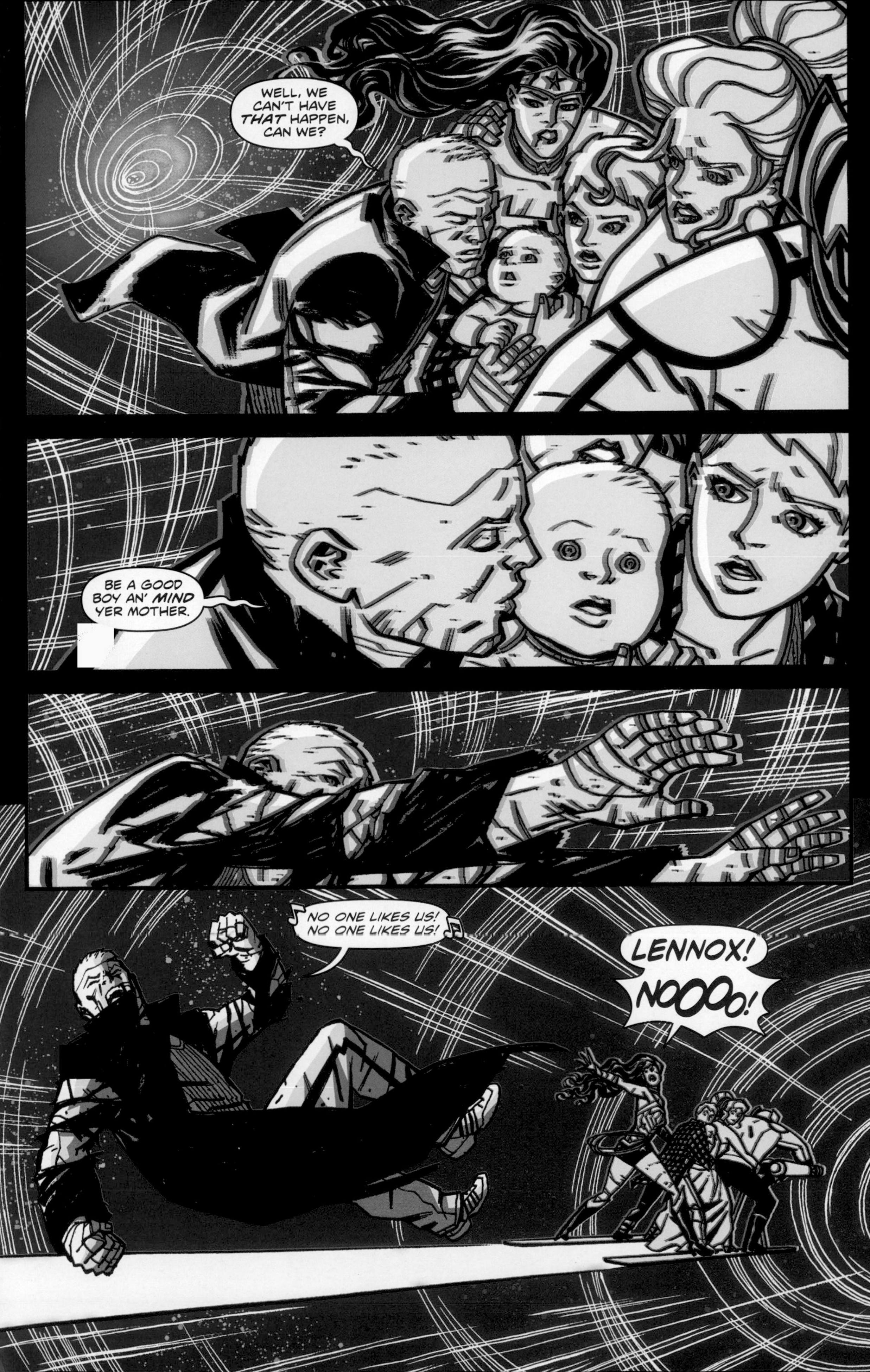
WELL, WE CAN'T HAVE THAT HAPPEN, CAN WE?
BE A GOOD BOY AN' MIND YER MOTHER.
NO ONE LIKES US! NO ONE LIKES US!
LENNOX! NOOOo!

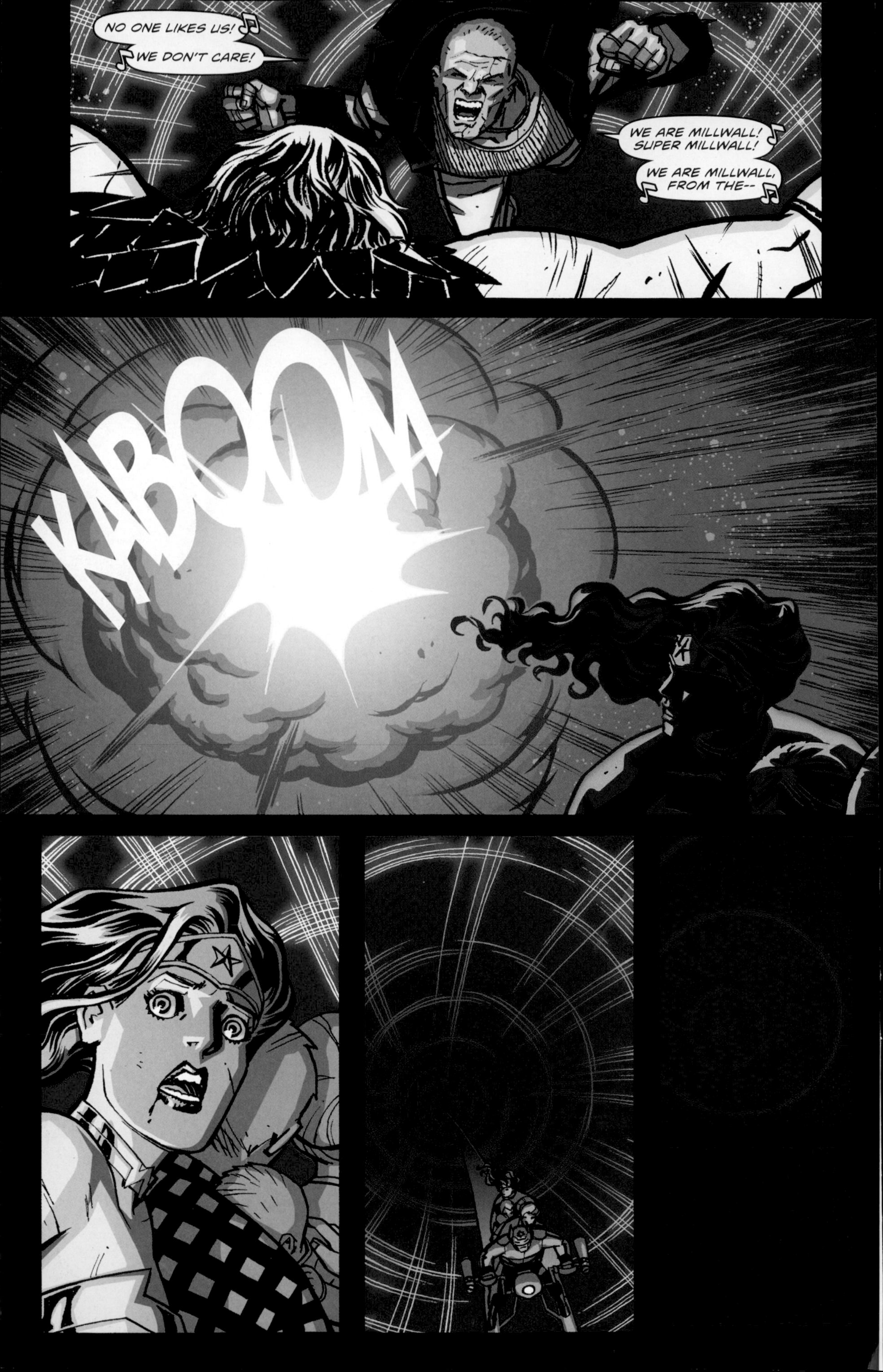
NO ONE LIKES US!
WE DON'T CARE!
WE ARE MILLWALL! SUPER MILLWALL!
WE ARE MILLWALL, FROM THE--
KABOOM

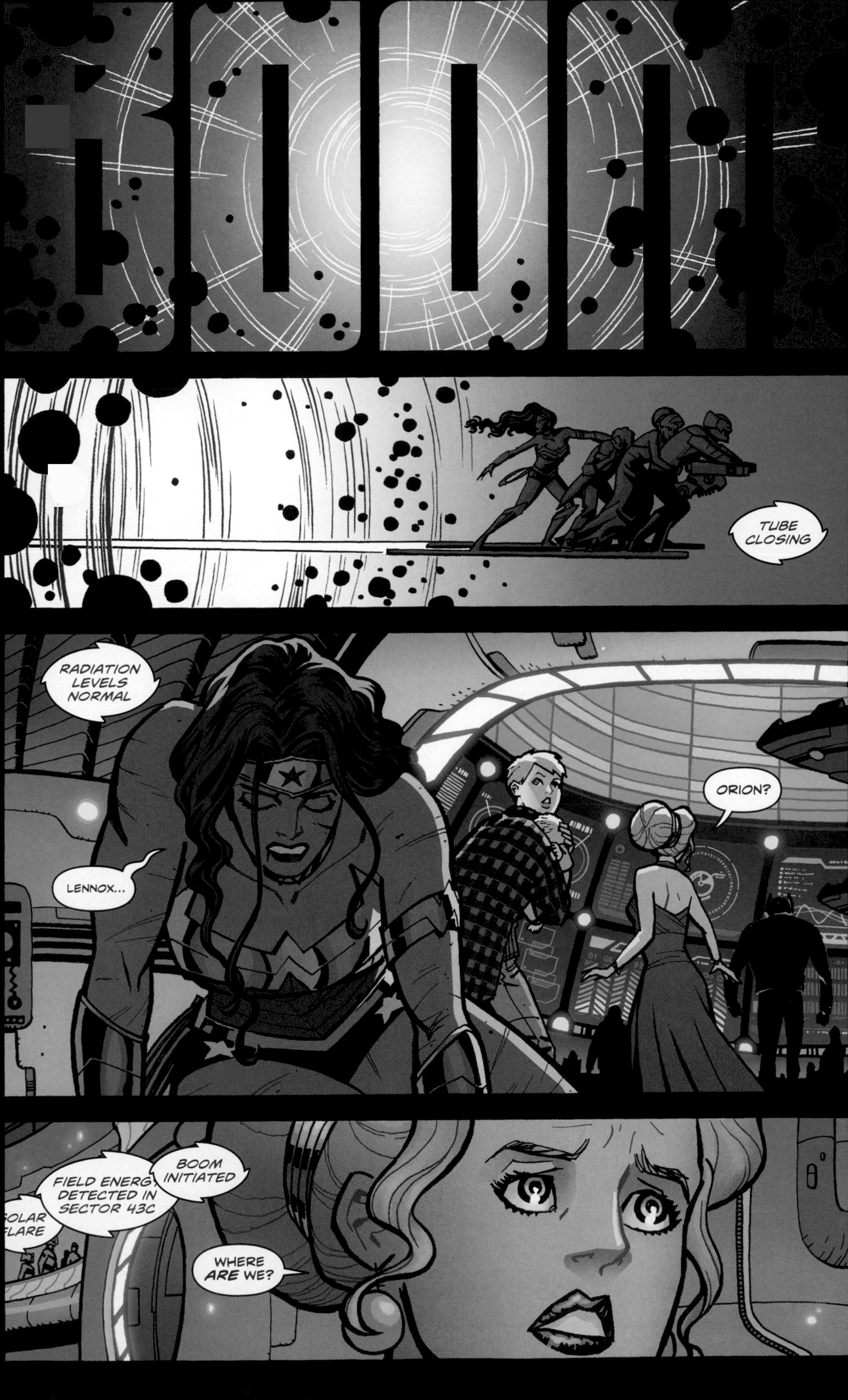
TUBE CLOSING
RADIATION LEVELS NORMAL
LENNOX...
ORION?
SOLAR FLARE
FIELD ENERG DETECTED IN SECTOR 43C
BOOM INITIATED
WHERE *ARE* WE?

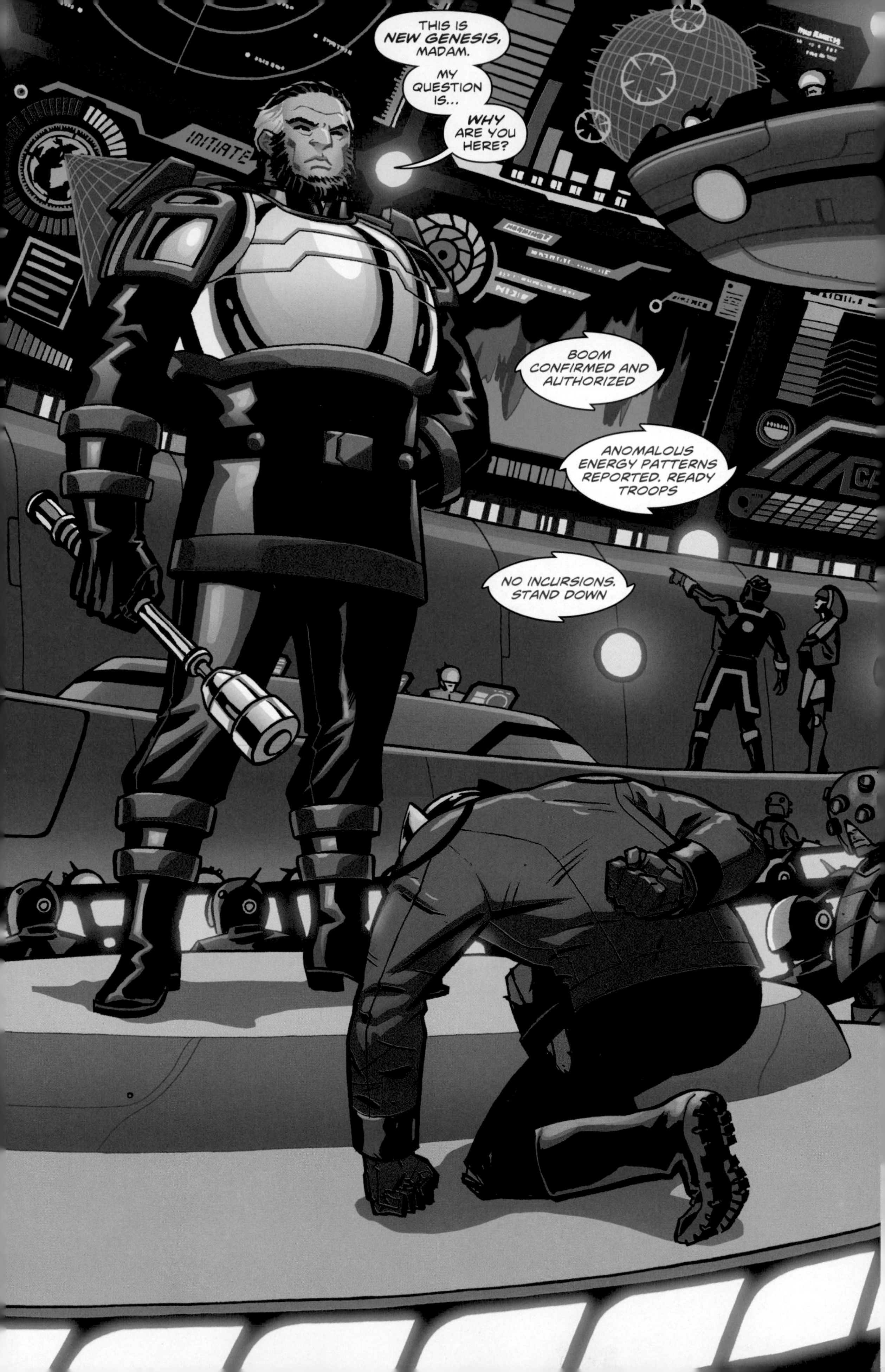
THIS IS NEW GENESIS, MADAM.
MY QUESTION IS...
WHY ARE YOU HERE?
BOOM CONFIRMED AND AUTHORIZED
ANOMALOUS ENERGY PATTERNS REPORTED. READY TROOPS
NO INCURSIONS. STAND DOWN

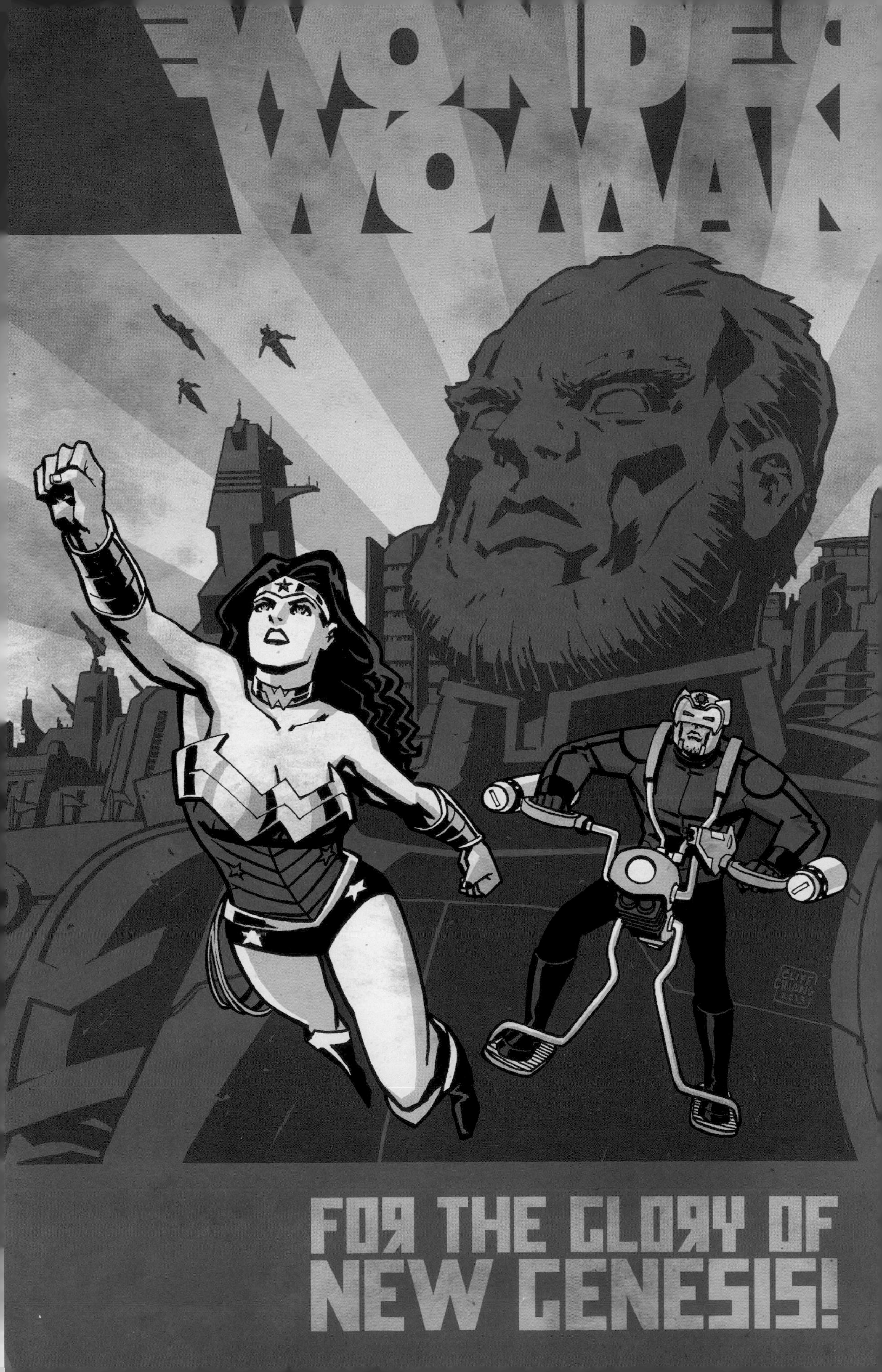
WONDER WOMAN
CLIFF CHIANG 2013
FOR THE GLORY OF
NEW GENESIS!

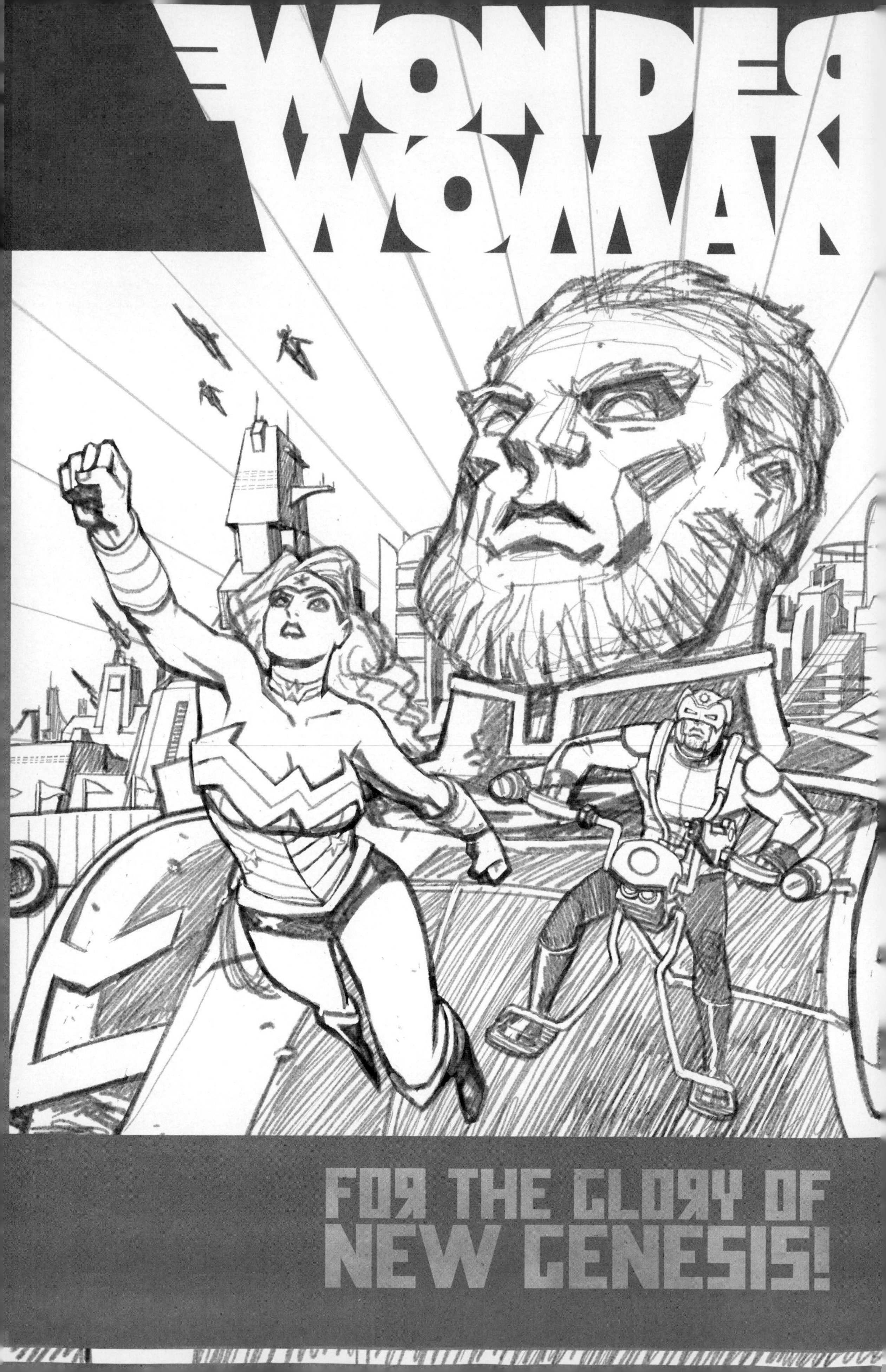
WONDER WOMAN
FOR THE GLORY OF
NEW GENESIS!

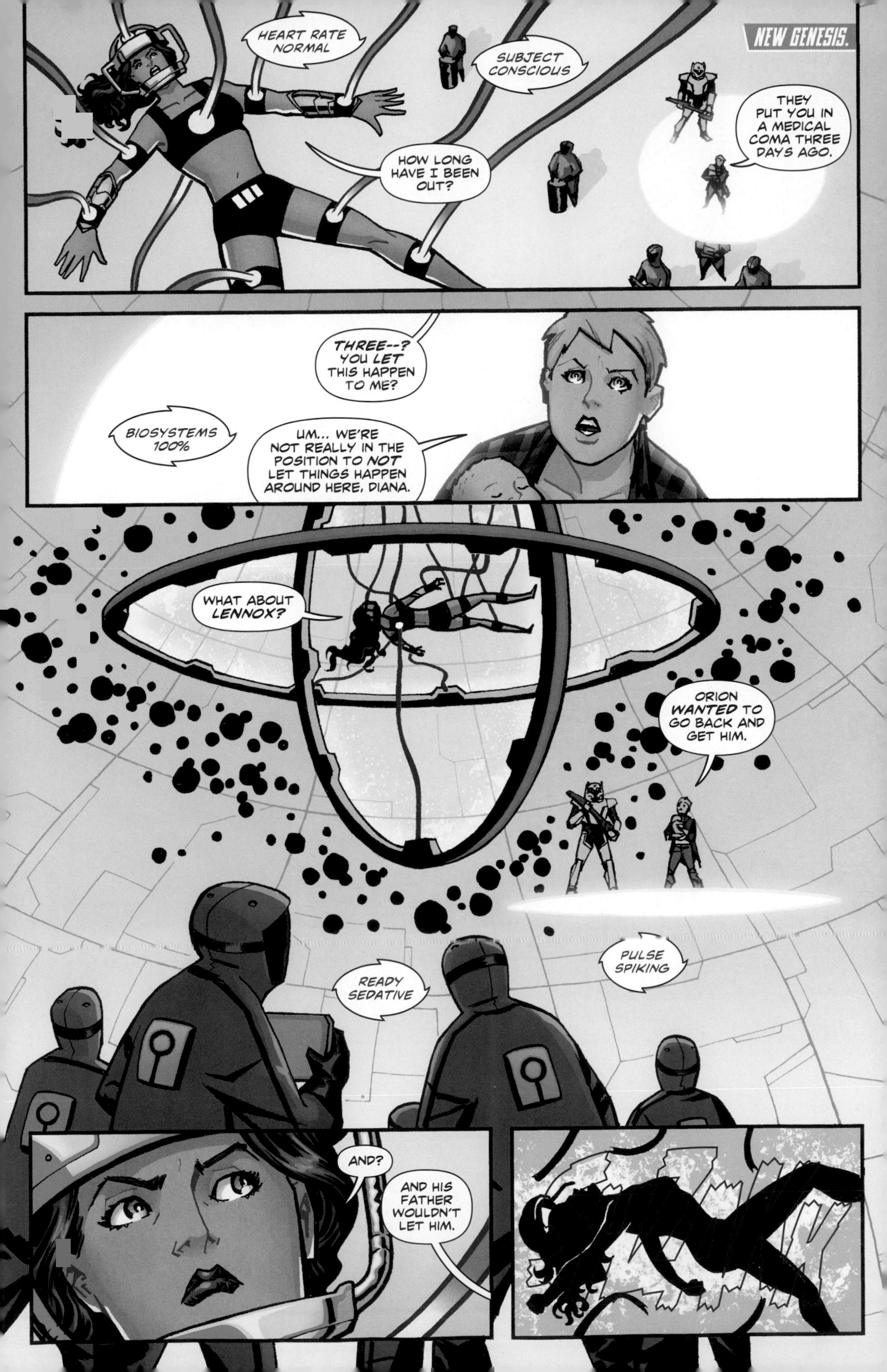
NEW GENESIS.
HEART RATE NORMAL
SUBJECT CONSCIOUS
HOW LONG HAVE I BEEN OUT?
THEY PUT YOU IN A MEDICAL COMA THREE DAYS AGO.
THREE--? YOU LET THIS HAPPEN TO ME?
BIOSYSTEMS 100%
UM... WE'RE NOT REALLY IN THE POSITION TO NOT LET THINGS HAPPEN AROUND HERE, DIANA.
WHAT ABOUT LENNOX?
ORION WANTED TO GO BACK AND GET HIM.
READY SEDATIVE
PULSE SPIKING
AND?
AND HIS FATHER WOULDN'T LET HIM.

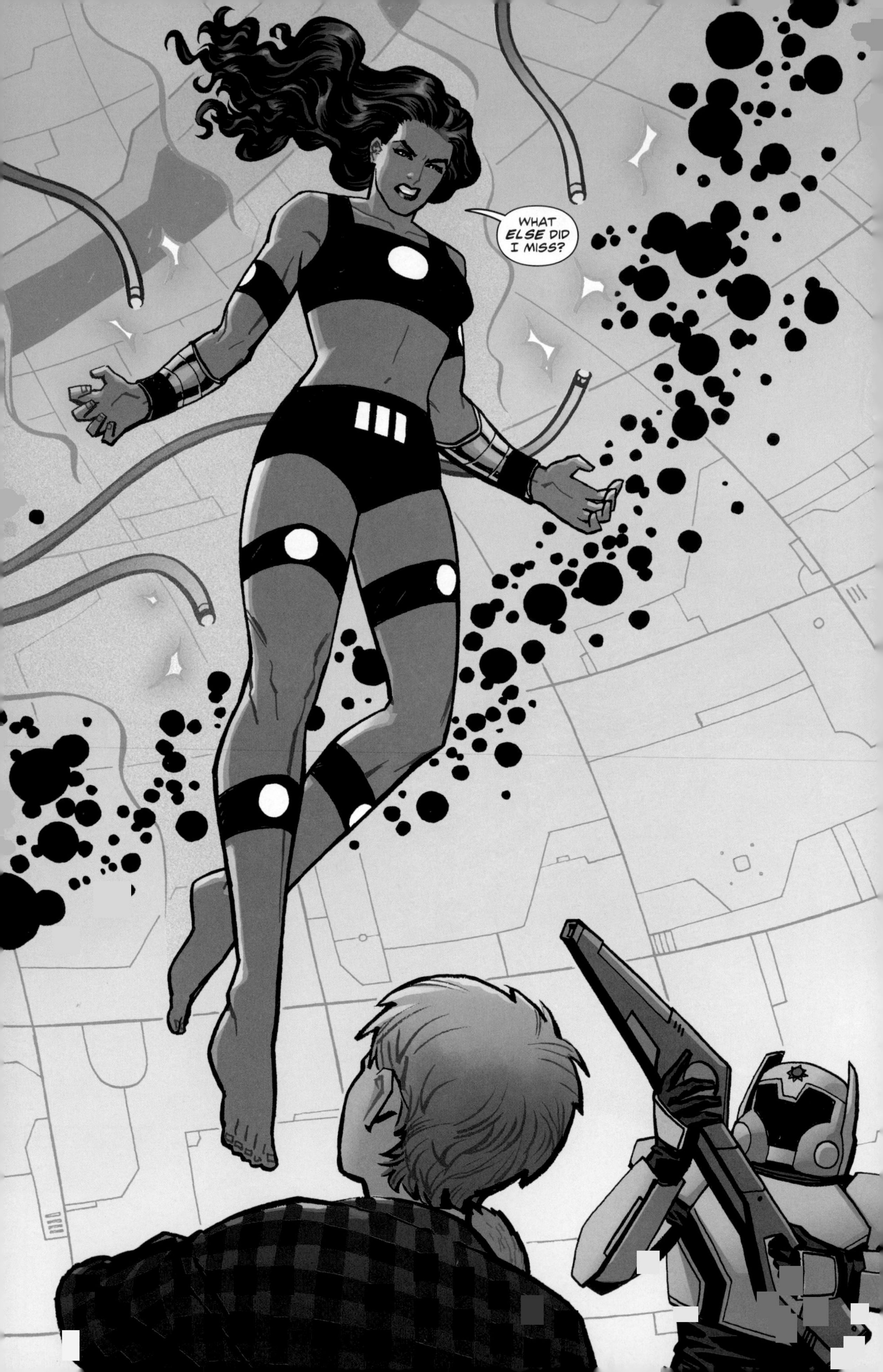
WHAT ELSE DID I MISS?

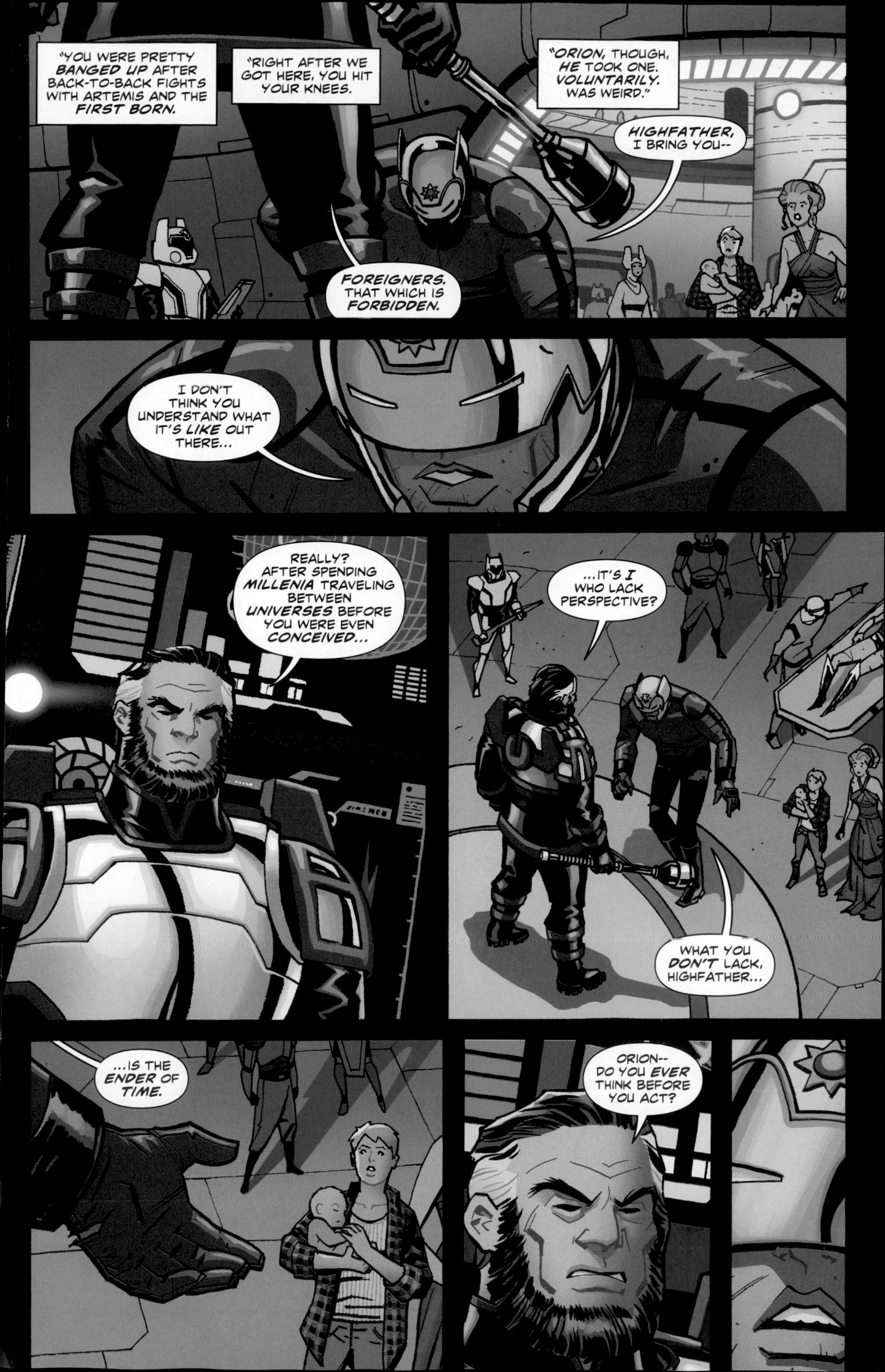
"YOU WERE PRETTY BANGED UP AFTER BACK-TO-BACK FIGHTS WITH ARTEMIS AND THE FIRST BORN.
"RIGHT AFTER WE GOT HERE, YOU HIT YOUR KNEES.
"ORION, THOUGH, HE TOOK ONE. VOLUNTARILY. WAS WEIRD."
HIGHFATHER, I BRING YOU--
FOREIGNERS. THAT WHICH IS FORBIDDEN.
I DON'T THINK YOU UNDERSTAND WHAT IT'S LIKE OUT THERE...
REALLY? AFTER SPENDING MILLENIA TRAVELING BETWEEN UNIVERSES BEFORE YOU WERE EVEN CONCEIVED...
...IT'S I WHO LACK PERSPECTIVE?
WHAT YOU DON'T LACK, HIGHFATHER...
...IS THE ENDER OF TIME.
ORION-- DO YOU EVER THINK BEFORE YOU ACT?

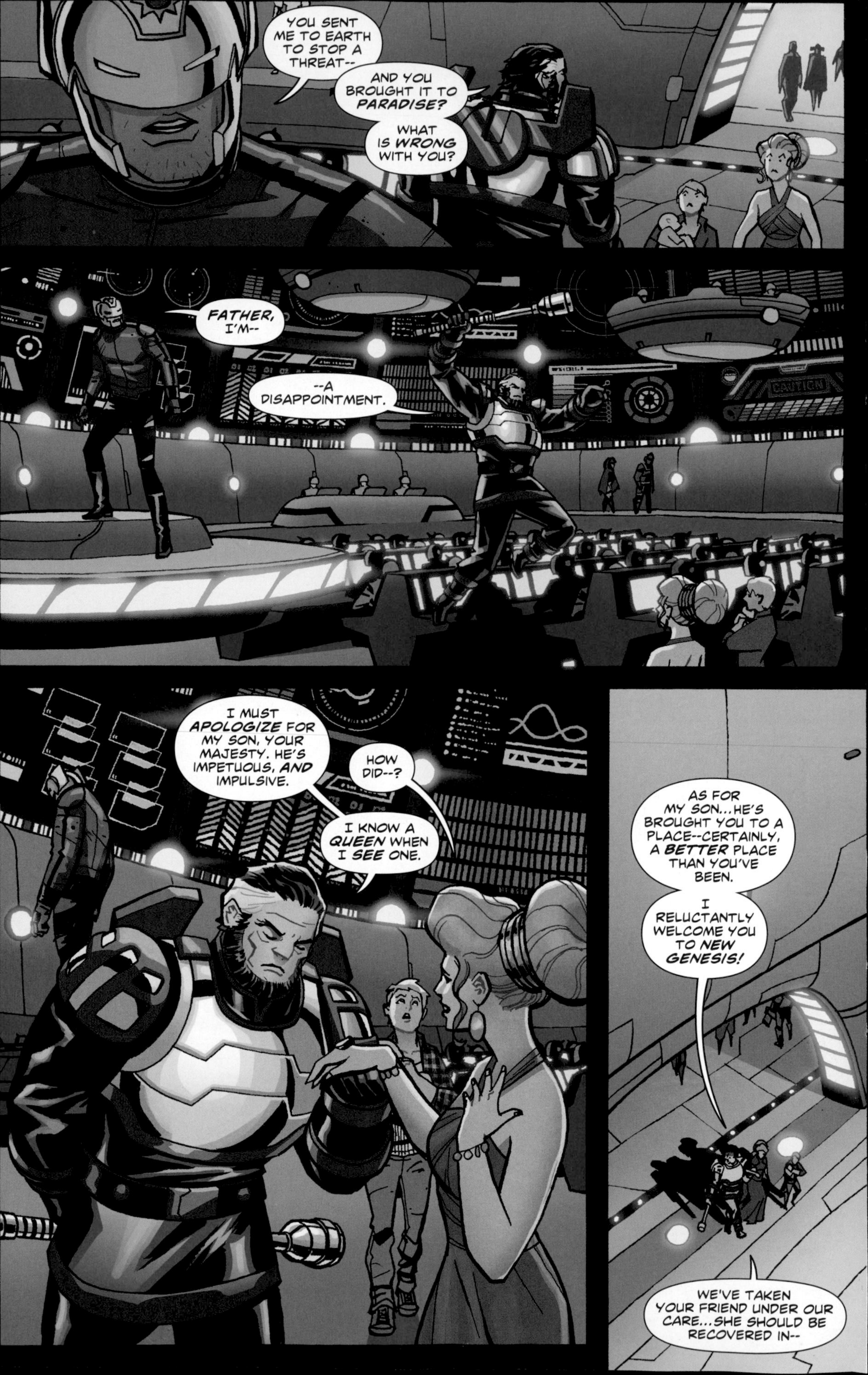
YOU SENT ME TO EARTH TO STOP A THREAT--
AND YOU BROUGHT IT TO PARADISE?
WHAT IS WRONG WITH YOU?
FATHER, I'M--
--A DISAPPOINTMENT.
CAUTION
I MUST APOLOGIZE FOR MY SON, YOUR MAJESTY. HE'S IMPETUOUS, AND IMPULSIVE.
HOW DID--?
I KNOW A QUEEN WHEN I SEE ONE.
AS FOR MY SON...HE'S BROUGHT YOU TO A PLACE--CERTAINLY, A BETTER PLACE THAN YOU'VE BEEN.
I RELUCTANTLY WELCOME YOU TO NEW GENESIS!
WE'VE TAKEN YOUR FRIEND UNDER OUR CARE...SHE SHOULD BE RECOVERED IN--

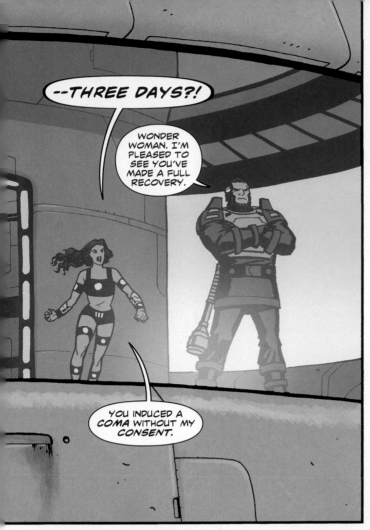

--THREE DAYS?!

WONDER WOMAN, I'M PLEASED TO SEE YOU'VE MADE A FULL RECOVERY.

YOU INDUCED A COMA WITHOUT MY CONSENT.

I APOLOGIZE...

FOR SAVING YOUR LIFE.

I'M SORRY. I AM GRATEFUL.

YOUR INTERNAL WOUNDS WERE SEVERE.

WHAT IS THIS PLACE?

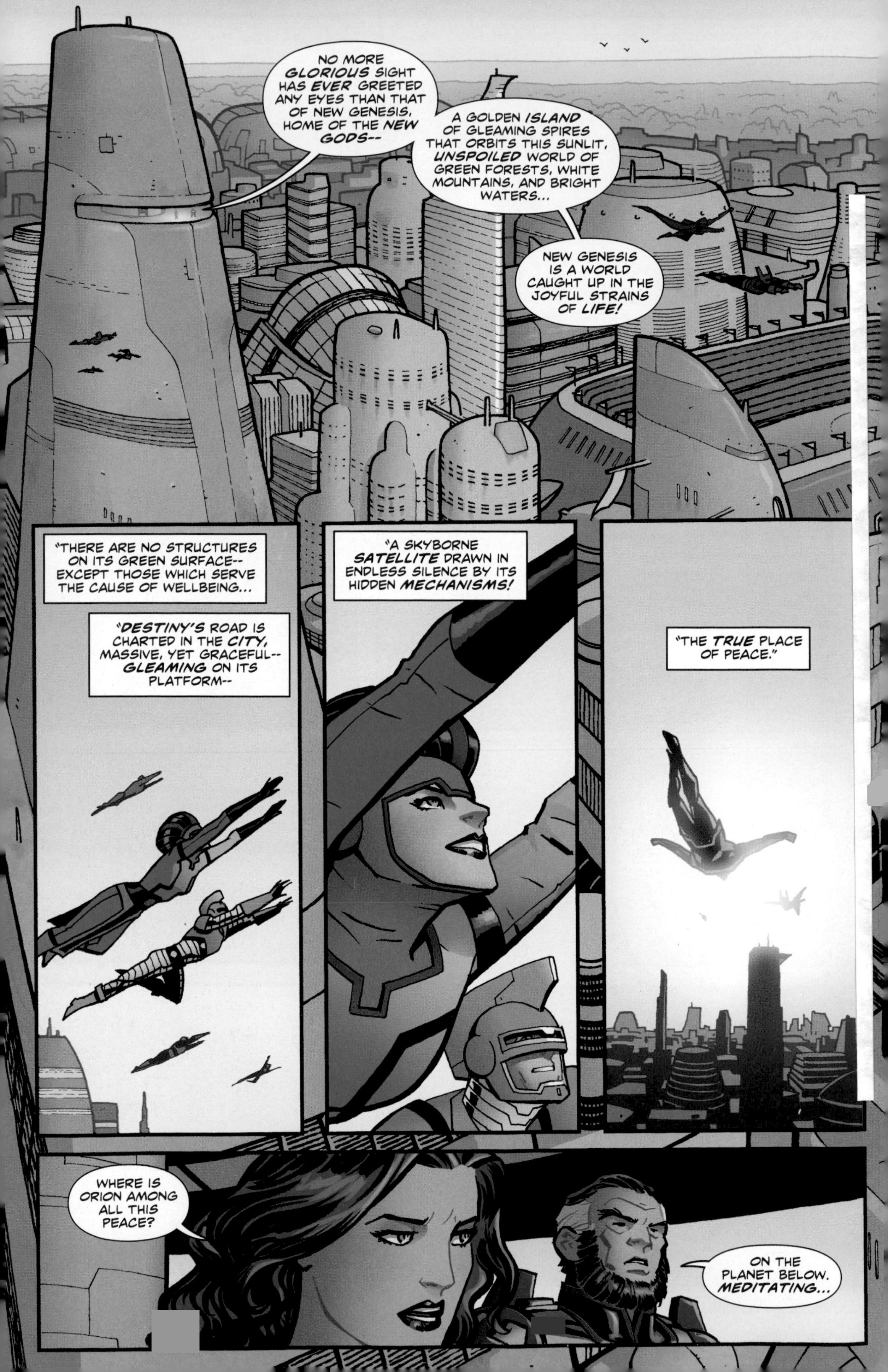
NO MORE GLORIOUS SIGHT HAS EVER GREETED ANY EYES THAN THAT OF NEW GENESIS, HOME OF THE NEW GODS--
A GOLDEN ISLAND OF GLEAMING SPIRES THAT ORBITS THIS SUNLIT, UNSPOILED WORLD OF GREEN FORESTS, WHITE MOUNTAINS, AND BRIGHT WATERS...
NEW GENESIS IS A WORLD CAUGHT UP IN THE JOYFUL STRAINS OF LIFE!
"THERE ARE NO STRUCTURES ON ITS GREEN SURFACE-- EXCEPT THOSE WHICH SERVE THE CAUSE OF WELLBEING...
"DESTINY'S ROAD IS CHARTED IN THE CITY, MASSIVE, YET GRACEFUL-- GLEAMING ON ITS PLATFORM--
"A SKYBORNE SATELLITE DRAWN IN ENDLESS SILENCE BY ITS HIDDEN MECHANISMS!
"THE TRUE PLACE OF PEACE."
WHERE IS ORION AMONG ALL THIS PEACE?
ON THE PLANET BELOW. MEDITATING...

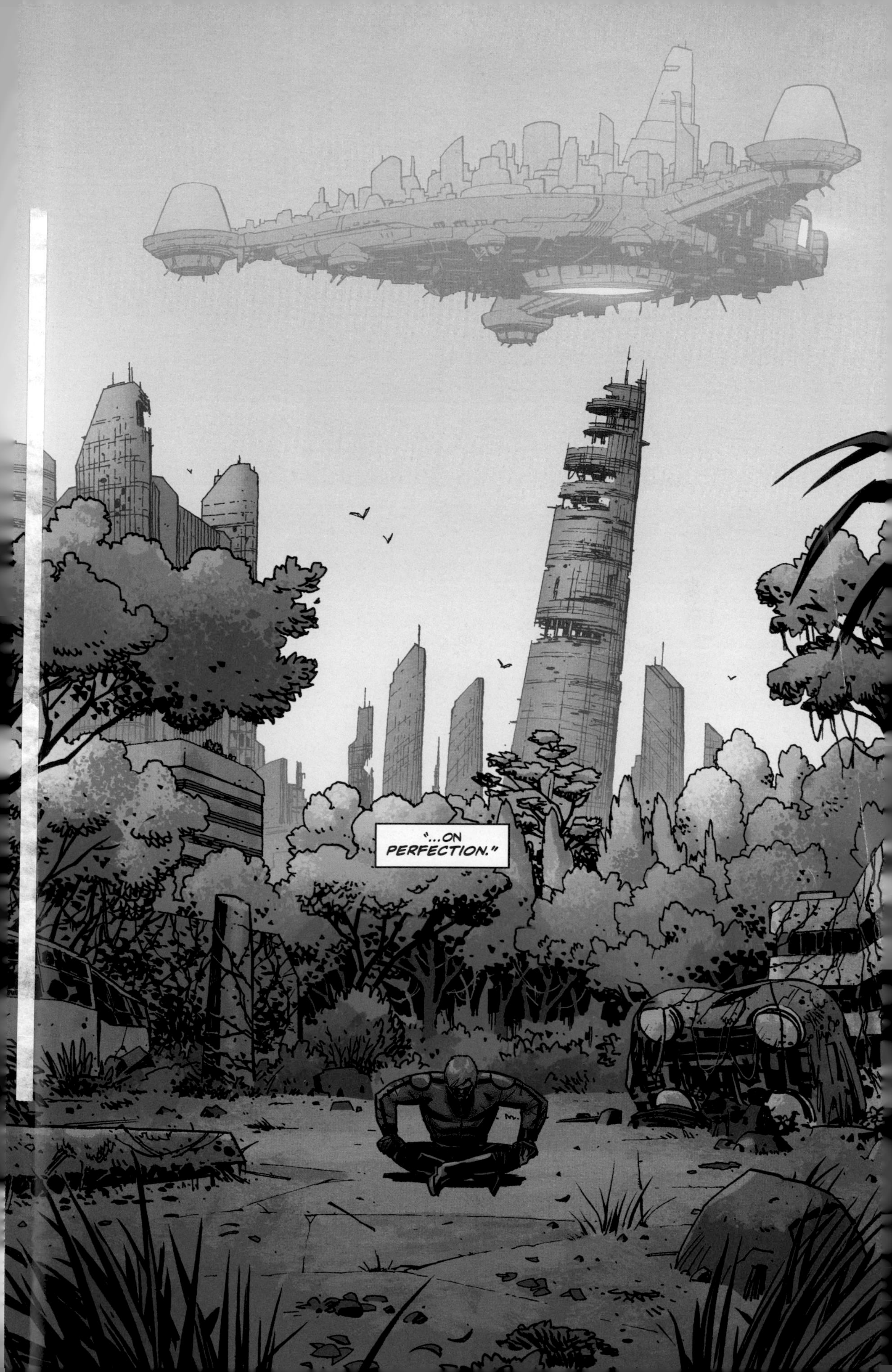
"...ON PERFECTION."

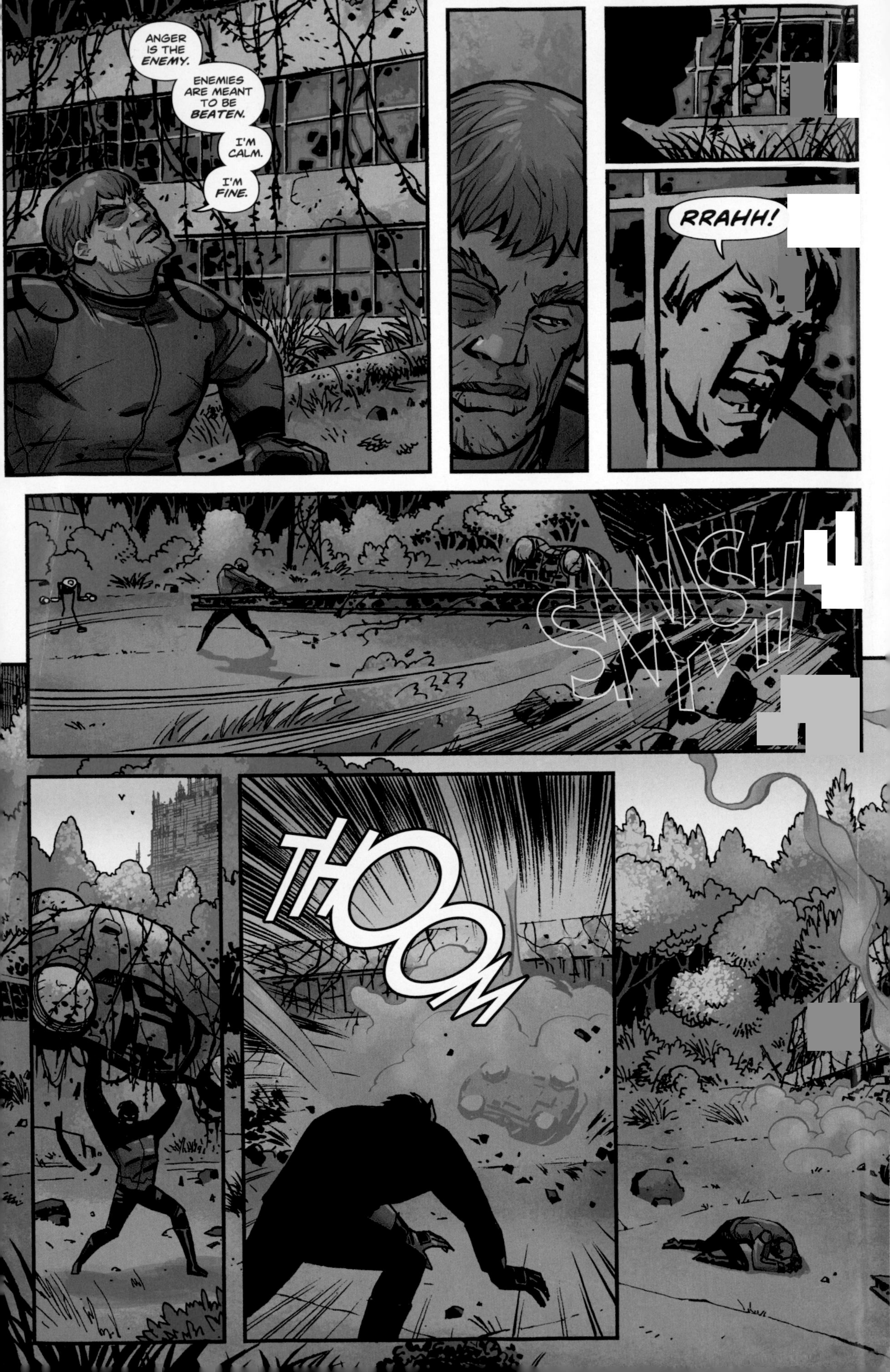
ANGER IS THE ENEMY.
ENEMIES ARE MEANT TO BE BEATEN.
I'M CALM.
I'M FINE.
RRAHH!
SWISH
THOOM

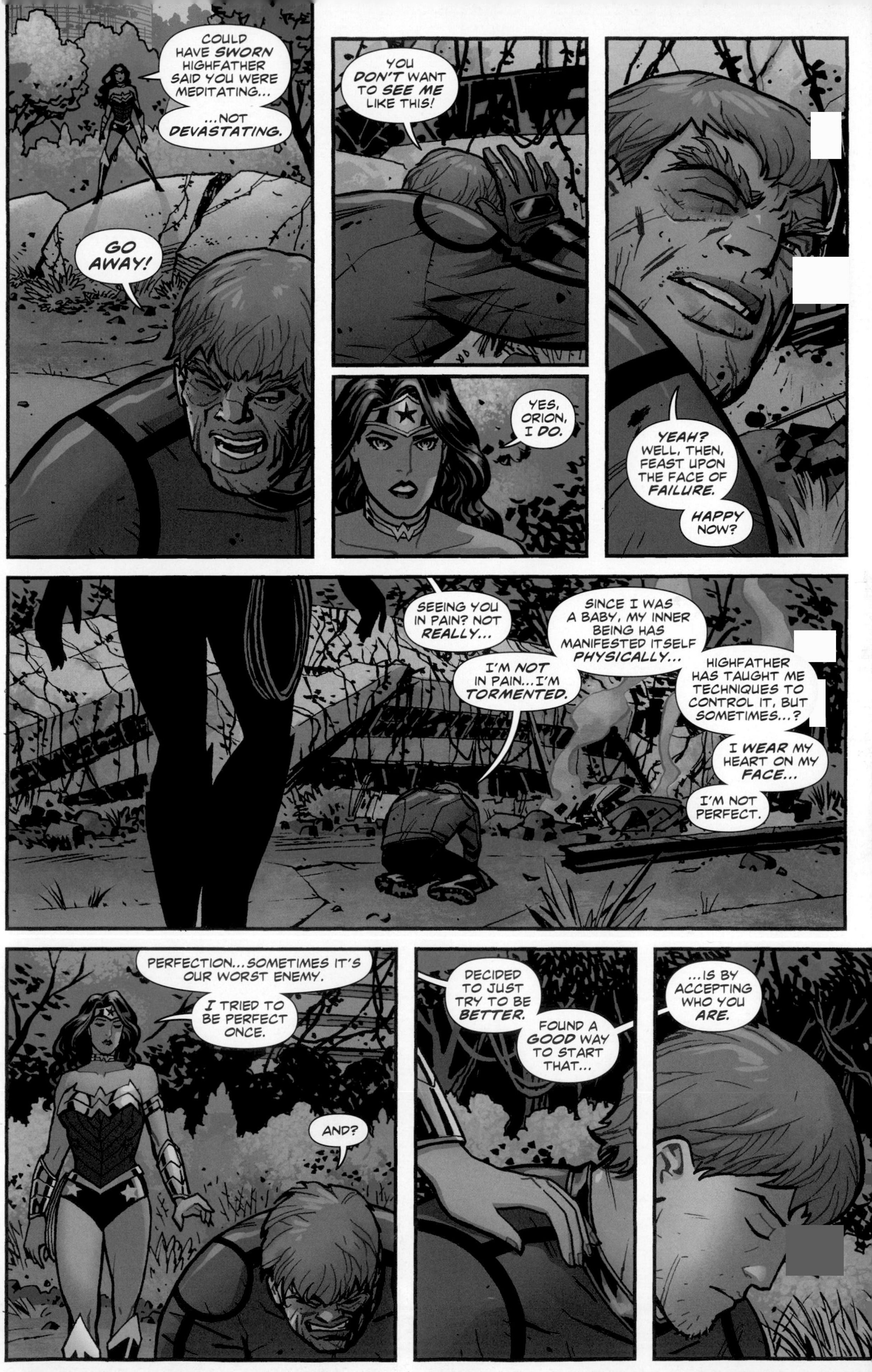
COULD HAVE SWORN HIGHFATHER SAID YOU WERE MEDITATING...
...NOT DEVASTATING.
GO AWAY!
YOU DON'T WANT TO SEE ME LIKE THIS!
YES, ORION, I DO.
YEAH? WELL, THEN, FEAST UPON THE FACE OF FAILURE.
HAPPY NOW?
SEEING YOU IN PAIN? NOT REALLY...
I'M NOT IN PAIN...I'M TORMENTED.
SINCE I WAS A BABY, MY INNER BEING HAS MANIFESTED ITSELF PHYSICALLY...
HIGHFATHER HAS TAUGHT ME TECHNIQUES TO CONTROL IT, BUT SOMETIMES...?
I WEAR MY HEART ON MY FACE...
I'M NOT PERFECT.
PERFECTION...SOMETIMES IT'S OUR WORST ENEMY.
I TRIED TO BE PERFECT ONCE.
AND?
DECIDED TO JUST TRY TO BE BETTER.
FOUND A GOOD WAY TO START THAT...
...IS BY ACCEPTING WHO YOU ARE.

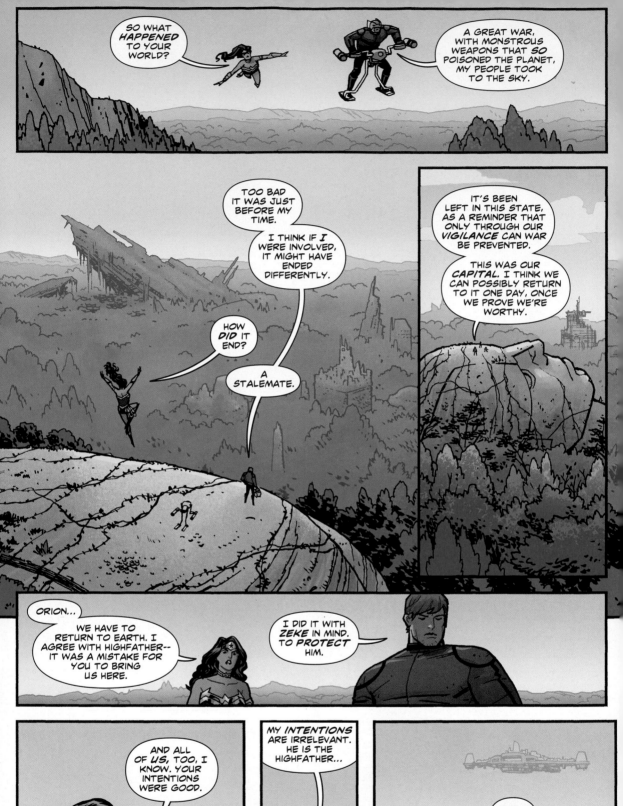

SO WHAT *HAPPENED* TO YOUR WORLD?

A GREAT WAR, WITH MONSTROUS WEAPONS THAT *SO* POISONED THE PLANET, MY PEOPLE TOOK TO THE SKY.

TOO BAD IT WAS JUST BEFORE MY TIME.

I THINK IF *I* WERE INVOLVED, IT MIGHT HAVE ENDED DIFFERENTLY.

HOW *DID* IT END?

A STALEMATE.

IT'S BEEN LEFT IN THIS STATE, AS A REMINDER THAT ONLY THROUGH OUR *VIGILANCE* CAN WAR BE PREVENTED.

THIS WAS OUR *CAPITAL.* I THINK WE CAN POSSIBLY RETURN TO IT ONE DAY, ONCE WE PROVE WE'RE WORTHY.

ORION...

WE HAVE TO RETURN TO EARTH. I AGREE WITH HIGHFATHER-- IT WAS A MISTAKE FOR YOU TO BRING US HERE.

I DID IT WITH *ZEKE* IN MIND. TO *PROTECT* HIM.

AND ALL OF *US,* TOO, I KNOW. YOUR INTENTIONS WERE GOOD.

MY *INTENTIONS* ARE IRRELEVANT. HE IS THE HIGHFATHER...

AND I AM HIS SON.

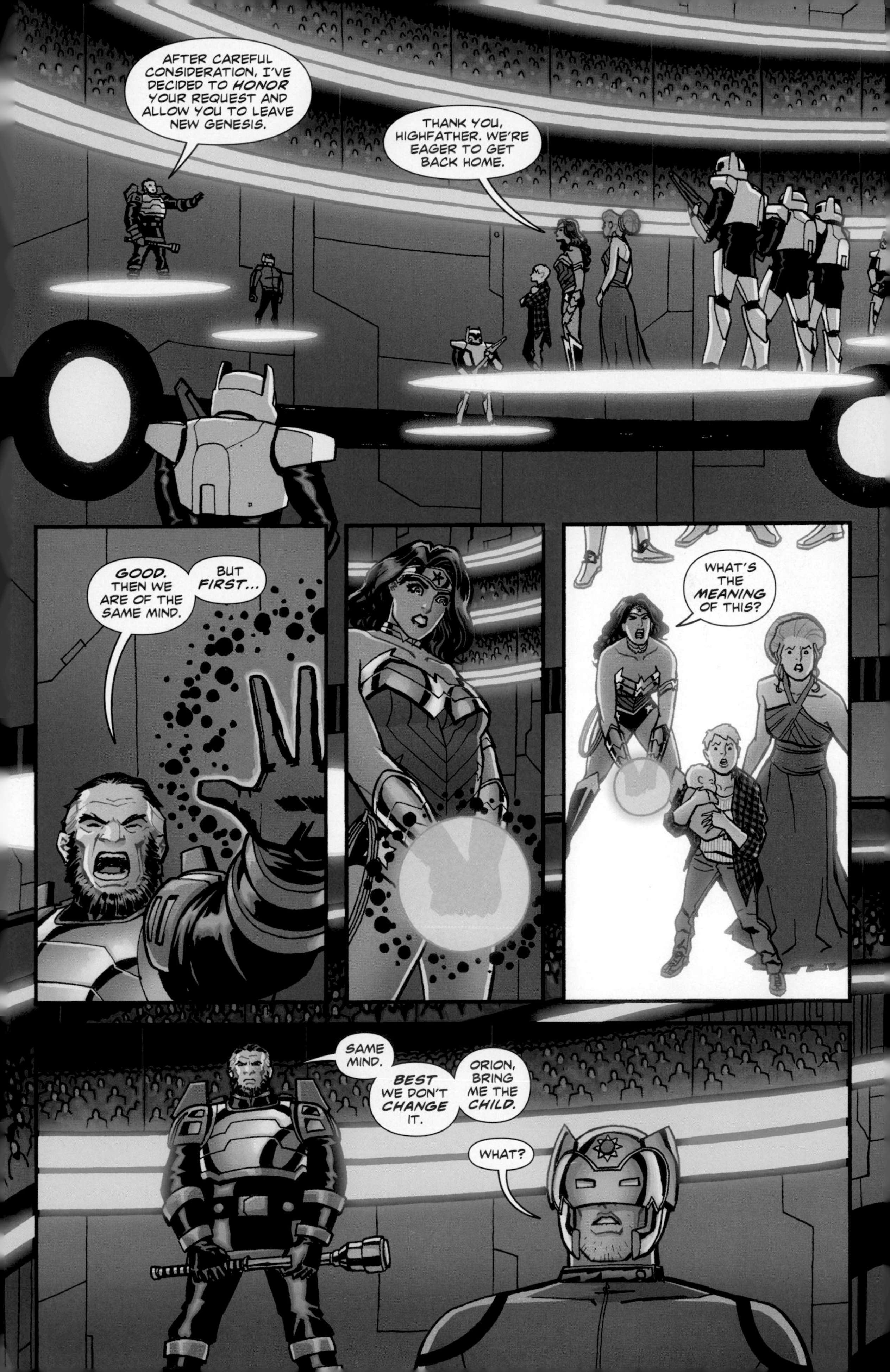
AFTER CAREFUL CONSIDERATION, I'VE DECIDED TO HONOR YOUR REQUEST AND ALLOW YOU TO LEAVE NEW GENESIS.
THANK YOU, HIGHFATHER. WE'RE EAGER TO GET BACK HOME.
GOOD. THEN WE ARE OF THE SAME MIND.
BUT FIRST...
WHAT'S THE MEANING OF THIS?
SAME MIND.
BEST WE DON'T CHANGE IT.
ORION, BRING ME THE CHILD.
WHAT?

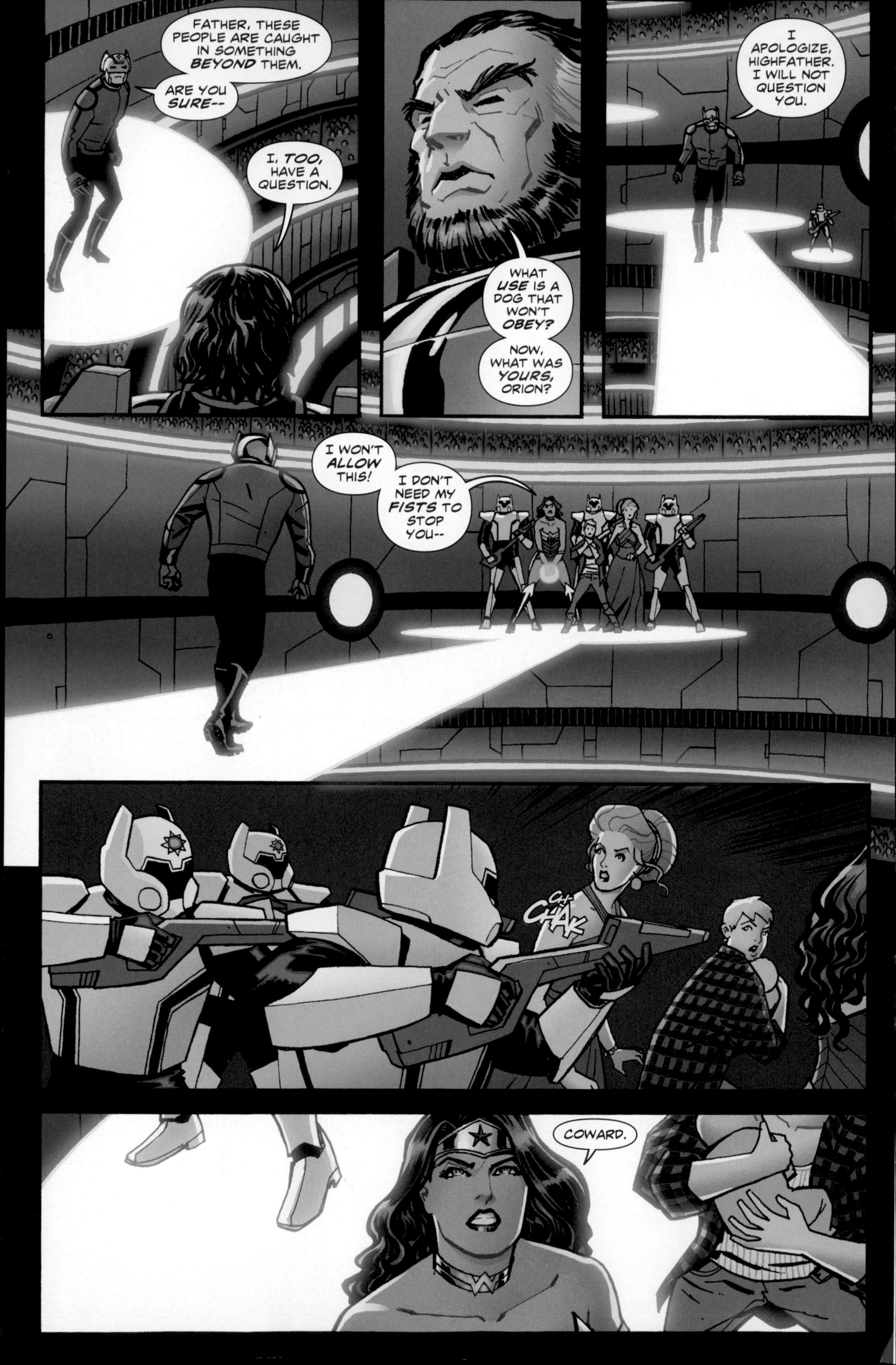
FATHER, THESE PEOPLE ARE CAUGHT IN SOMETHING BEYOND THEM.
ARE YOU SURE--
I, TOO, HAVE A QUESTION.
WHAT USE IS A DOG THAT WON'T OBEY?
NOW, WHAT WAS YOURS, ORION?
I APOLOGIZE, HIGHFATHER. I WILL NOT QUESTION YOU.
I WON'T ALLOW THIS!
I DON'T NEED MY FISTS TO STOP YOU--
CH-CHAK
COWARD.

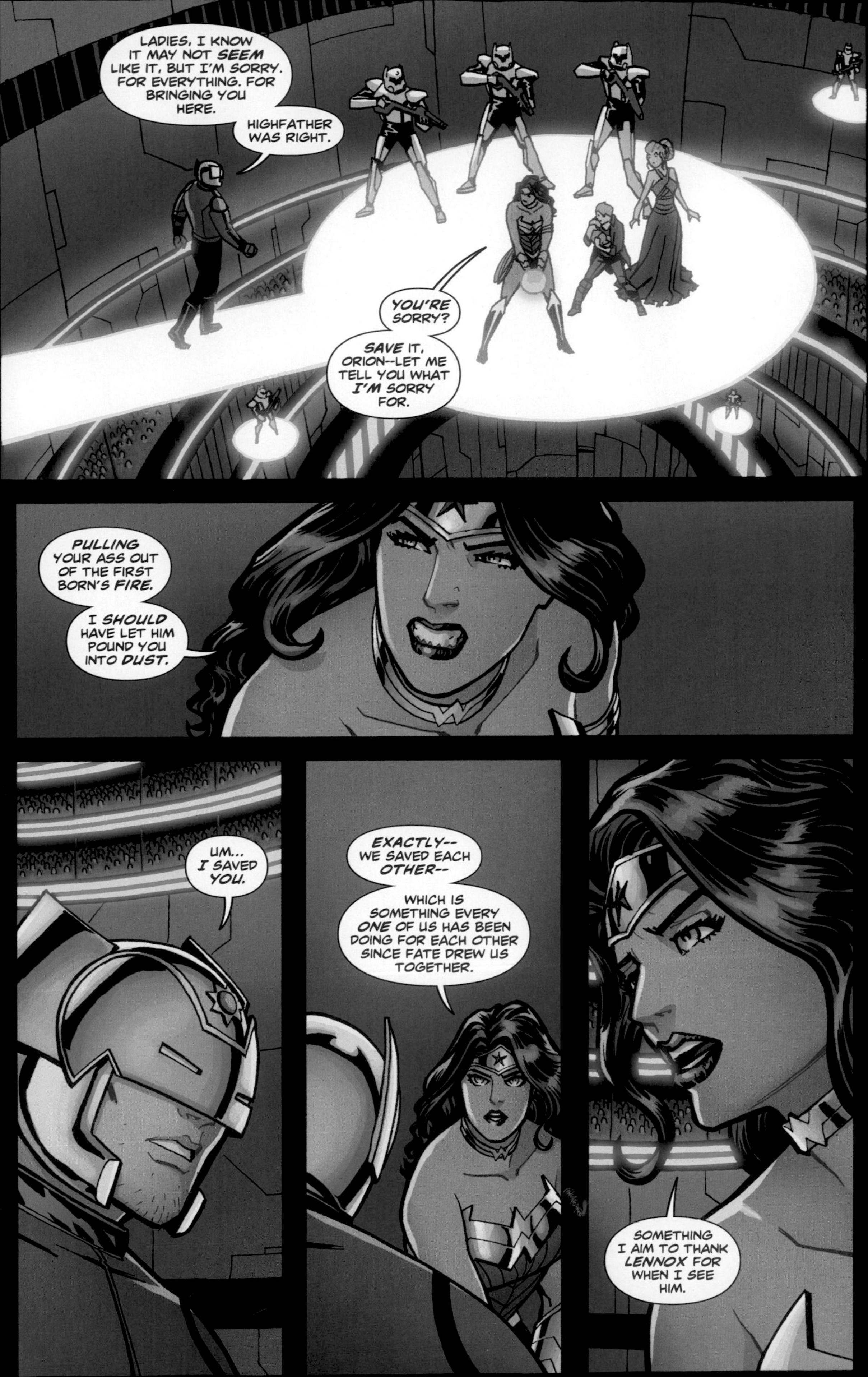
LADIES, I KNOW IT MAY NOT SEEM LIKE IT, BUT I'M SORRY. FOR EVERYTHING. FOR BRINGING YOU HERE.
HIGHFATHER WAS RIGHT.
YOU'RE SORRY?
SAVE IT, ORION--LET ME TELL YOU WHAT I'M SORRY FOR.
PULLING YOUR ASS OUT OF THE FIRST BORN'S FIRE.
I SHOULD HAVE LET HIM POUND YOU INTO DUST.
UM... I SAVED YOU.
EXACTLY-- WE SAVED EACH OTHER--
WHICH IS SOMETHING EVERY ONE OF US HAS BEEN DOING FOR EACH OTHER SINCE FATE DREW US TOGETHER.
SOMETHING I AIM TO THANK LENNOX FOR WHEN I SEE HIM.

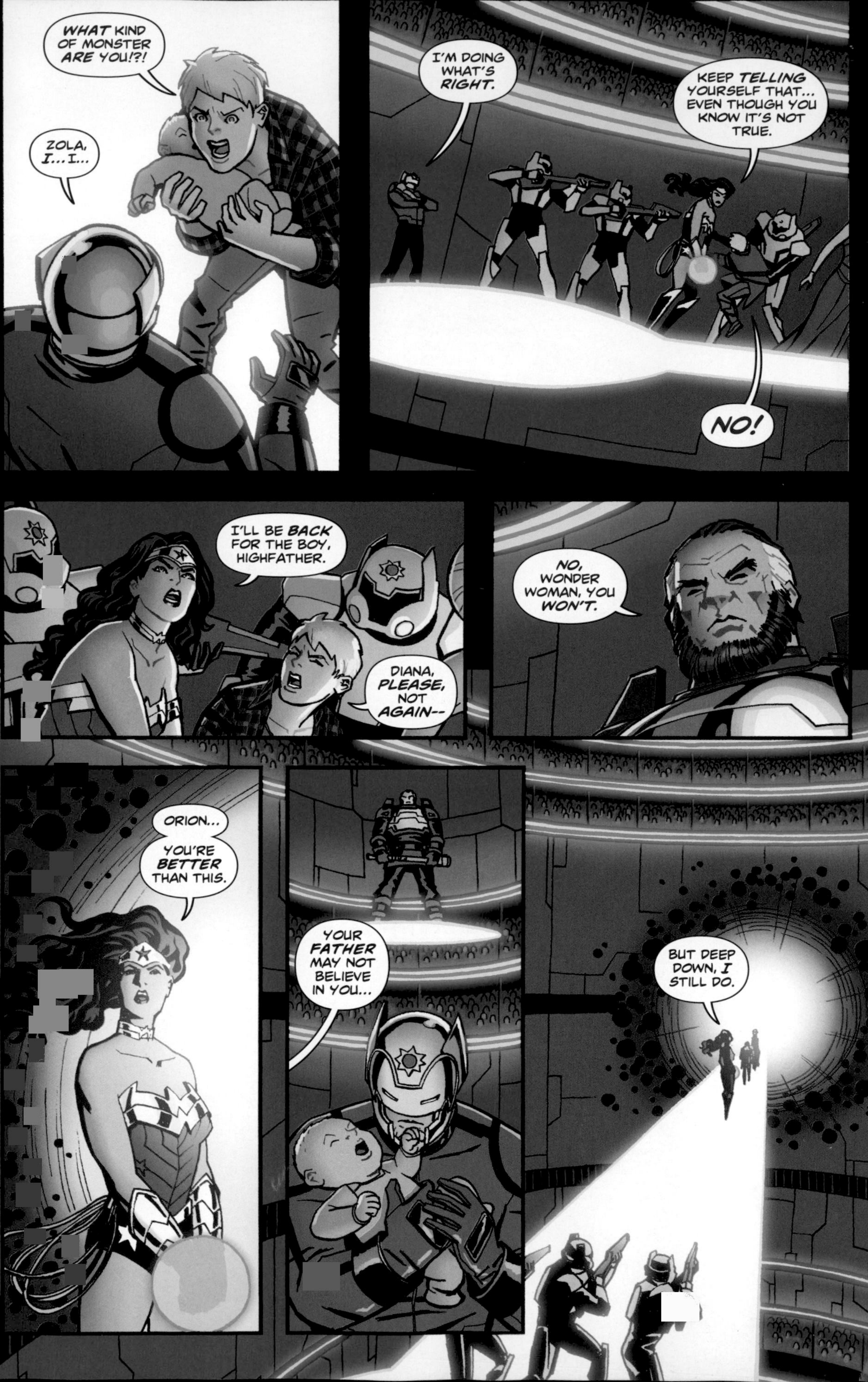
WHAT KIND OF MONSTER ARE YOU!?!
ZOLA, I... I...
I'M DOING WHAT'S RIGHT.
KEEP TELLING YOURSELF THAT... EVEN THOUGH YOU KNOW IT'S NOT TRUE.
NO!
I'LL BE BACK FOR THE BOY, HIGHFATHER.
DIANA, PLEASE, NOT AGAIN--
NO, WONDER WOMAN, YOU WON'T.
ORION...
YOU'RE BETTER THAN THIS.
YOUR FATHER MAY NOT BELIEVE IN YOU...
BUT DEEP DOWN, I STILL DO.

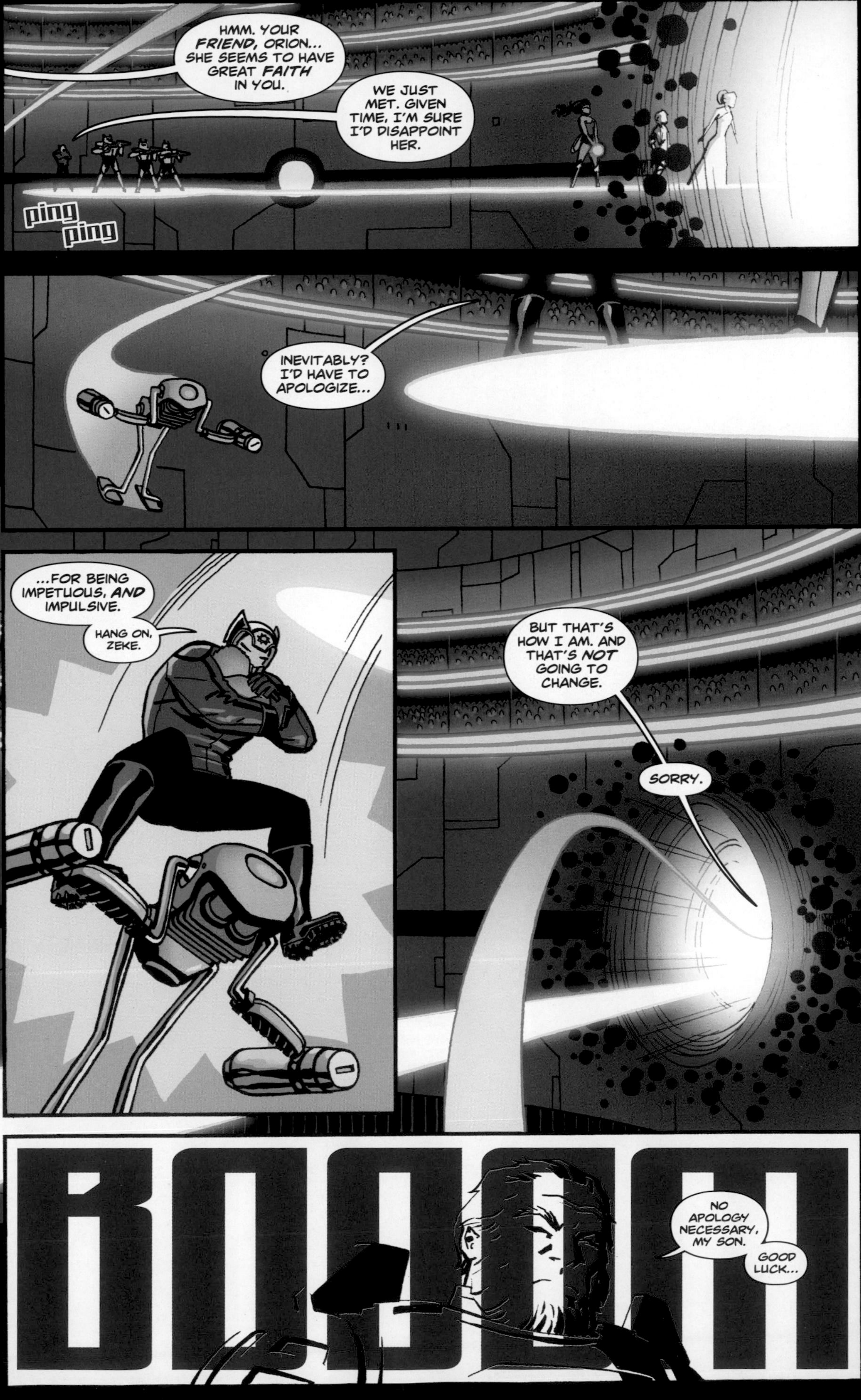
HMM. YOUR FRIEND, ORION... SHE SEEMS TO HAVE GREAT FAITH IN YOU.
WE JUST MET. GIVEN TIME, I'M SURE I'D DISAPPOINT HER.
ping ping
INEVITABLY? I'D HAVE TO APOLOGIZE...
...FOR BEING IMPETUOUS, AND IMPULSIVE.
HANG ON, ZEKE.
BUT THAT'S HOW I AM. AND THAT'S NOT GOING TO CHANGE.
SORRY.
BOOOM
NO APOLOGY NECESSARY, MY SON.
GOOD LUCK...

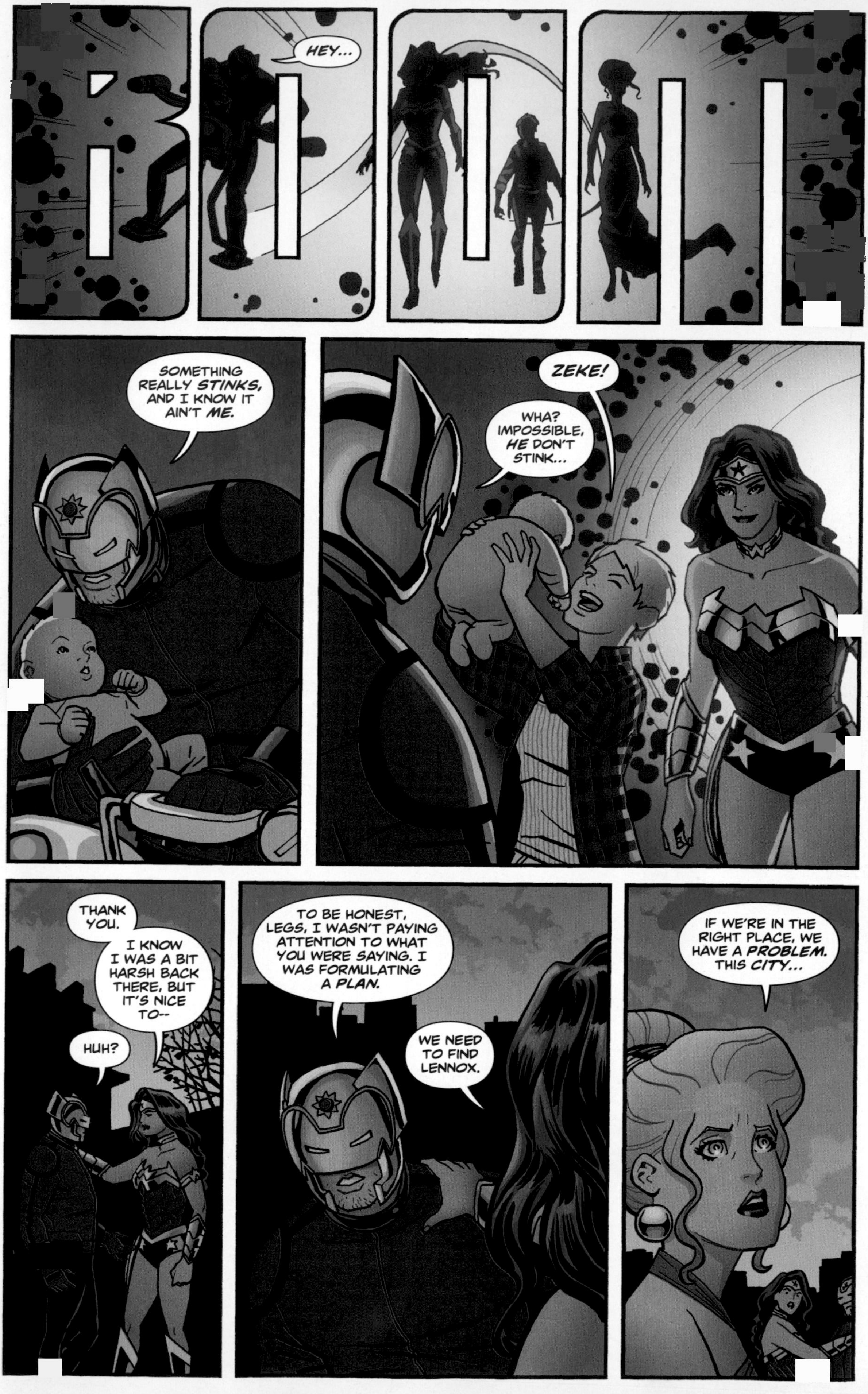
HEY...
SOMETHING REALLY STINKS, AND I KNOW IT AIN'T ME.
ZEKE!
WHA? IMPOSSIBLE, HE DON'T STINK...
THANK YOU.
I KNOW I WAS A BIT HARSH BACK THERE, BUT IT'S NICE TO--
HUH?
TO BE HONEST, LEGS, I WASN'T PAYING ATTENTION TO WHAT YOU WERE SAYING. I WAS FORMULATING A PLAN.
WE NEED TO FIND LENNOX.
IF WE'RE IN THE RIGHT PLACE, WE HAVE A PROBLEM. THIS CITY...

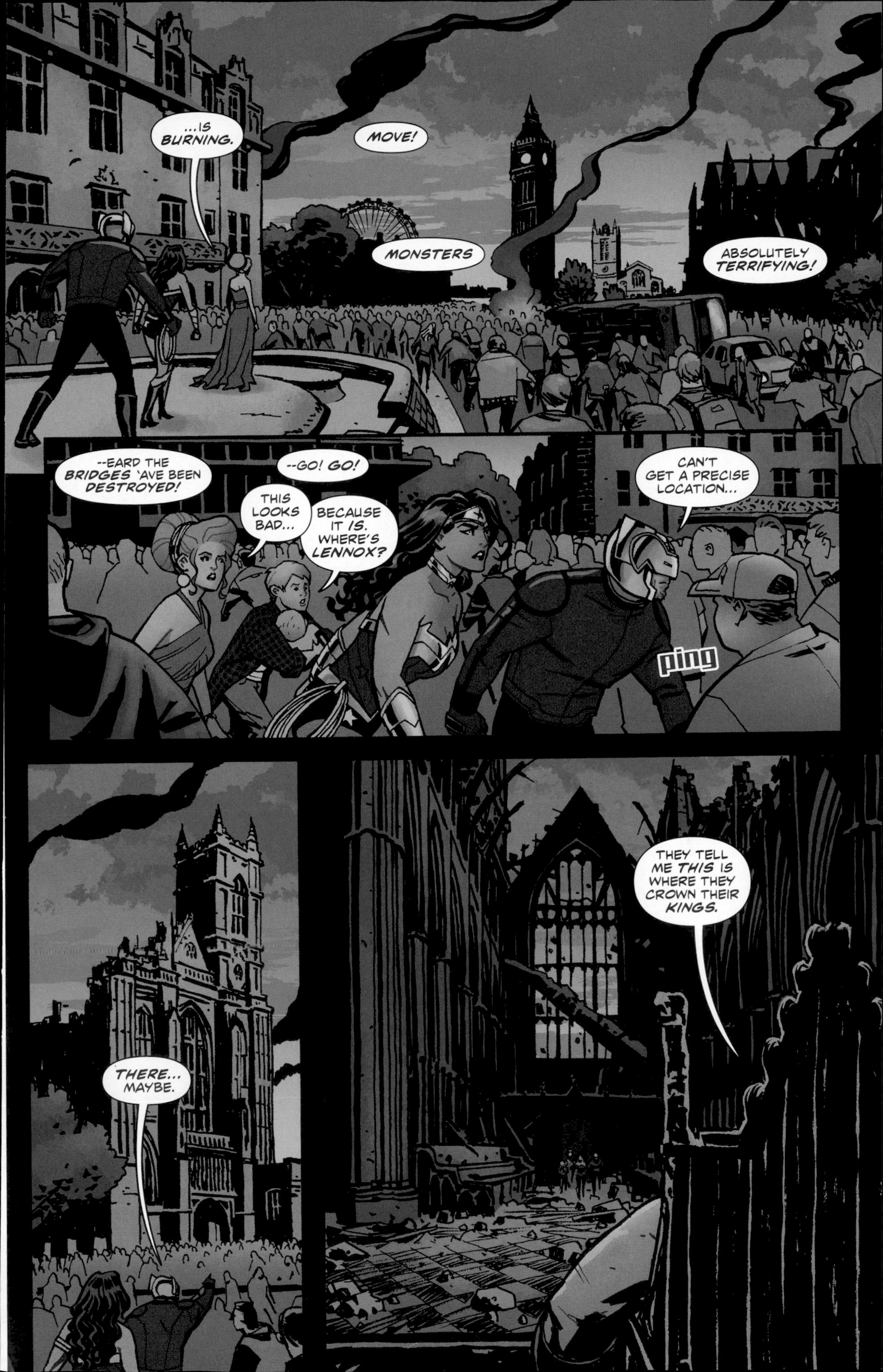
...IS BURNING.
MOVE!
MONSTERS
ABSOLUTELY TERRIFYING!
--EARD THE BRIDGES 'AVE BEEN DESTROYED!
--GO! GO!
THIS LOOKS BAD...
BECAUSE IT IS. WHERE'S LENNOX?
CAN'T GET A PRECISE LOCATION...
ping
THERE... MAYBE.
THEY TELL ME THIS IS WHERE THEY CROWN THEIR KINGS.

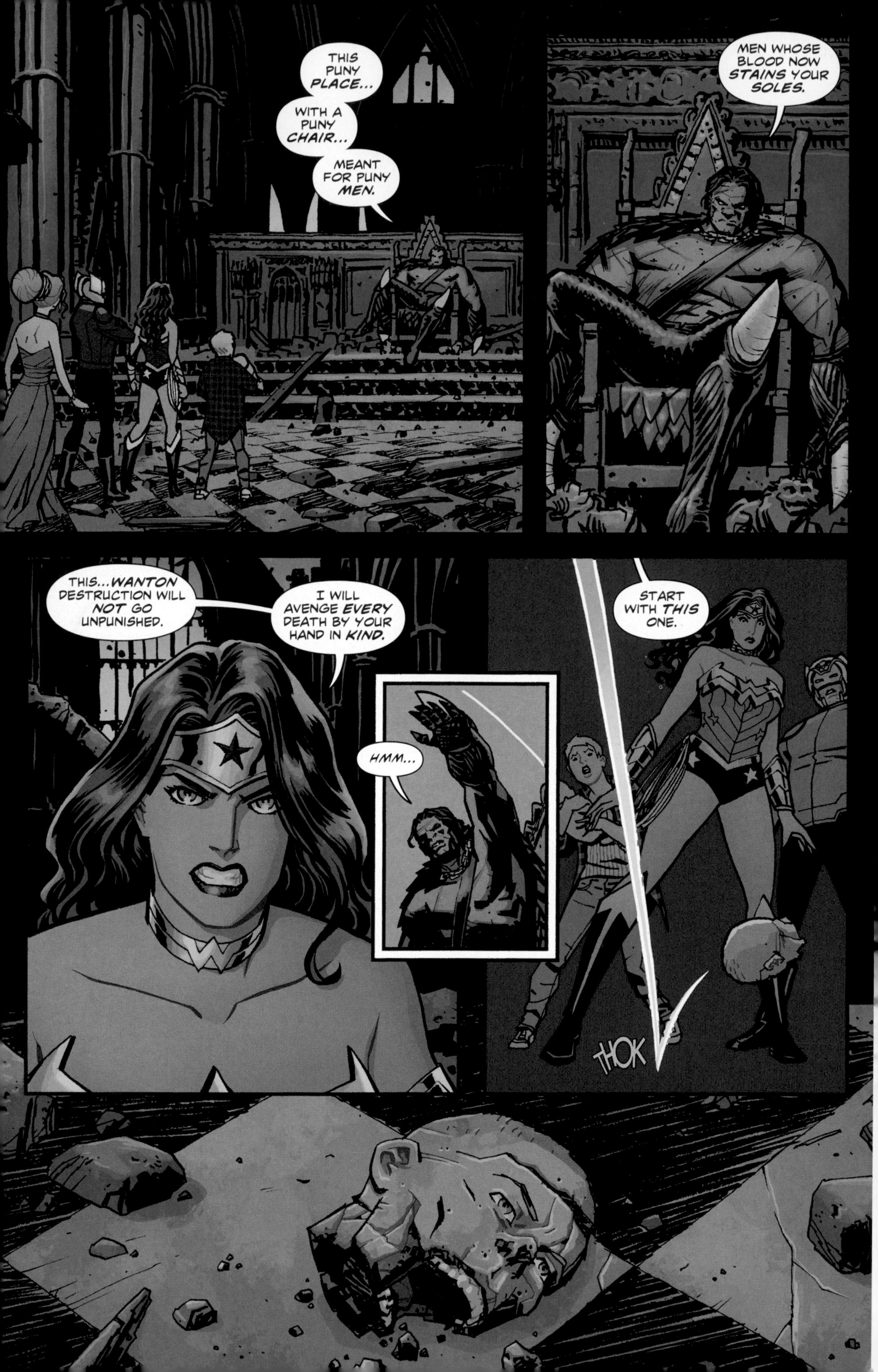
THIS PUNY PLACE...
WITH A PUNY CHAIR...
MEANT FOR PUNY MEN.
MEN WHOSE BLOOD NOW STAINS YOUR SOLES.
THIS...WANTON DESTRUCTION WILL NOT GO UNPUNISHED.
I WILL AVENGE EVERY DEATH BY YOUR HAND IN KIND.
HMM...
START WITH THIS ONE.
THOK

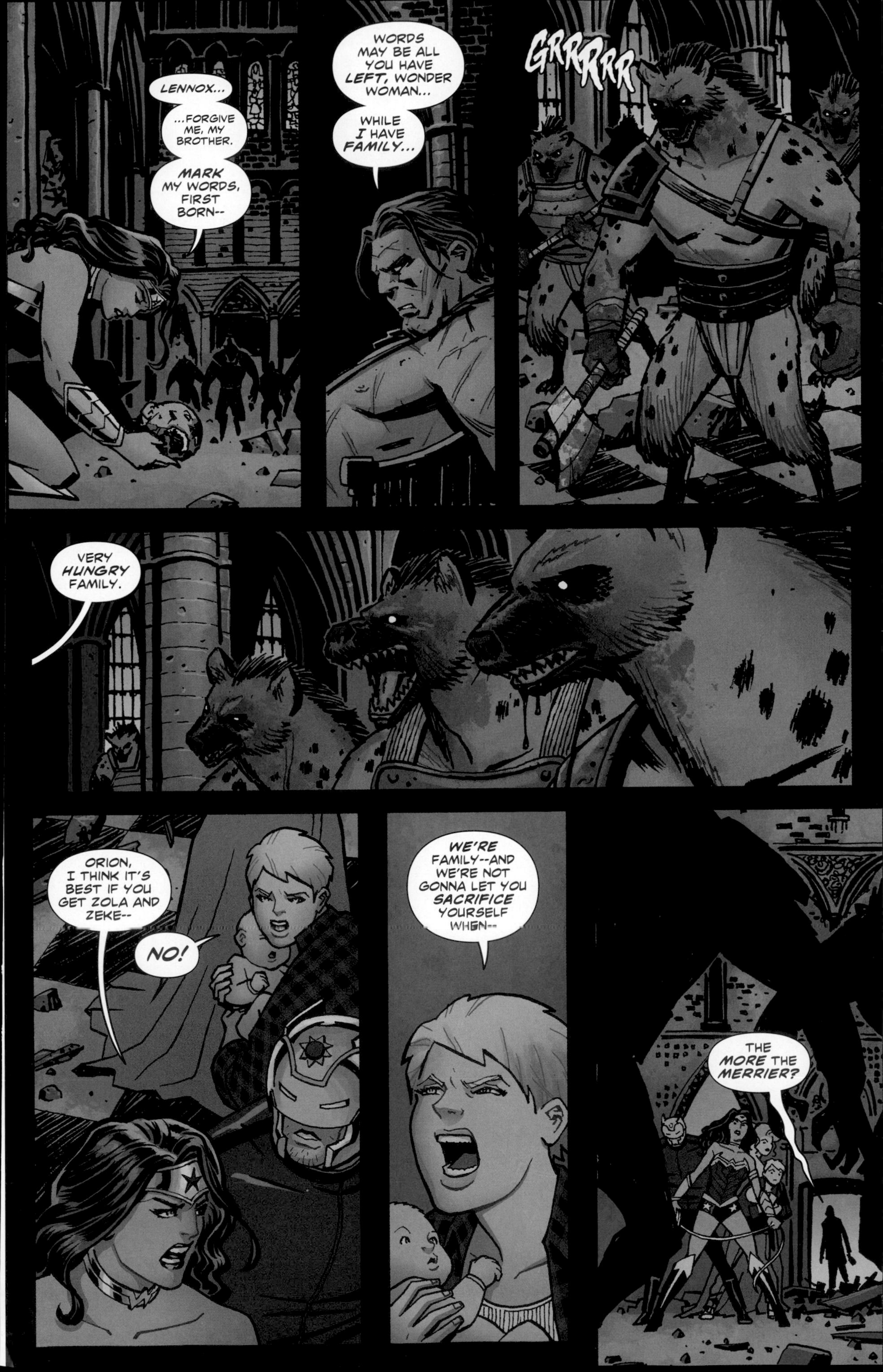
LENNOX...
...FORGIVE ME, MY BROTHER.
MARK MY WORDS, FIRST BORN--
WORDS MAY BE ALL YOU HAVE LEFT, WONDER WOMAN...
WHILE I HAVE FAMILY...
GRRRRRR
VERY HUNGRY FAMILY.
ORION, I THINK IT'S BEST IF YOU GET ZOLA AND ZEKE--
NO!
WE'RE FAMILY--AND WE'RE NOT GONNA LET YOU SACRIFICE YOURSELF WHEN--
THE MORE THE MERRIER?

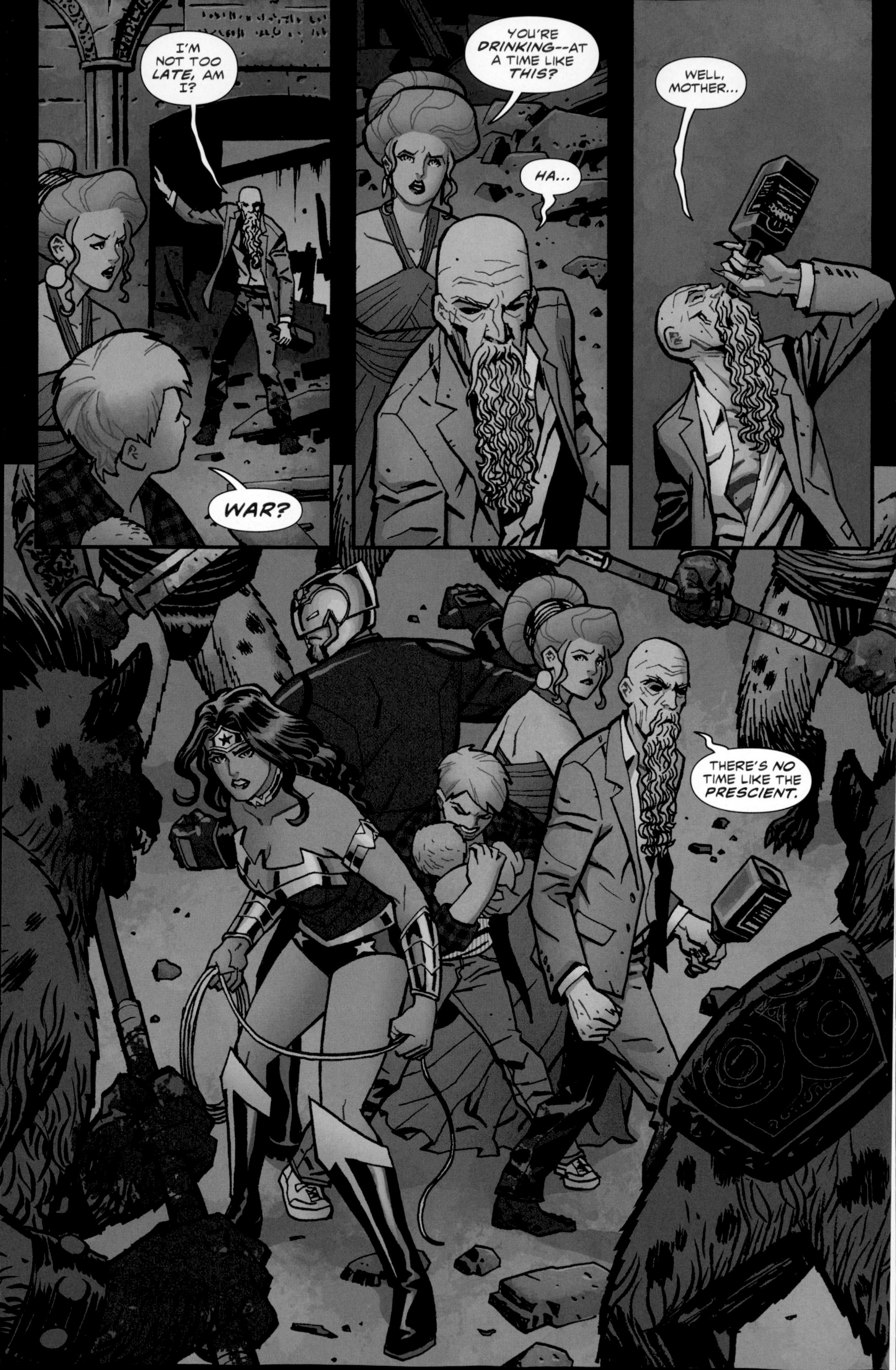
I'M NOT TOO LATE, AM I?
WAR?
YOU'RE DRINKING--AT A TIME LIKE THIS?
HA...
WELL, MOTHER...
THERE'S NO TIME LIKE THE PRESCIENT.

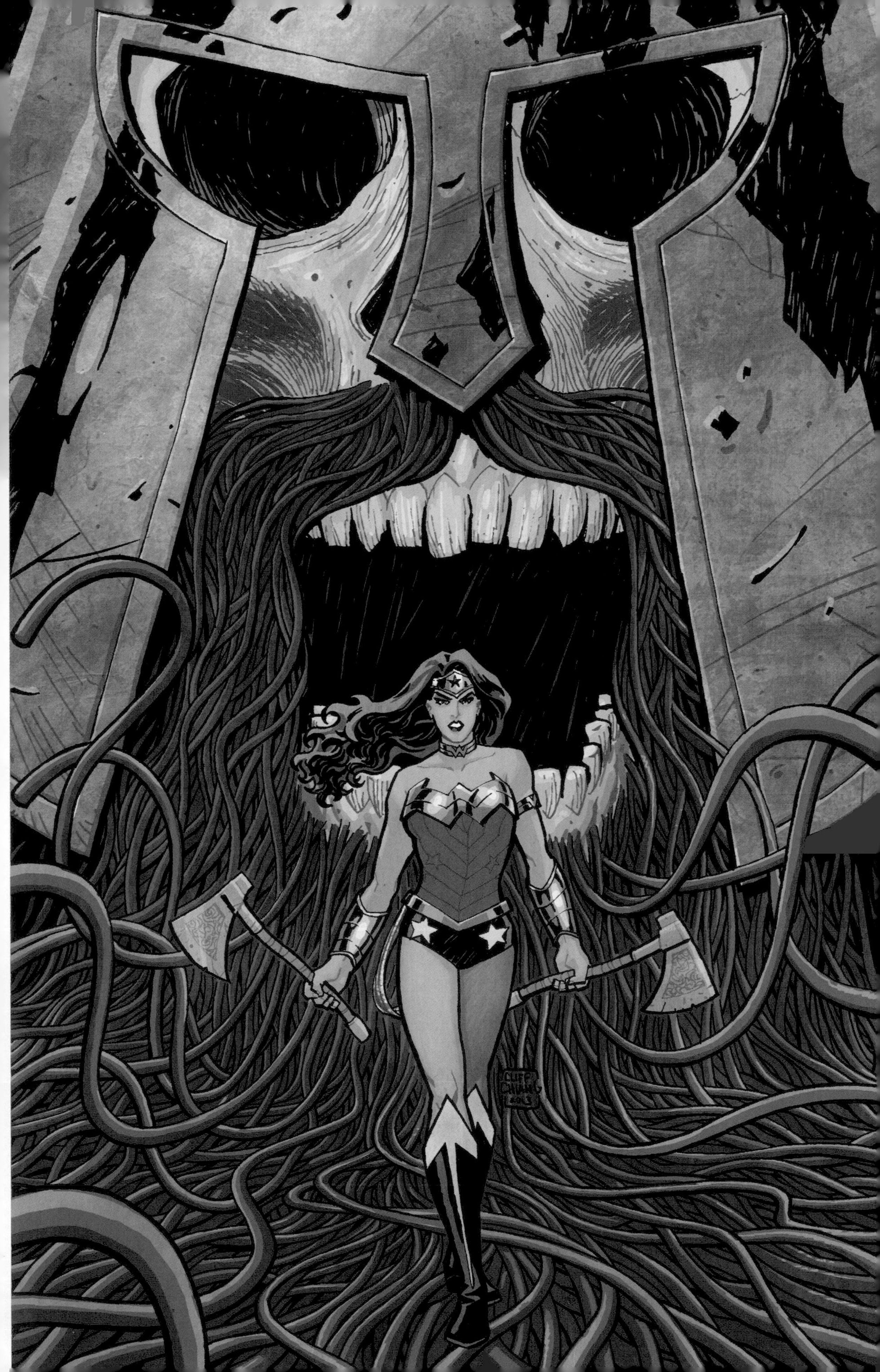

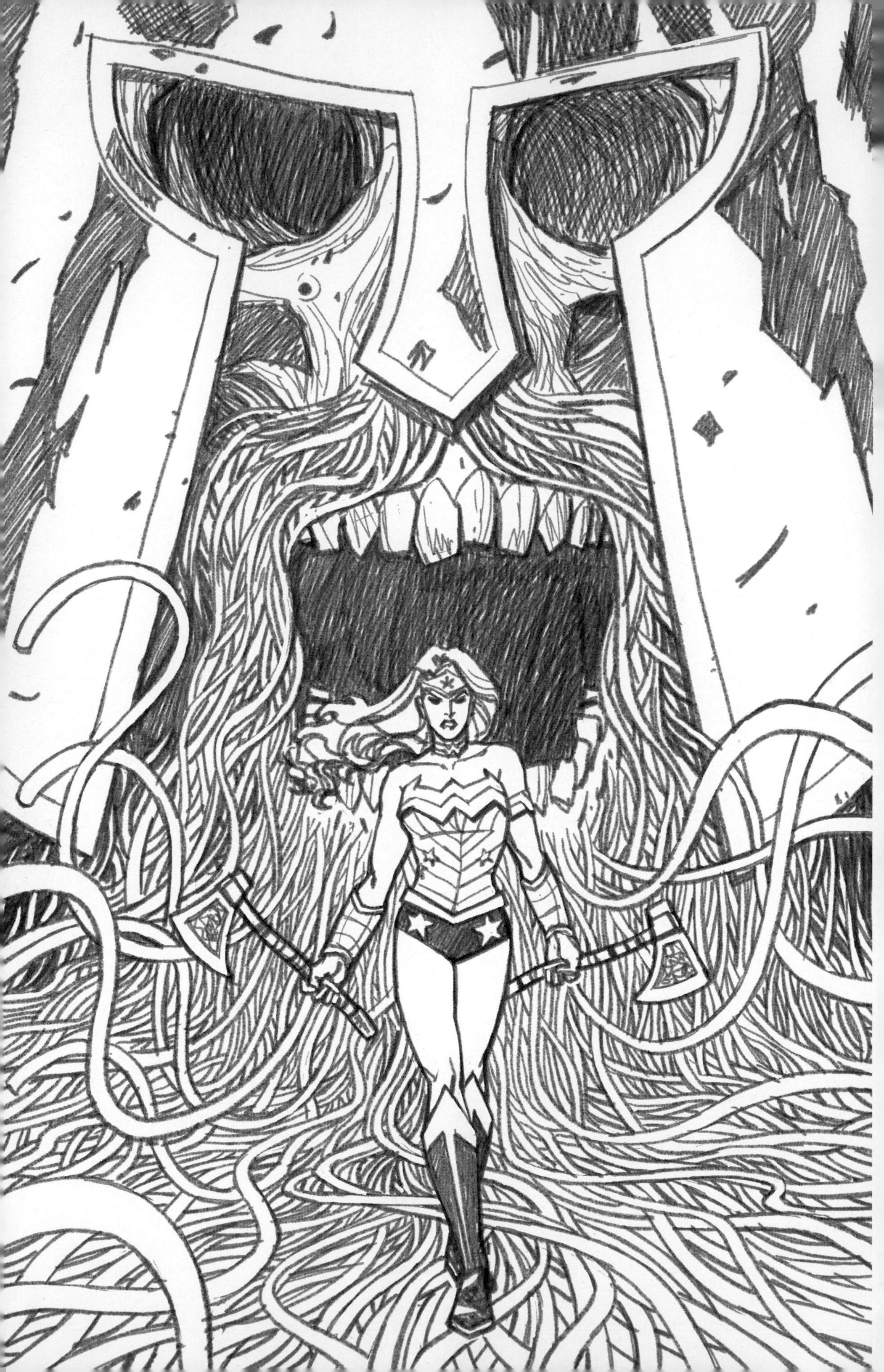

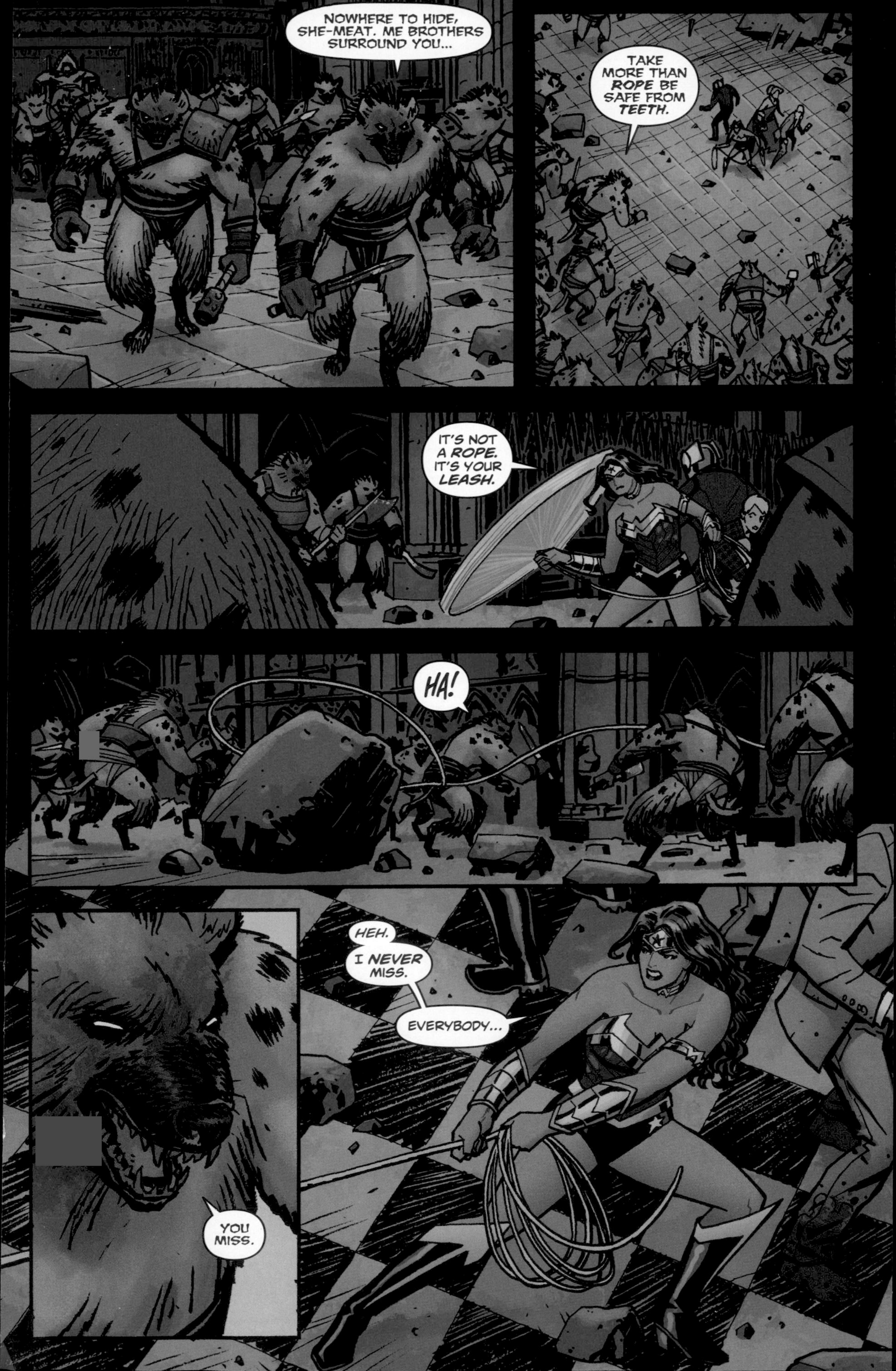
NOWHERE TO HIDE, SHE-MEAT. ME BROTHERS SURROUND YOU...
TAKE MORE THAN ROPE BE SAFE FROM TEETH.
IT'S NOT A ROPE. IT'S YOUR LEASH.
HA!
HEH.
I NEVER MISS.
EVERYBODY...
YOU MISS.

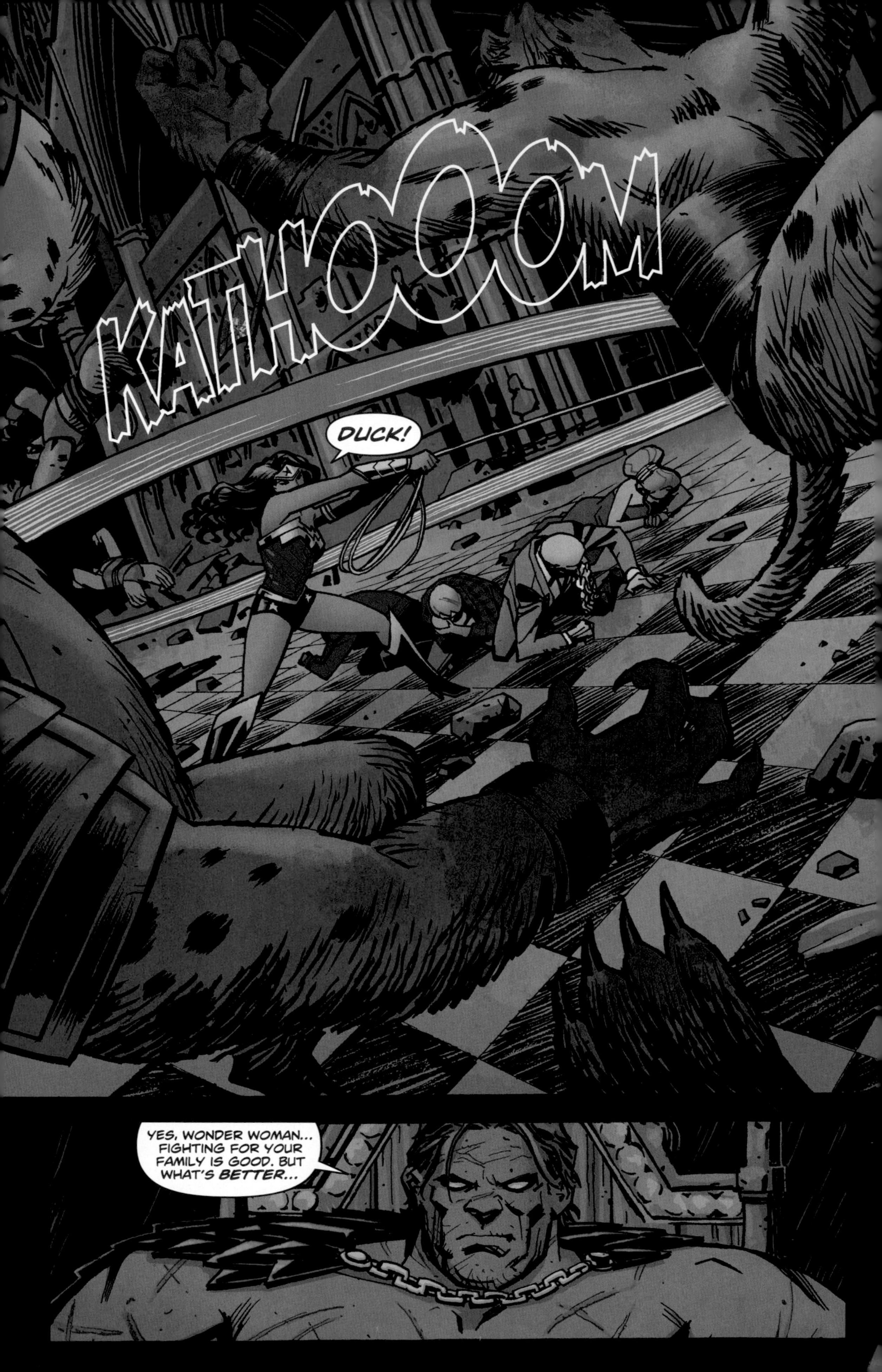
KATHOOOM
DUCK!
YES, WONDER WOMAN... FIGHTING FOR YOUR FAMILY IS GOOD. BUT WHAT'S *BETTER*...

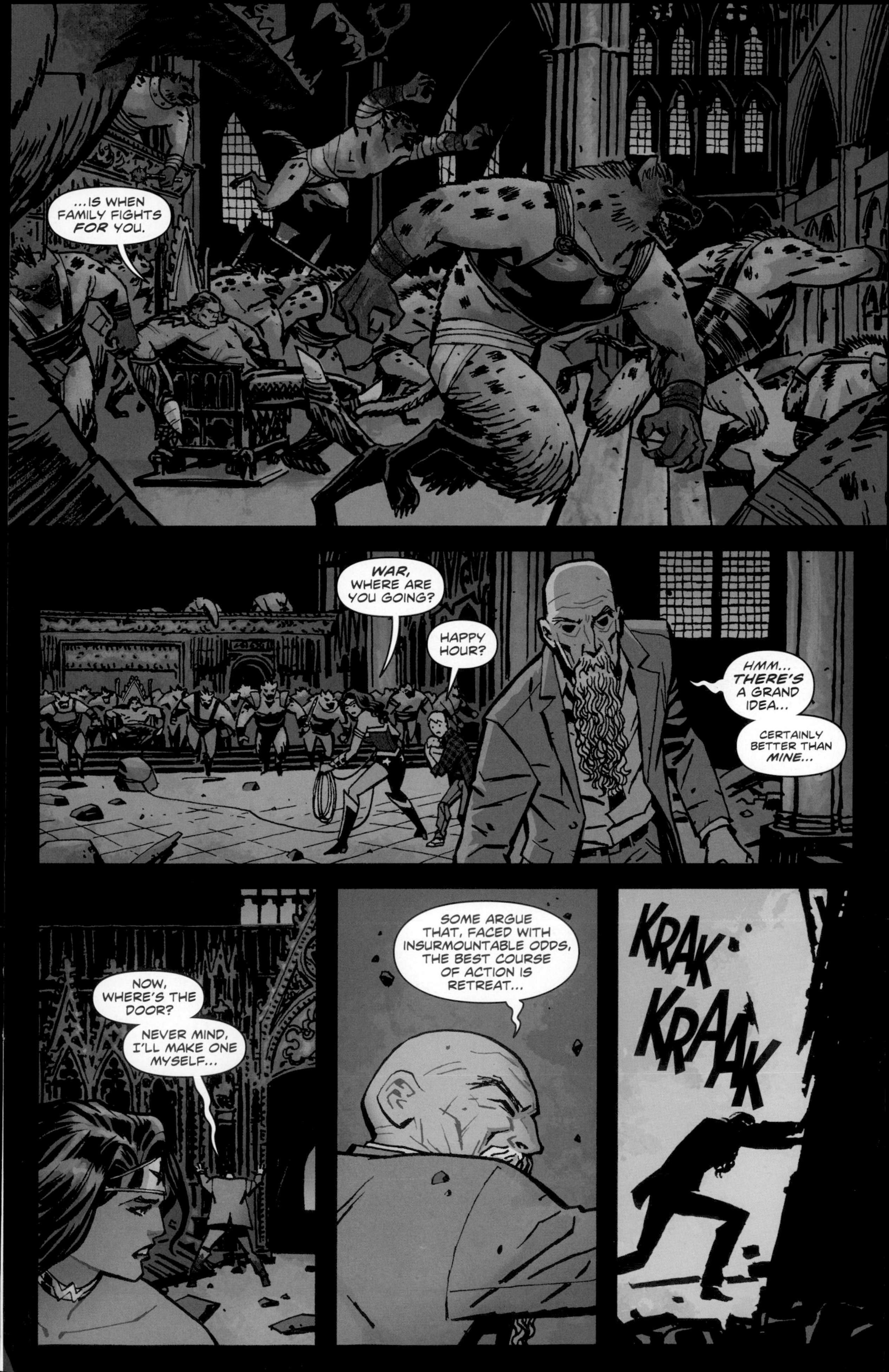
...IS WHEN FAMILY FIGHTS FOR YOU.
WAR, WHERE ARE YOU GOING?
HAPPY HOUR?
HMM... THERE'S A GRAND IDEA...
CERTAINLY BETTER THAN MINE...
NOW, WHERE'S THE DOOR?
NEVER MIND, I'LL MAKE ONE MYSELF...
SOME ARGUE THAT, FACED WITH INSURMOUNTABLE ODDS, THE BEST COURSE OF ACTION IS RETREAT...
KRAK
KRAAAK

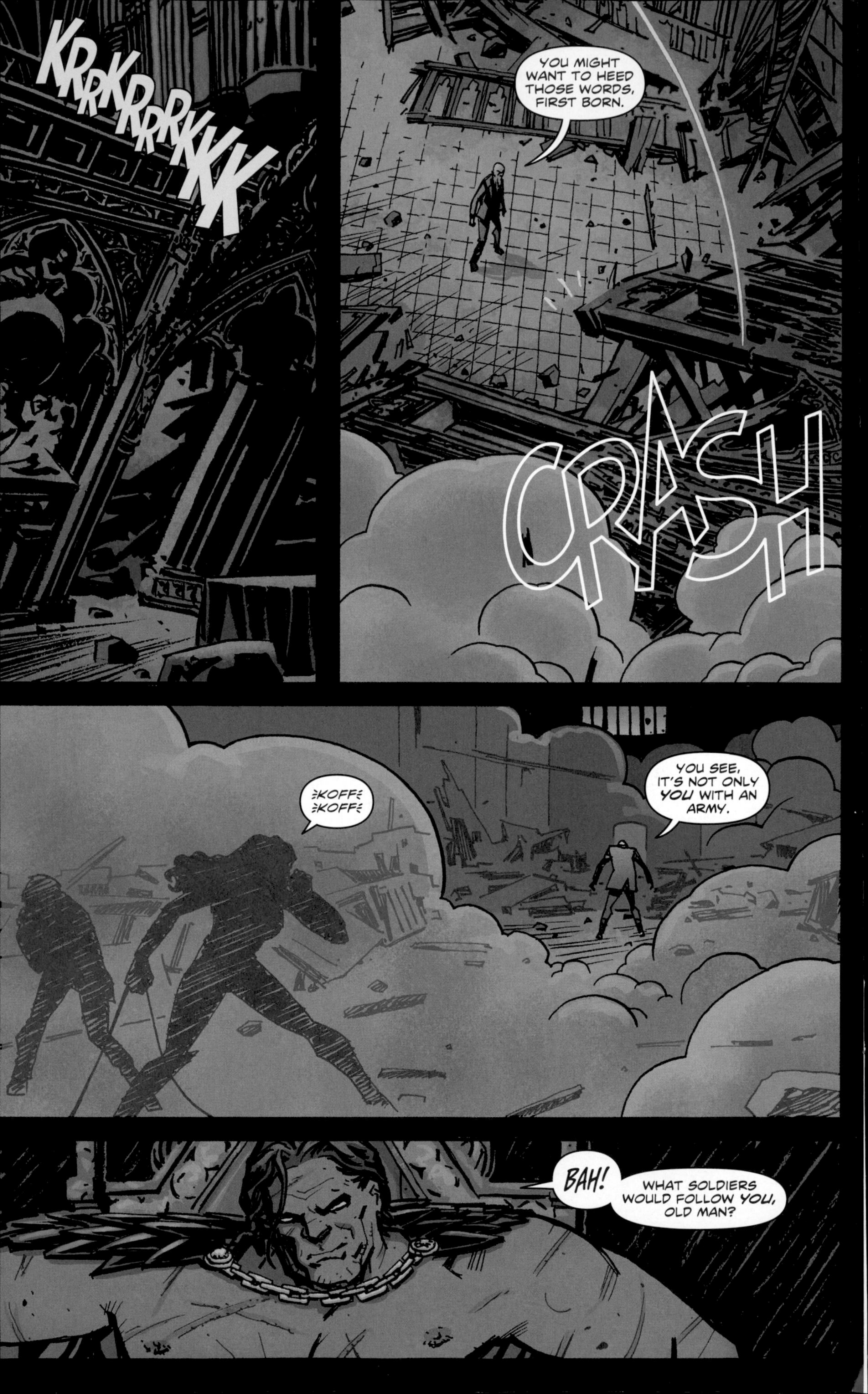
KRRKRRRKKK
YOU MIGHT WANT TO HEED THOSE WORDS, FIRST BORN.
CRASH
KOFF KOFF
YOU SEE, IT'S NOT ONLY YOU WITH AN ARMY.
BAH!
WHAT SOLDIERS WOULD FOLLOW YOU, OLD MAN?

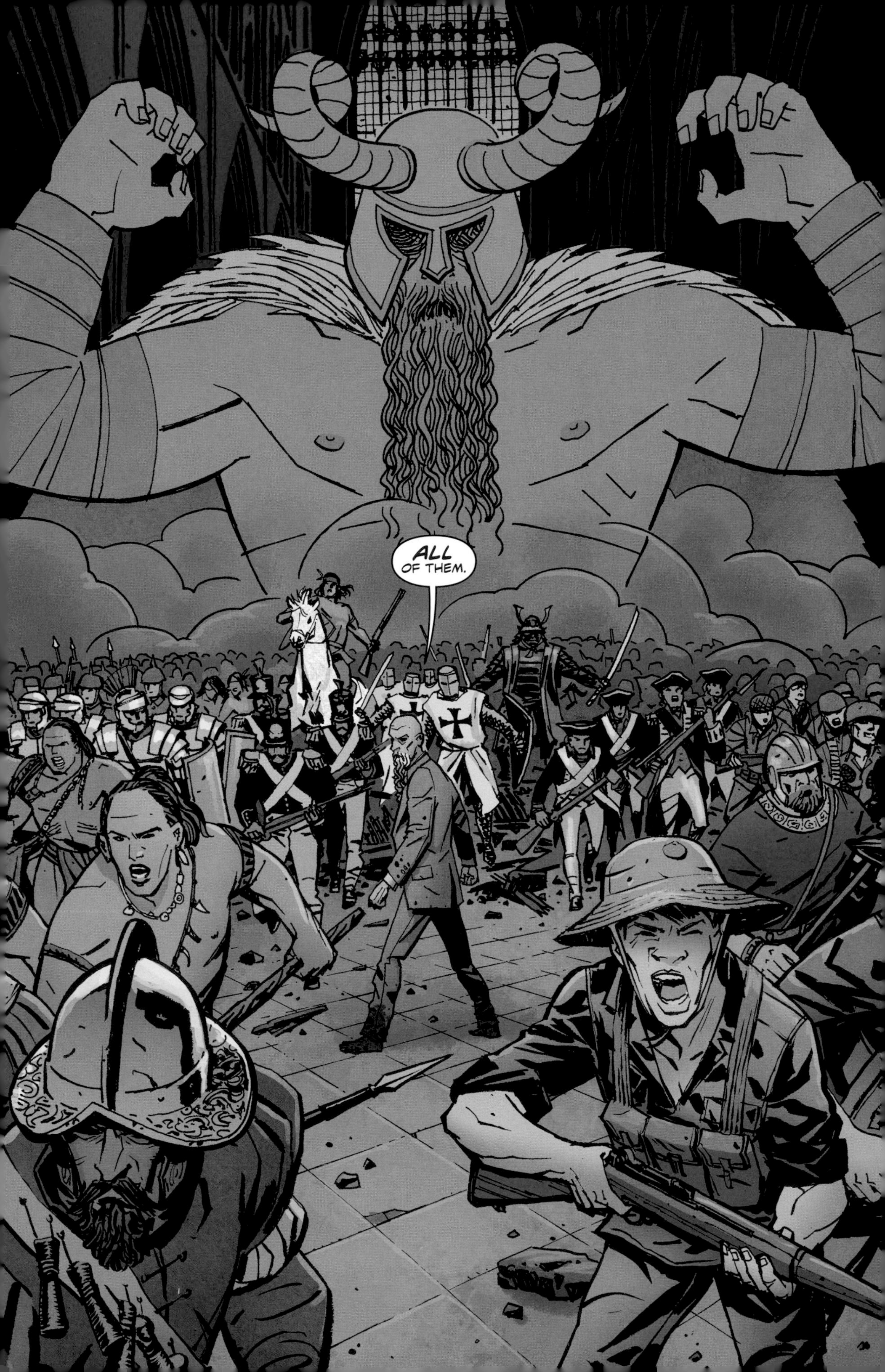
ALL OF THEM.

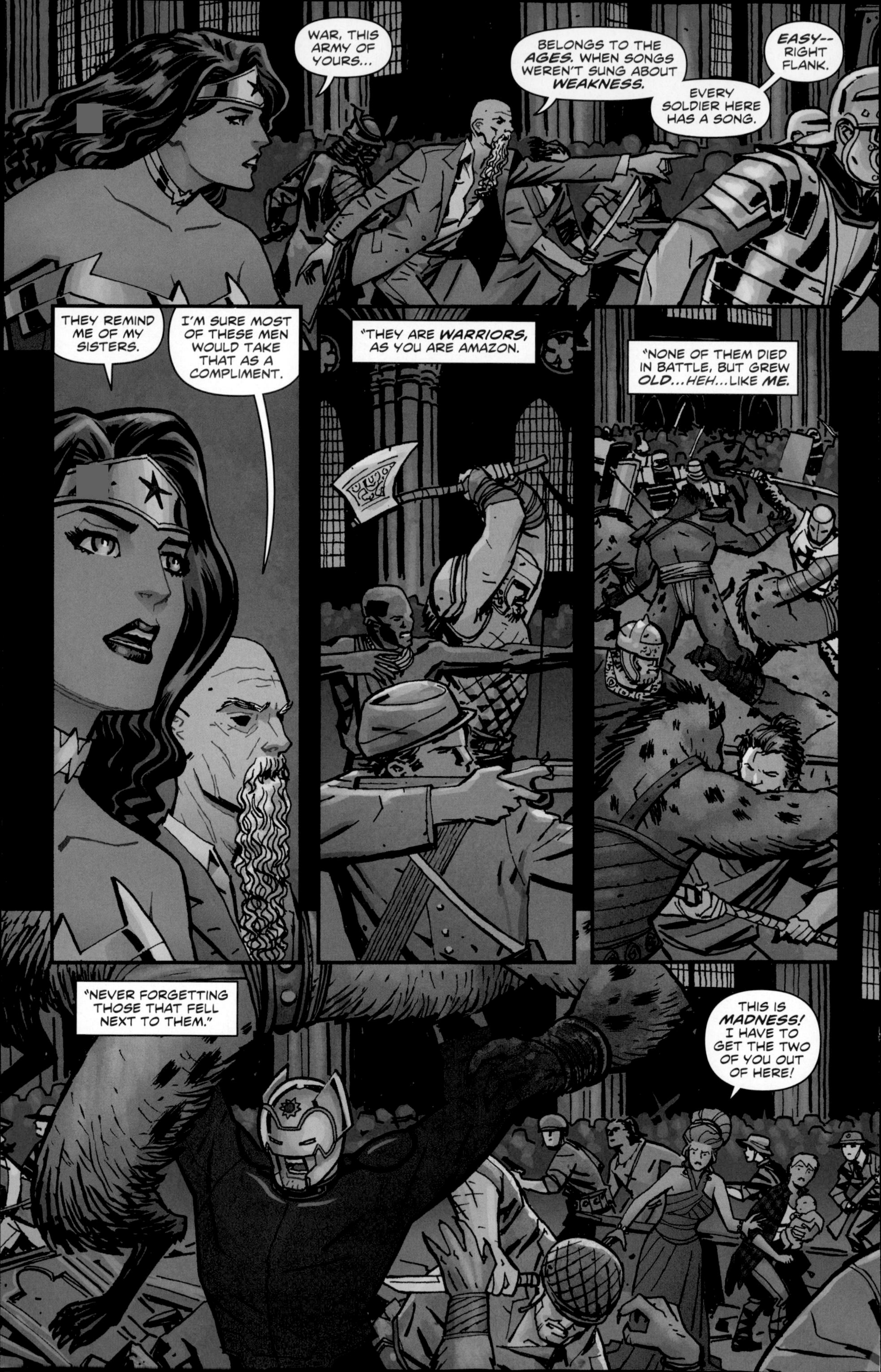
WAR, THIS ARMY OF YOURS...
BELONGS TO THE AGES. WHEN SONGS WEREN'T SUNG ABOUT WEAKNESS.
EVERY SOLDIER HERE HAS A SONG.
EASY-- RIGHT FLANK.
THEY REMIND ME OF MY SISTERS.
I'M SURE MOST OF THESE MEN WOULD TAKE THAT AS A COMPLIMENT.
"THEY ARE WARRIORS, AS YOU ARE AMAZON.
"NONE OF THEM DIED IN BATTLE, BUT GREW OLD...HEH...LIKE ME.
"NEVER FORGETTING THOSE THAT FELL NEXT TO THEM."
THIS IS MADNESS! I HAVE TO GET THE TWO OF YOU OUT OF HERE!

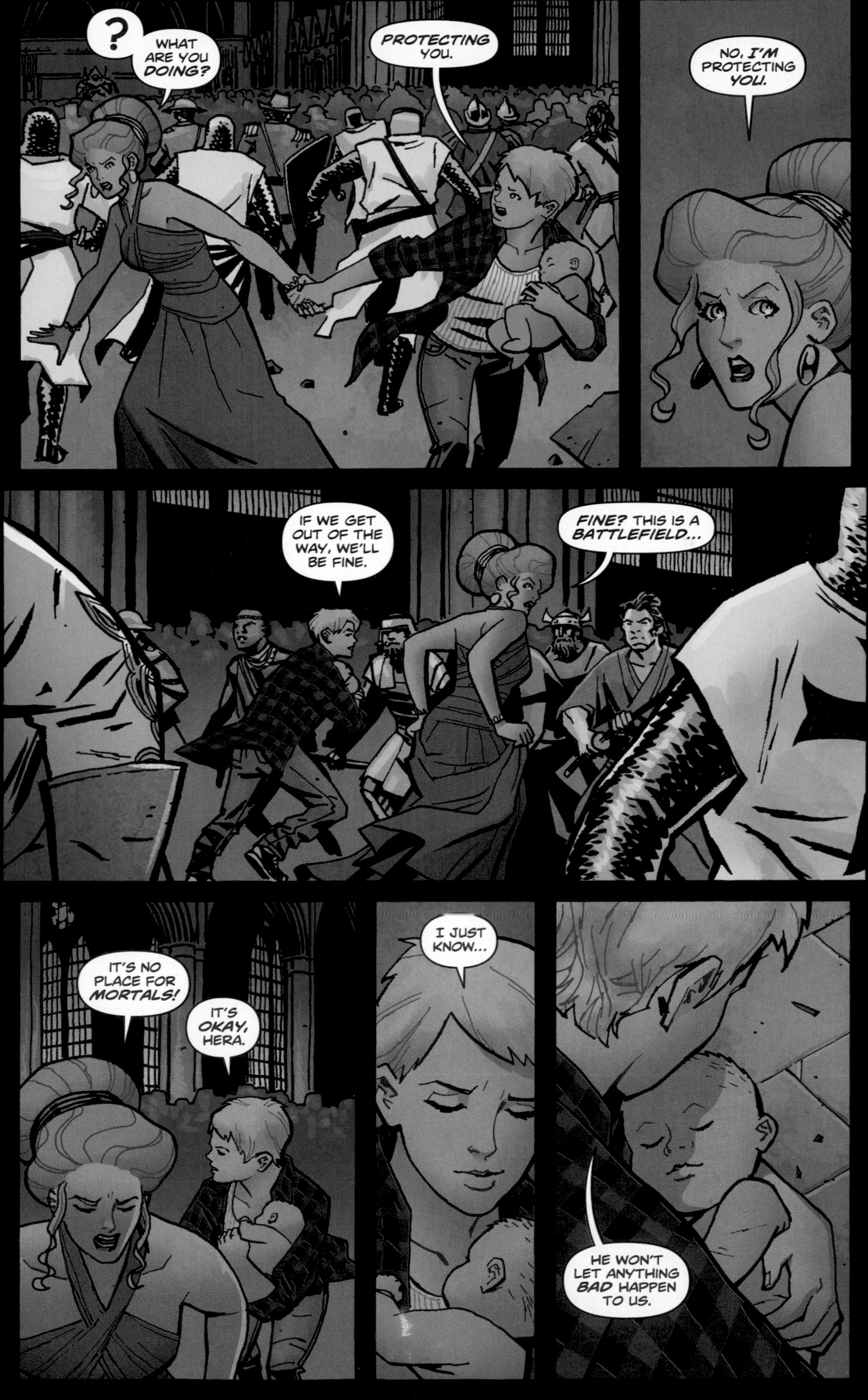
?
WHAT ARE YOU DOING?
PROTECTING YOU.
NO, I'M PROTECTING YOU.
IF WE GET OUT OF THE WAY, WE'LL BE FINE.
FINE? THIS IS A BATTLEFIELD...
IT'S NO PLACE FOR MORTALS!
IT'S OKAY, HERA.
I JUST KNOW...
HE WON'T LET ANYTHING BAD HAPPEN TO US.

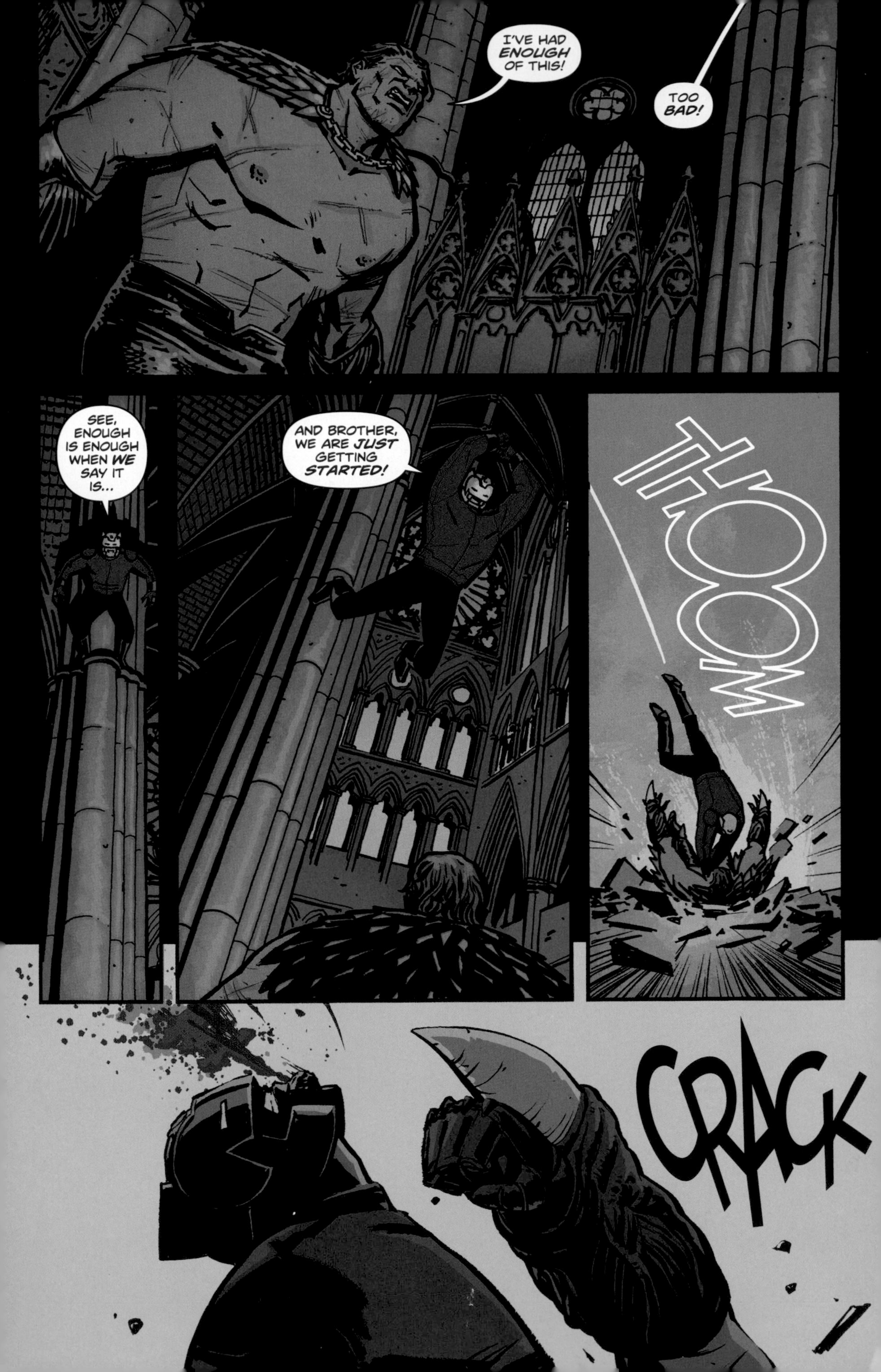
I'VE HAD ENOUGH OF THIS!
TOO BAD!
SEE, ENOUGH IS ENOUGH WHEN WE SAY IT IS...
AND BROTHER, WE ARE JUST GETTING STARTED!
THOOOM
CRACK

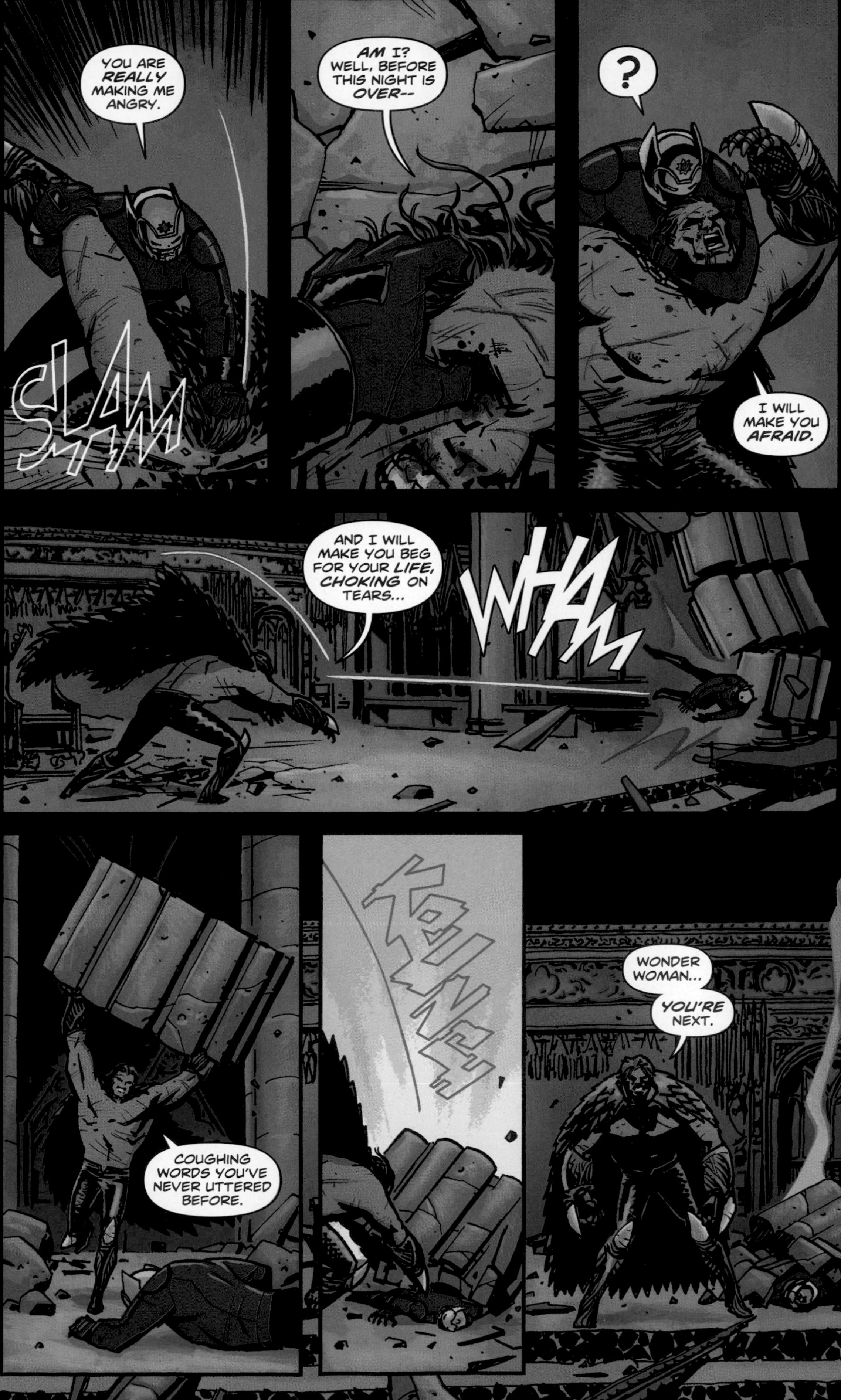
YOU ARE REALLY MAKING ME ANGRY.
SLAM
AM I? WELL, BEFORE THIS NIGHT IS OVER--
?
I WILL MAKE YOU AFRAID.
AND I WILL MAKE YOU BEG FOR YOUR LIFE, CHOKING ON TEARS...
WHAM
COUGHING WORDS YOU'VE NEVER UTTERED BEFORE.
KALUNCH
WONDER WOMAN...
YOU'RE NEXT.

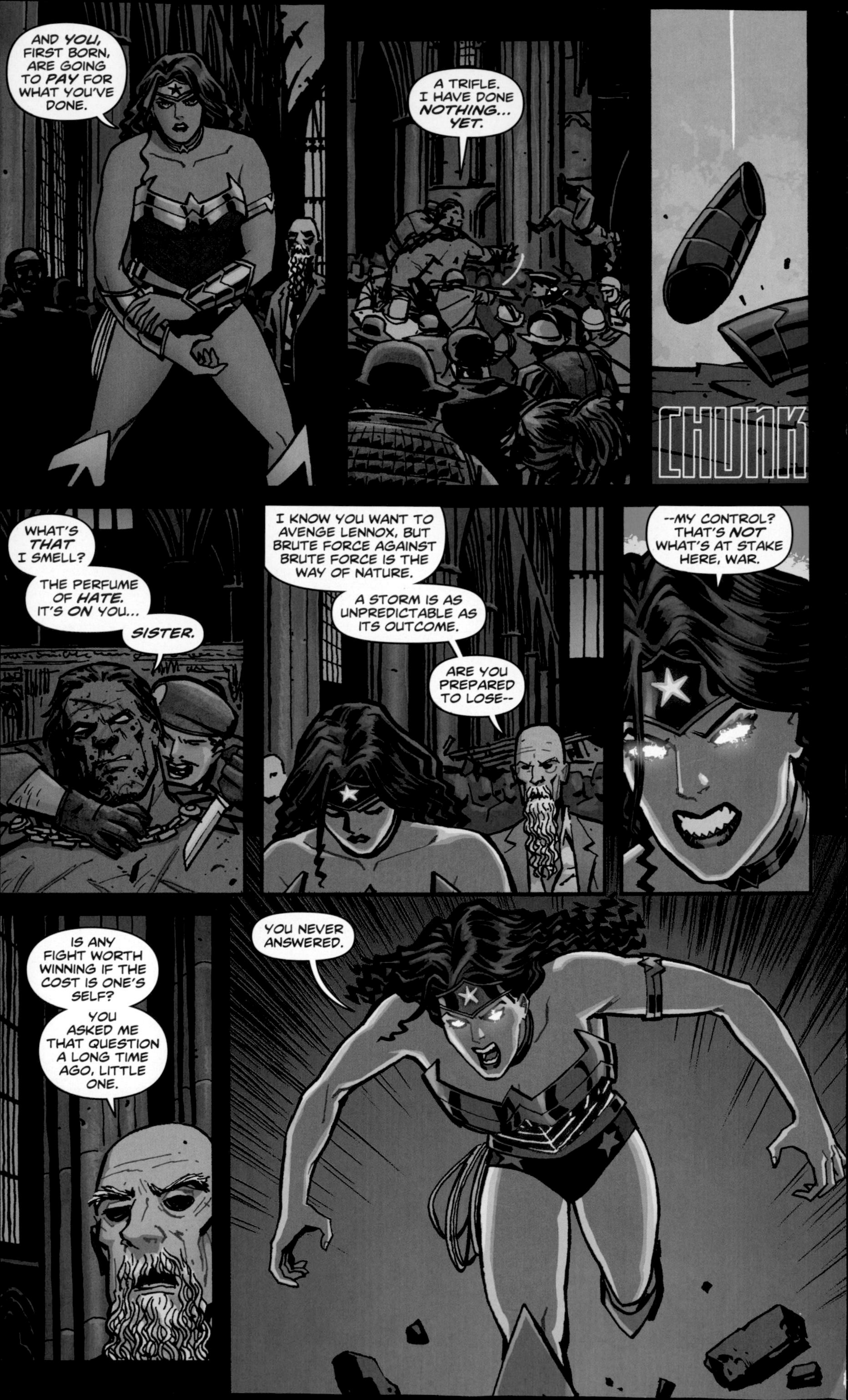
AND YOU, FIRST BORN, ARE GOING TO PAY FOR WHAT YOU'VE DONE.
A TRIFLE. I HAVE DONE NOTHING... YET.
CHUNK
WHAT'S THAT I SMELL?
THE PERFUME OF HATE. IT'S ON YOU...
SISTER.
I KNOW YOU WANT TO AVENGE LENNOX, BUT BRUTE FORCE AGAINST BRUTE FORCE IS THE WAY OF NATURE.
A STORM IS AS UNPREDICTABLE AS ITS OUTCOME.
ARE YOU PREPARED TO LOSE--
--MY CONTROL? THAT'S NOT WHAT'S AT STAKE HERE, WAR.
IS ANY FIGHT WORTH WINNING IF THE COST IS ONE'S SELF?
YOU ASKED ME THAT QUESTION A LONG TIME AGO, LITTLE ONE.
YOU NEVER ANSWERED.

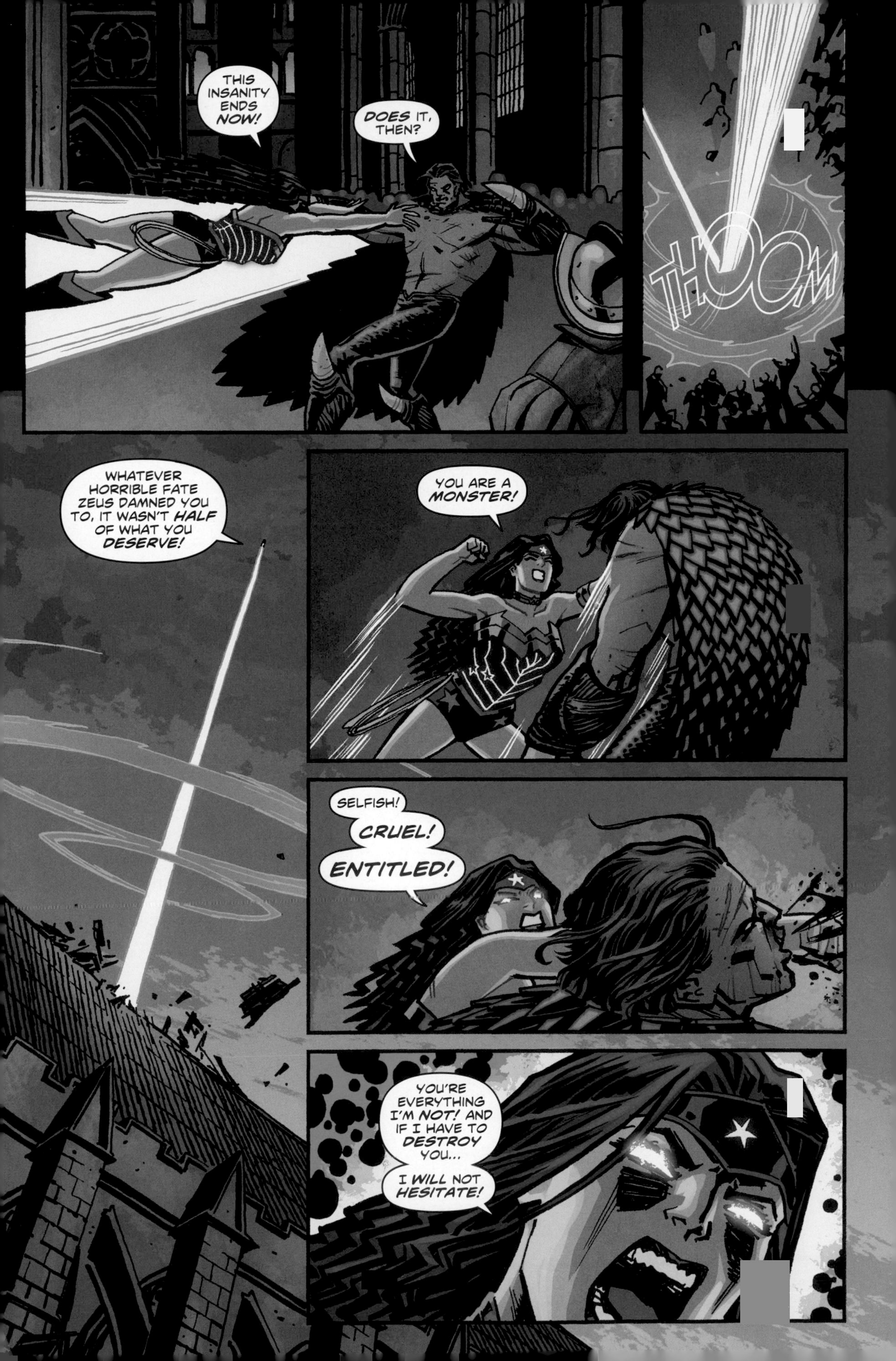

THIS INSANITY ENDS NOW!
DOES IT, THEN?
THOOM
WHATEVER HORRIBLE FATE ZEUS DAMNED YOU TO, IT WASN'T HALF OF WHAT YOU DESERVE!
YOU ARE A MONSTER!
SELFISH!
CRUEL!
ENTITLED!
YOU'RE EVERYTHING I'M NOT! AND IF I HAVE TO DESTROY YOU...
I WILL NOT HESITATE!

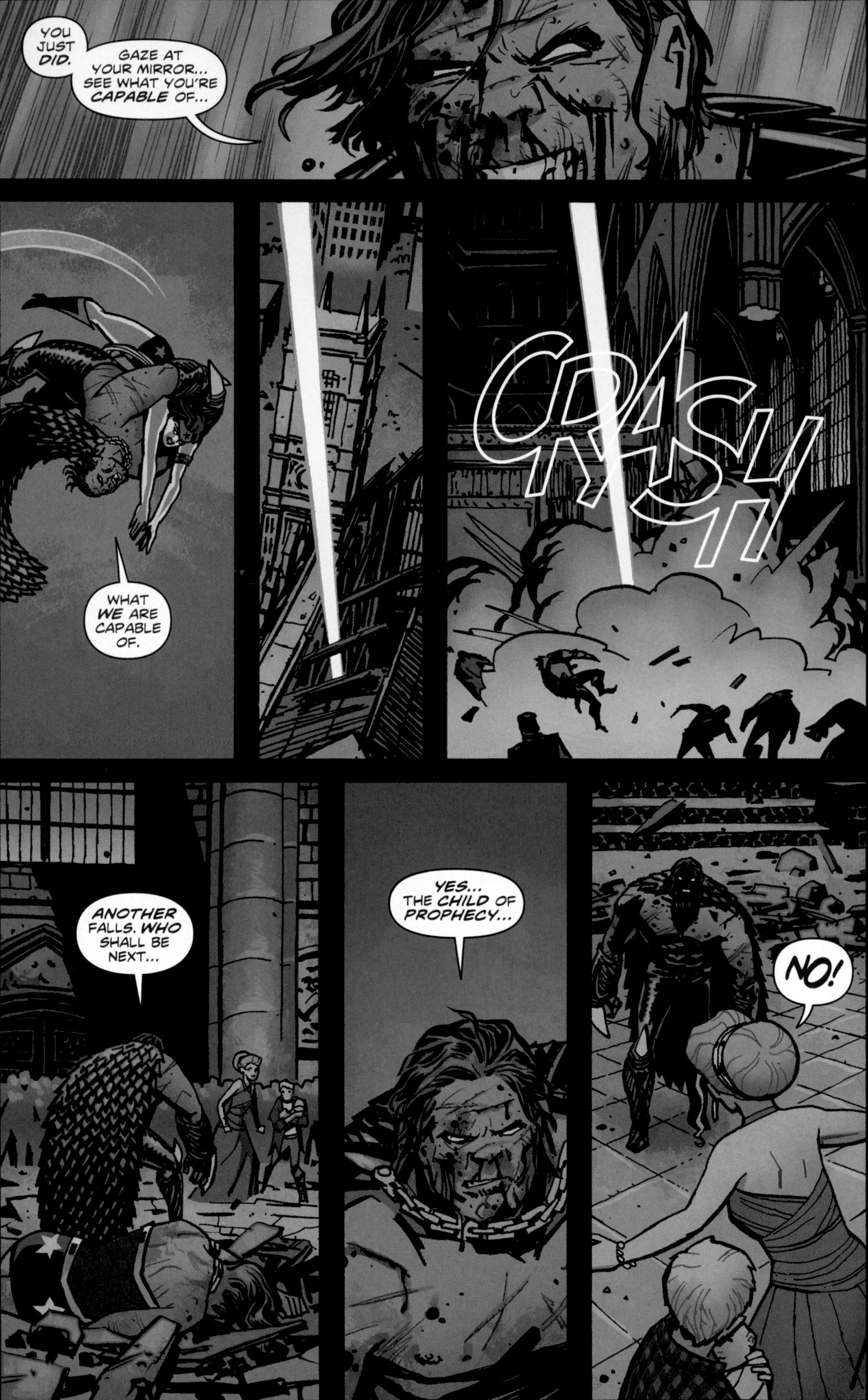
YOU JUST DID.
GAZE AT YOUR MIRROR... SEE WHAT YOU'RE CAPABLE OF...
WHAT WE ARE CAPABLE OF.
CRASH
ANOTHER FALLS. WHO SHALL BE NEXT...
YES... THE CHILD OF PROPHECY...
NO!

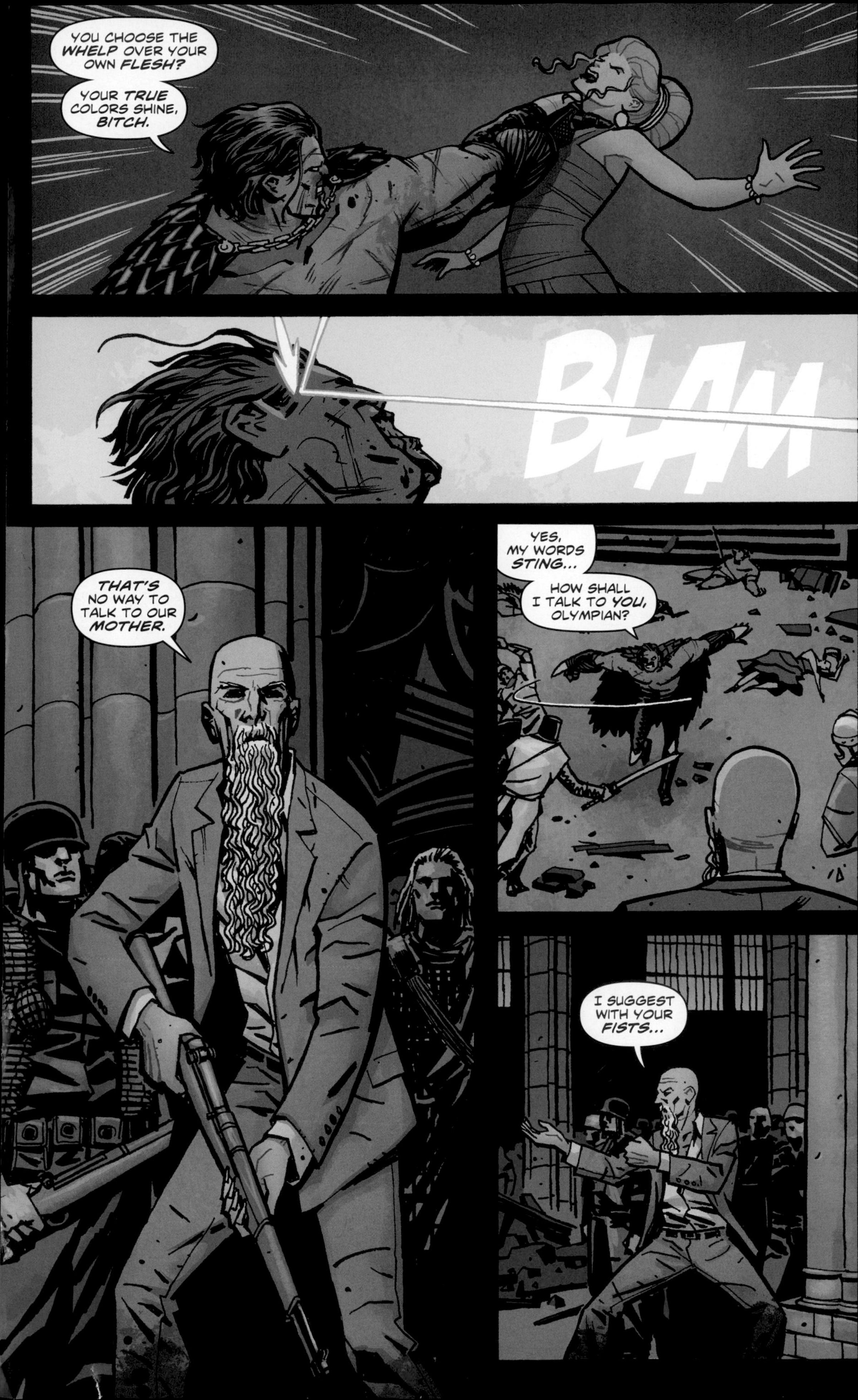

YOU CHOOSE THE WHELP OVER YOUR OWN FLESH?
YOUR TRUE COLORS SHINE, BITCH.
BLAM
THAT'S NO WAY TO TALK TO OUR MOTHER.
YES, MY WORDS STING...
HOW SHALL I TALK TO YOU, OLYMPIAN?
I SUGGEST WITH YOUR FISTS...

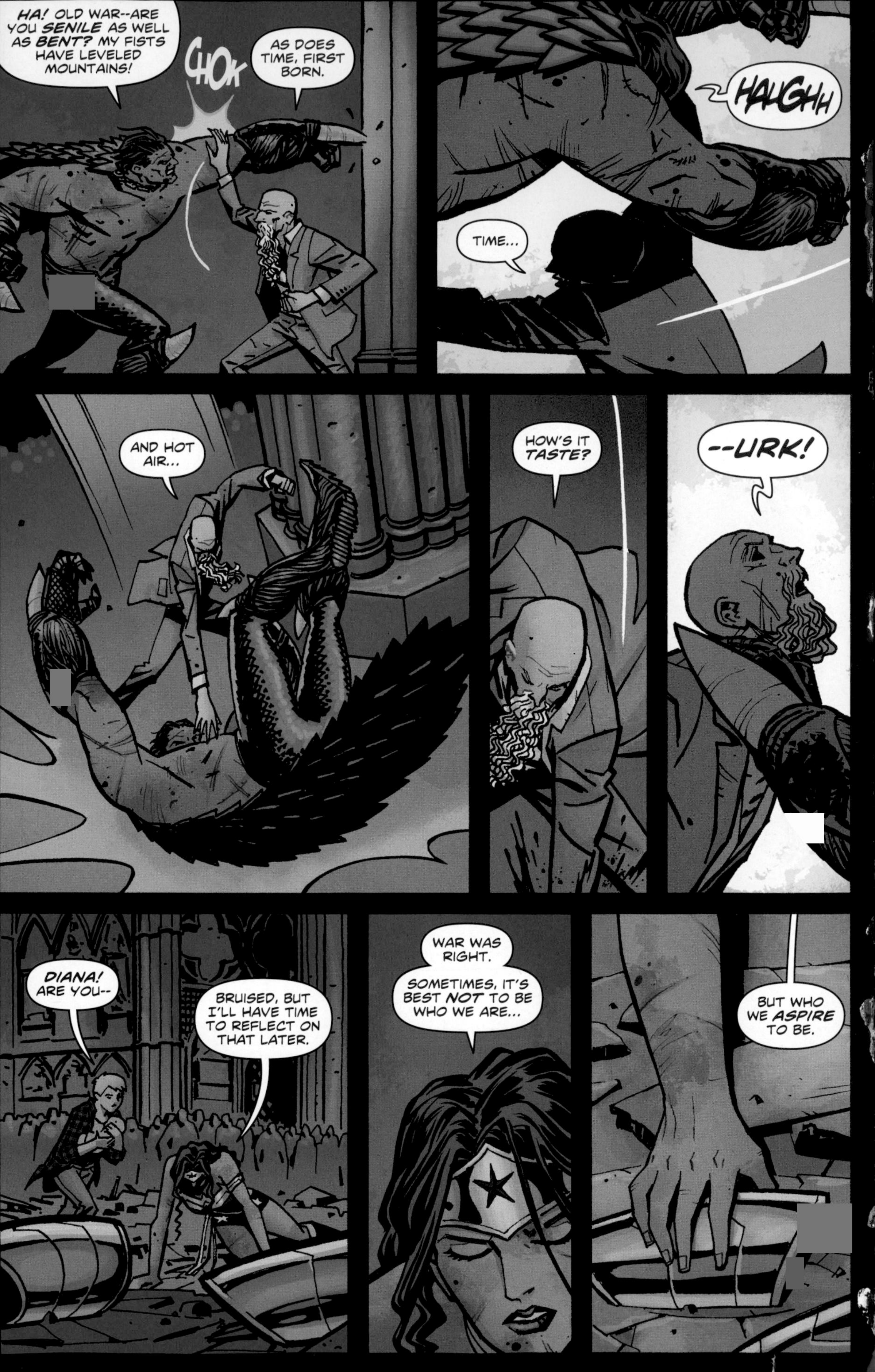
HA! OLD WAR--ARE YOU SENILE AS WELL AS BENT? MY FISTS HAVE LEVELED MOUNTAINS!
CHOK
AS DOES TIME, FIRST BORN.
HAUGHH
TIME...
AND HOT AIR...
HOW'S IT TASTE?
--URK!
DIANA! ARE YOU--
BRUISED, BUT I'LL HAVE TIME TO REFLECT ON THAT LATER.
WAR WAS RIGHT.
SOMETIMES, IT'S BEST NOT TO BE WHO WE ARE...
BUT WHO WE ASPIRE TO BE.

HOW *BLIND* OF ME! BELIEVING THE *CHILD* WAS MY *ONLY* KEY TO OLYMPUS...

≥KAK≤

WHEN I HOLD ANOTHER BY ITS *THROAT.*

I WILL *DESTROY* OLYMPUS FROM WITHIN. I WILL TAKE MY BIRTHRIGHT-- THE *SOLE* THRONE!

BUT *FIRST,* I WILL TAKE *YOURS...*

I WILL BE THE *GOD* OF WAR.

ZZZKKK

AND ALL I NEED TO DO IS *SQUEEZE...*

HUAAARGHH

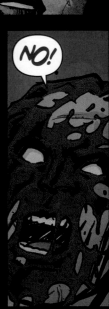

NO!

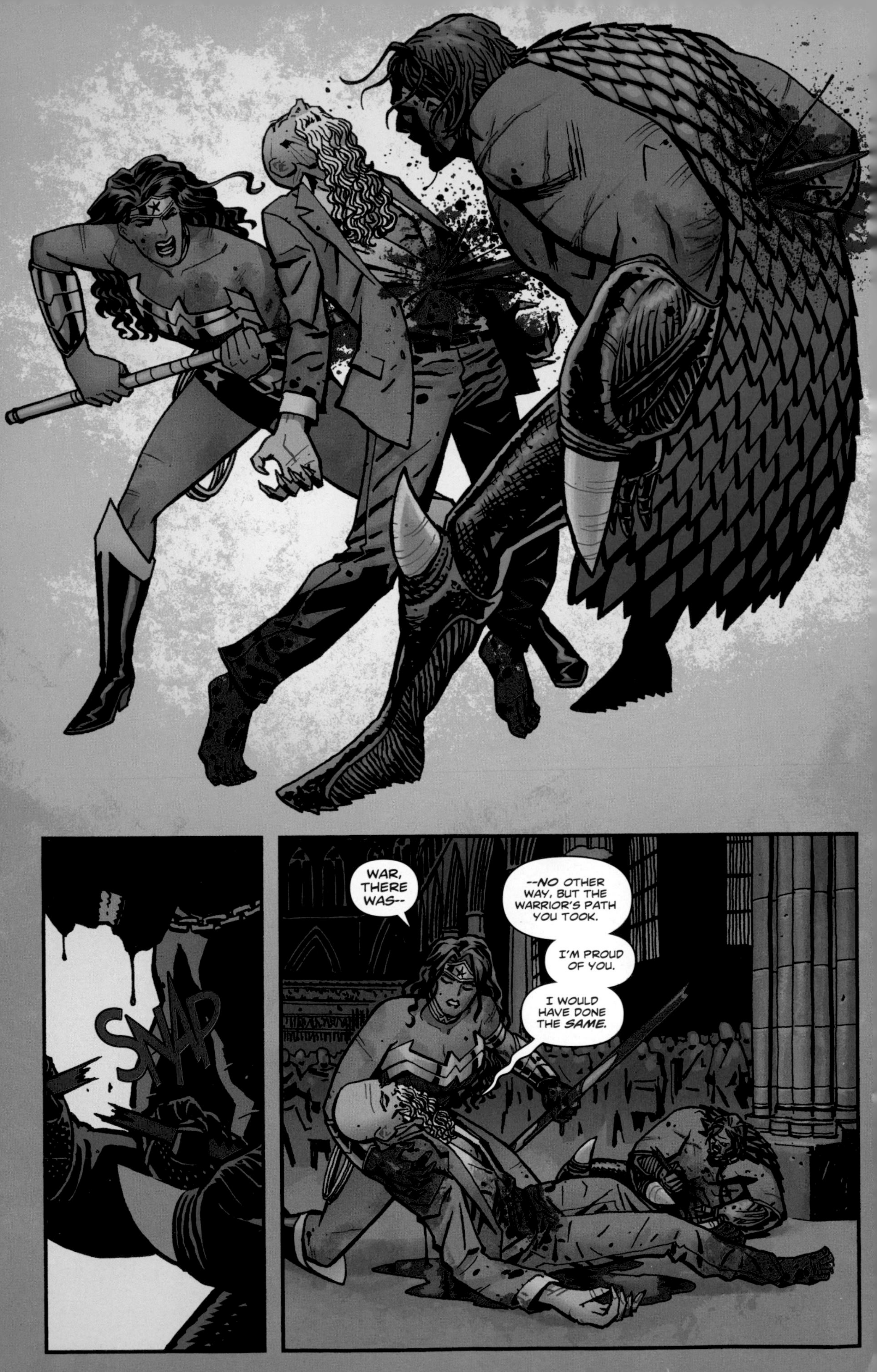
SNAP
WAR, THERE WAS--
--NO OTHER WAY, BUT THE WARRIOR'S PATH YOU TOOK.
I'M PROUD OF YOU.
I WOULD HAVE DONE THE *SAME*.

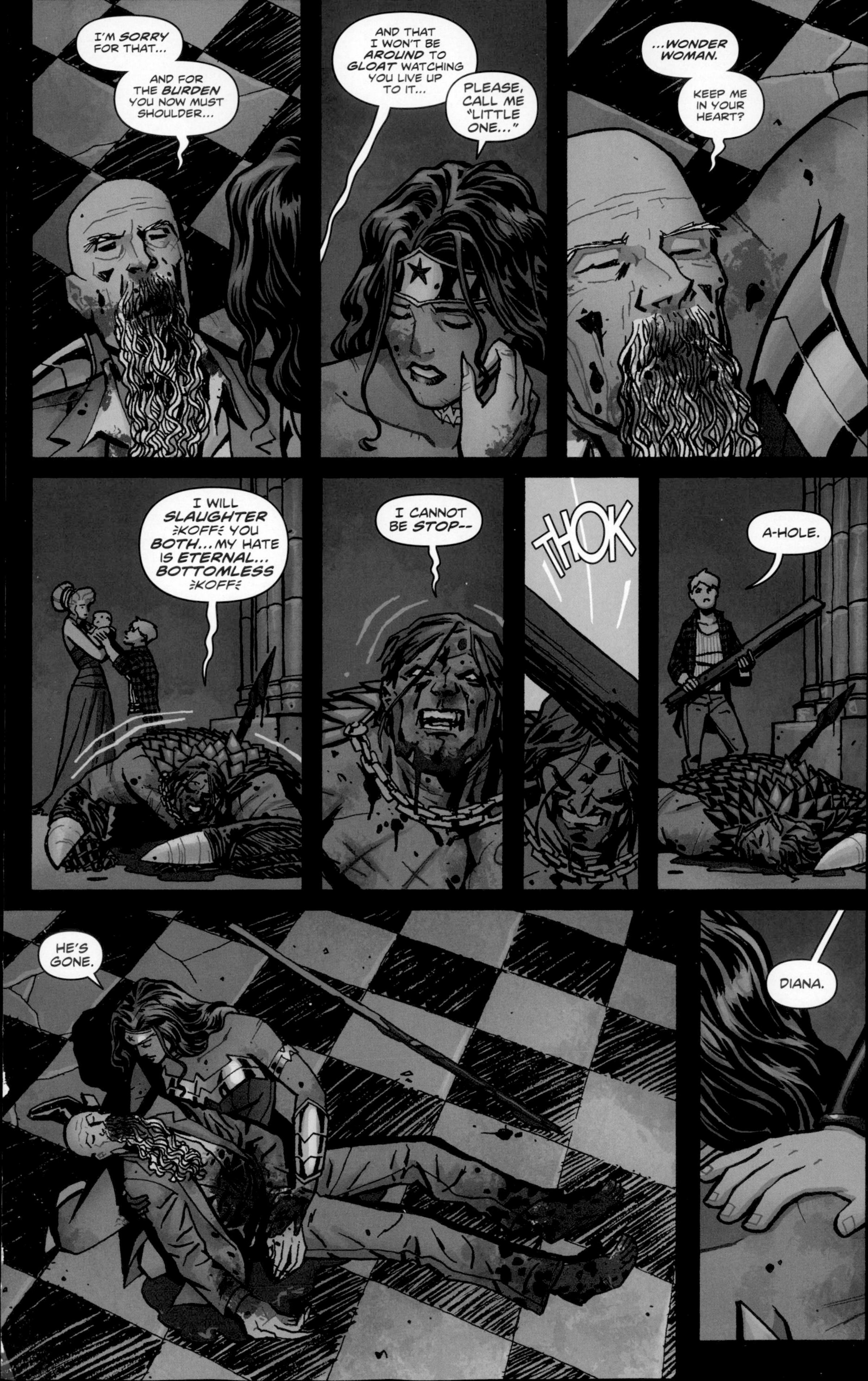
I'M SORRY FOR THAT...
AND FOR THE BURDEN YOU NOW MUST SHOULDER...
AND THAT I WON'T BE AROUND TO GLOAT WATCHING YOU LIVE UP TO IT...
PLEASE, CALL ME "LITTLE ONE..."
...WONDER WOMAN.
KEEP ME IN YOUR HEART?
I WILL SLAUGHTER *KOFF* YOU BOTH... MY HATE IS ETERNAL... BOTTOMLESS *KOFF*
I CANNOT BE STOP--
THOK
A-HOLE.
HE'S GONE.
DIANA.

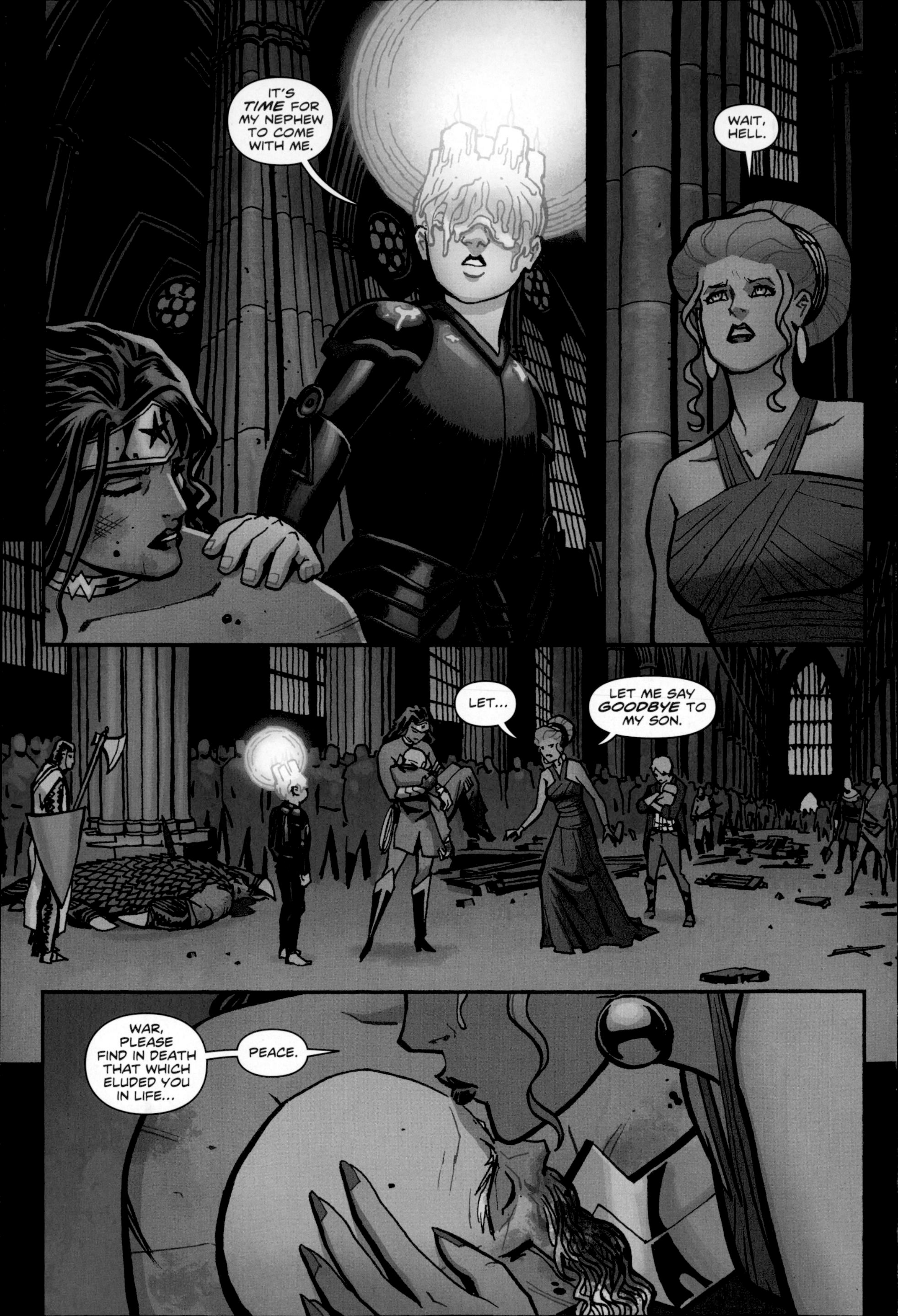
IT'S *TIME* FOR MY NEPHEW TO COME WITH ME.
WAIT, HELL.
LET...
LET ME SAY *GOODBYE* TO MY SON.
WAR, PLEASE FIND IN DEATH THAT WHICH ELUDED YOU IN LIFE...
PEACE.

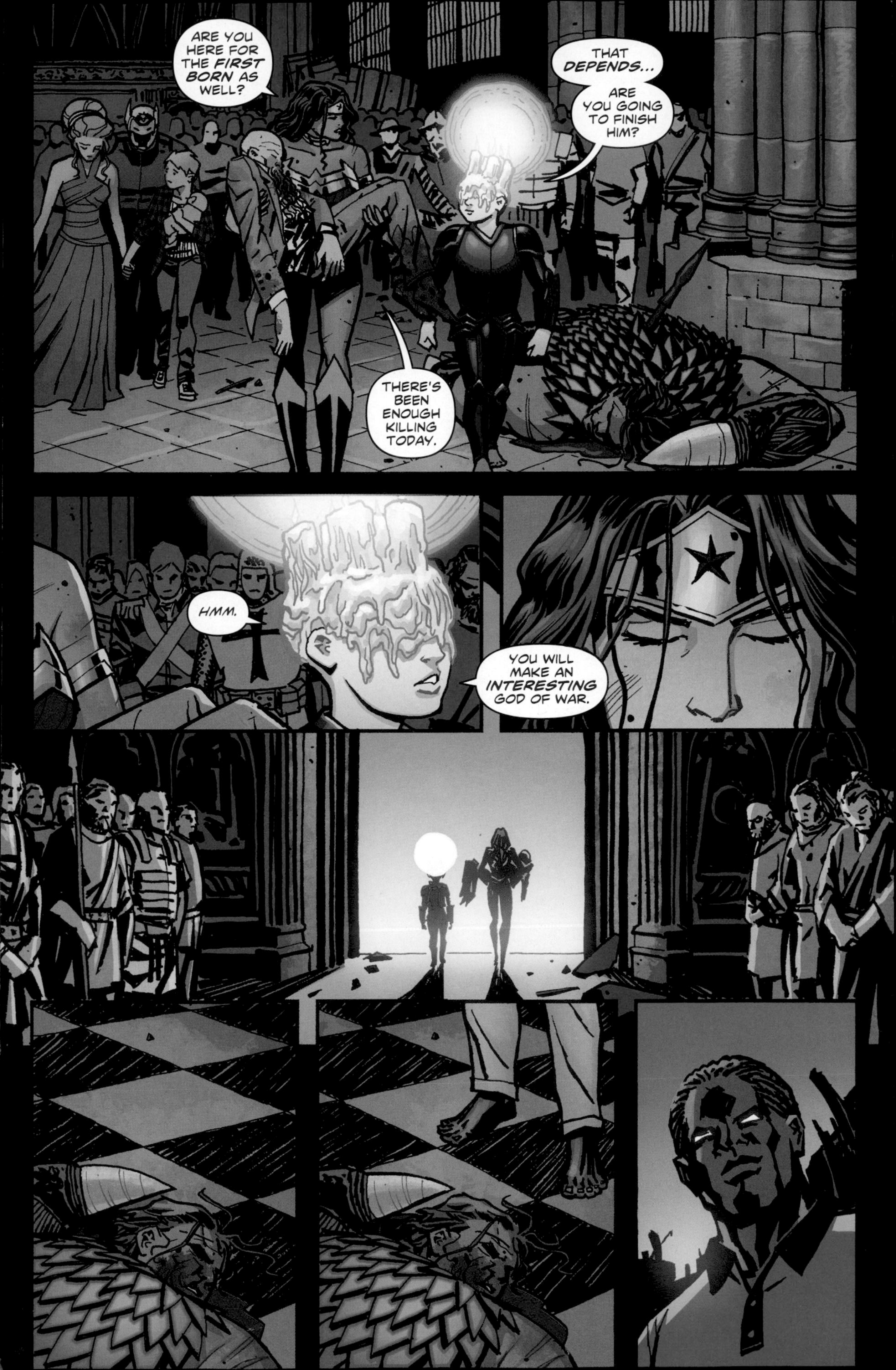
ARE YOU HERE FOR THE *FIRST BORN* AS WELL?
THAT *DEPENDS...*
ARE YOU GOING TO FINISH HIM?
THERE'S BEEN ENOUGH KILLING TODAY.
HMM.
YOU WILL MAKE AN *INTERESTING* GOD OF WAR.

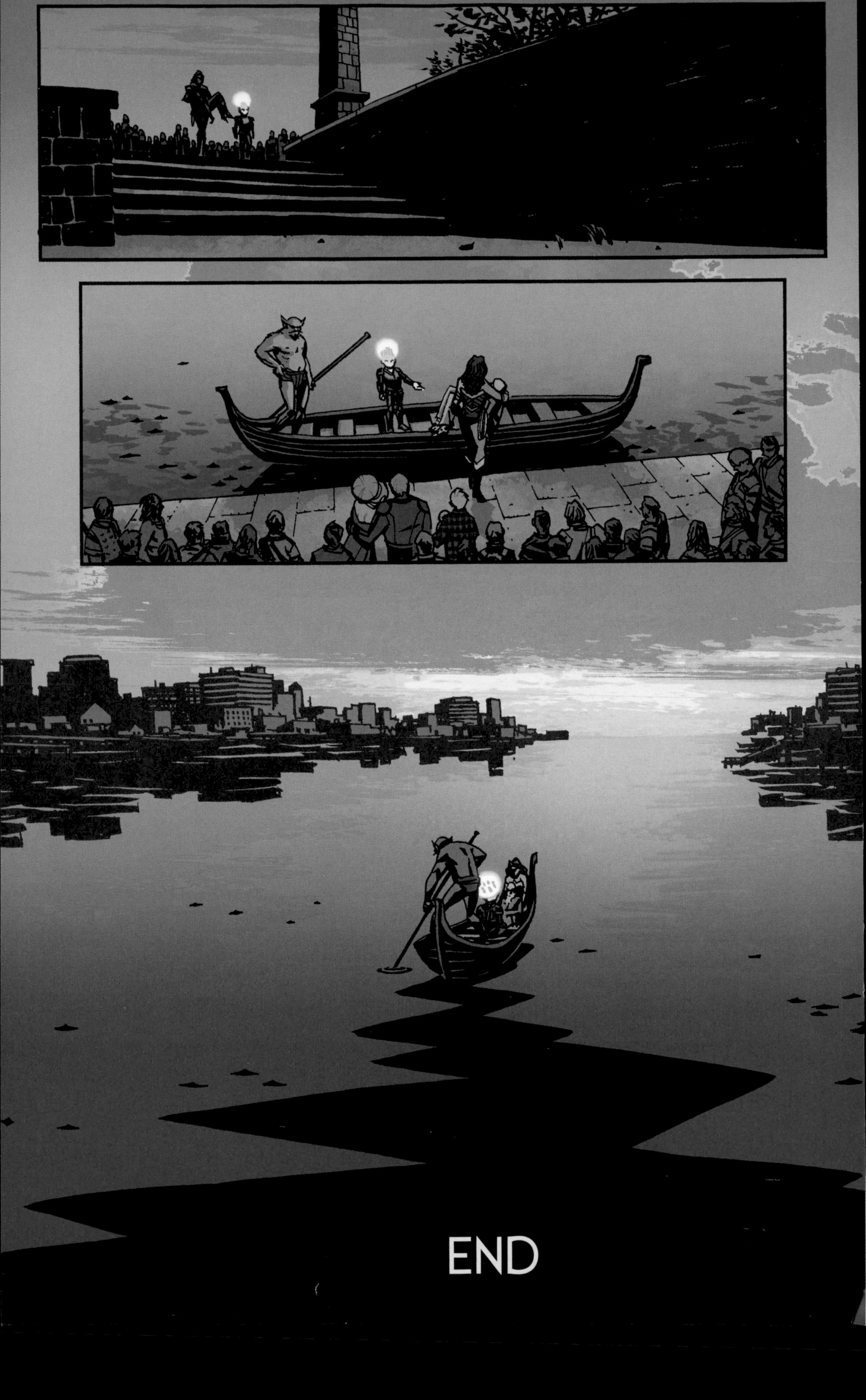
END

WONDER WOMAN

ISSUE #19 PENCILS BY GORAN SUDŽUKA

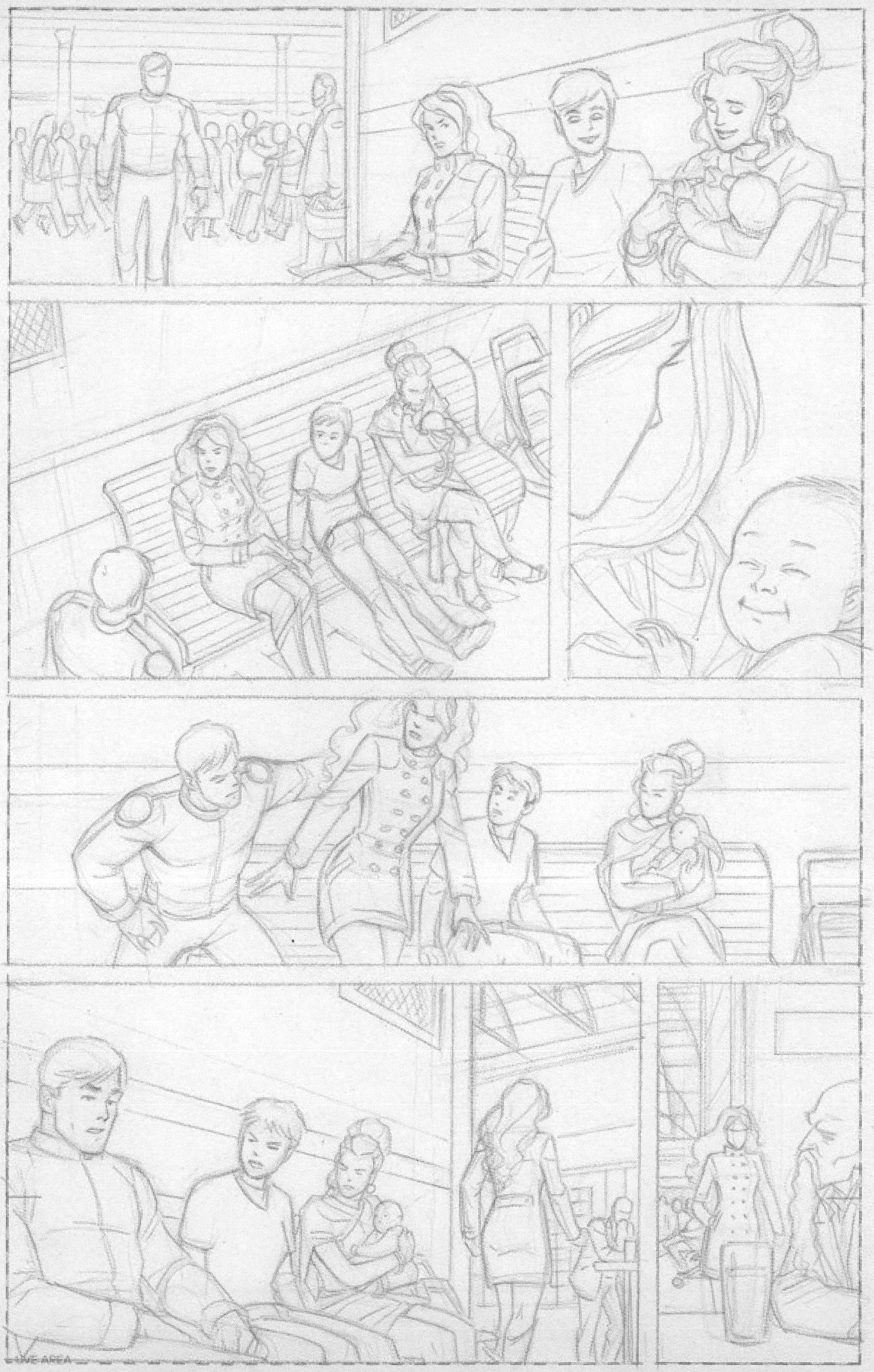
LIVE AREA

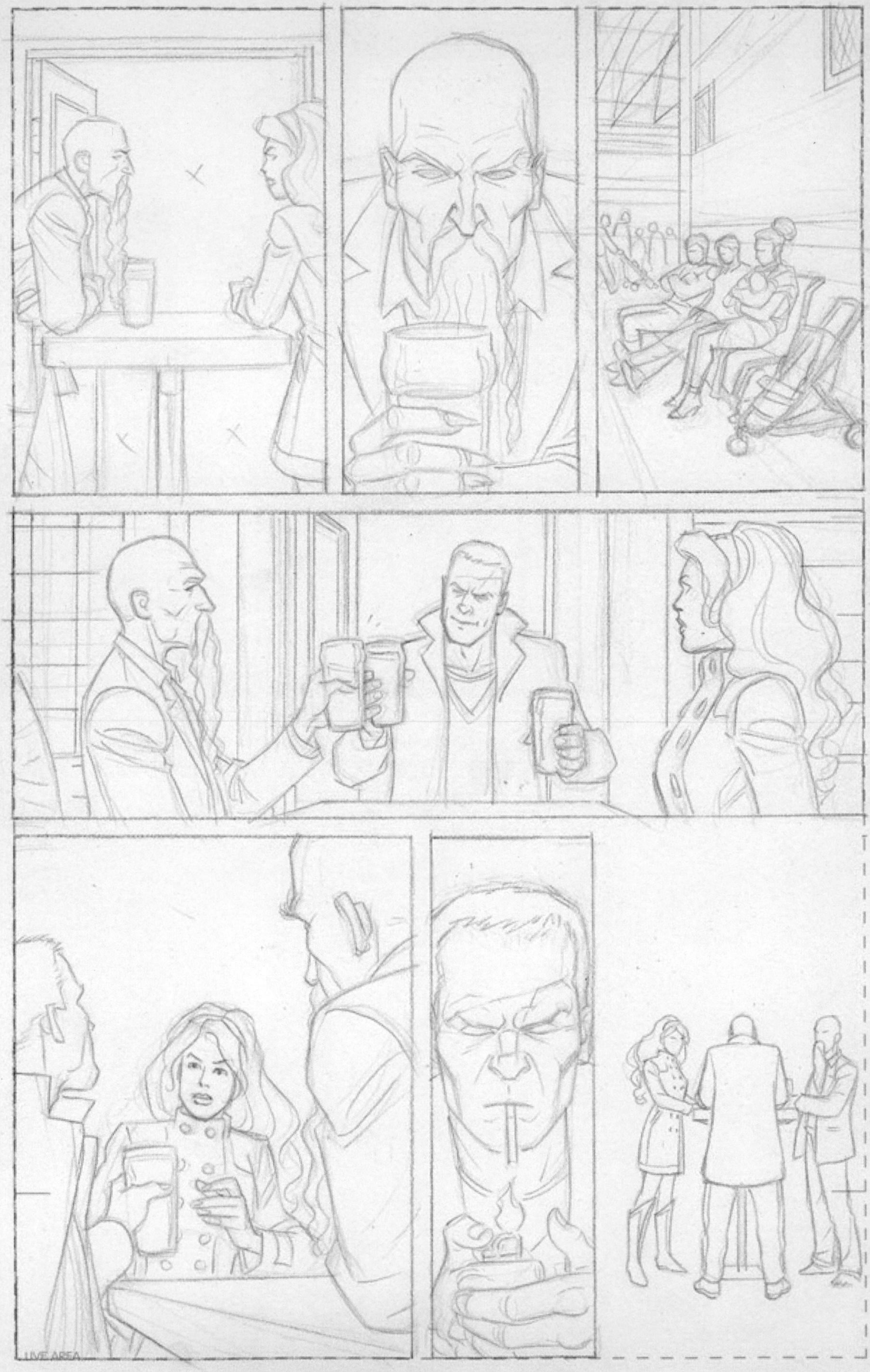
LIVE AREA

WONDER WOMAN 23 PLOT

We pick up right where we left off...

PAGE 1
Hyena man taunts WW, WW throws lasso, which main Hyena man dodges, but WW was aiming for a giant piece of rubble.

PAGE 2
WW swings lasso and takes out all nearby Hyena men. First Born laughs. "My family is bigger than yours."

PAGE 3
Reveal hordes of Hyena men around FB, moving towards group.

PAGE 4
War walks away from the group, mumbling to himself. He really seems like a doddering old man here. War knocks over either a wall or a column-- something that can create a lot of dust-- which it does. Dust fills the air, obscuring everything. FB laughs at War and his dust. "You can't hide from me, old man."

PAGE 5

Splash page. "Who's hiding?" Behind War is an army of warriors from all human history. Cavemen with clubs, Spartans, Goths, Romans, Crusaders, Redcoats, Nazis, WWII Marines, Viet Cong, etc.-- along with all their weaponry. It's epic.

PAGE 6

Hyena men and soldiers fight, as WW and War bond. I mean, he's going to have to tell her that he's proud of what she became, right? 4 panels. Last panel transition: Orion protects Hera and Zola (who grabs Hera's hand) from Hyena men.

PAGE 7

Hera and Zola bond, as they both try to protect each other. Zola pulls Hera in one direction, while Hera pulls in the other. Hera: "What do you think you're doing?" Zola: "Protecting you!" Hera: "No, I'M protecting YOU." They move past War's army towards abbey exit. Zola confides to Hera "Something tells me we're gonna be OK" – referring to Zeke, who is asleep.

PAGES 8-9

The Firstborn/Orion showdown. This has to be extremely brutal, with loads of dirty wrestling moves; eye gouges, bake rakes, low blows-- a real slobberknocker. Unlike last time, the First Born triumphs. Orion is powered by anger, War is powered by hate. Battle takes out back of church. Hate wins. FB crawls out of rubble.
Winded, he stands over Orion... as WW's cuffs hit the ground.

PAGE 10

FB swats soldiers away and makes his way towards War & WW. (What really has FB's attention is War; by killing him, he will take his throne. Our crew don't know this. It seems he's coming for WW.) War questions WW's strategy in fighting the First Born; brute strength vs. brute strength. WW assures him she knows what she's doing. "That doesn't make it smart," War counters. (Perhaps he'll also point out that WW is revealing to the world just how powerful she is. She'll counter that with, "Perhaps it needs to."

PAGES 11-13

The two-fisted meat-beating battle between WW & the FB. Go nuts. The thing is, everything she does, FB can take; it's almost as if he's conditioned to pain. One thing that does happen is WW begins to tire... and that's when FB strikes back. She's just an impediment to him-- War is the prize he wants. He makes quick work of WW. Before he can kill her, FB gets blasted with some machine gun fire (or something). It's War, holding the gun.

PAGE 14

FB threatens War. (War's army defends him-- if you can fit it in.) What's important is for Hera and Zola to rush to WW's aid. WW is beating herself up over her strategy, but there's no time for that! Get the cuffs on her.

PAGE 15
War puts up a good fight, but FB is just too much. He tells War he's going to kill him, fulfill the prophecy, take his throne, and then kill all the others. FB grabs War, and is going to kill him-- he'll get War's thrown, and take down Olympus from within. War sure looks done for... WW and War eye contact?... Fb is gloating... We need to see an energy flash from the cuffs...

PAGE 16
Let's go crazy... War pukes blood on FB's face. FB angrily whispers, "No..." Pull back. We see WW has driven a pike (or her sword) through War's back and into the FB. War hangs, dead. FB breaks the spear off, as WW catches War's body. (Or WW pulls the sword out.)

PAGES 17-18
WW cradles War... tender moment. He's proud of her, but also very sorry for the burden he's given her. He also tells her that he wasn't the first, and she won't be the last. While this is going on, an angry FB falls to his knees. WW is crying. He's like a dog that won't quit fighting, he's swinging at the air, desperately trying to get at War and kill him. Now, he can either run out of energy and pass out, or maybe Hera and Zola whack him, and knock him out. It can go either way.

War dies.

Just so you know, I think she would kill him dead while he's in FB's clutches, thereby ending the threat. And the melodrama.

(Also, should we do a dorky Highlander shtick and have some sort of energy plasma swirl around WW to show she's the God of War now? My gut says no, but it's been wrong before...)

PAGES 19-20

As WW cradles a dead War, a hand appears on her shoulder; it's Hades, & he's there for his brother. Might as well have his boat there too, maybe sailing on mist and haze. WW picks up War and takes him to the boat-- or War "floats" to the boat, if you'd like Hades & WW to hold hands. We should have a Hera moment too, as War was her son. Something along the lines of "He'll know something he's never known before... peace." The FB is passed along the way, and WW asks about him. Hades tells her he's not dead, but if she'd like to finish him... "No. There's been enough killing today."

WW and Hades sail away (with our crew too?) and we see that they were being watched by Apollo. He walks over to the FB, and smiles. The boat sails away. (I figure this will be accompanied by WW & Hades V/O, and he calls her the God of War.)

WONDER WOMAN

ISSUE #23 PENCILS BY CLIFF CHIANG

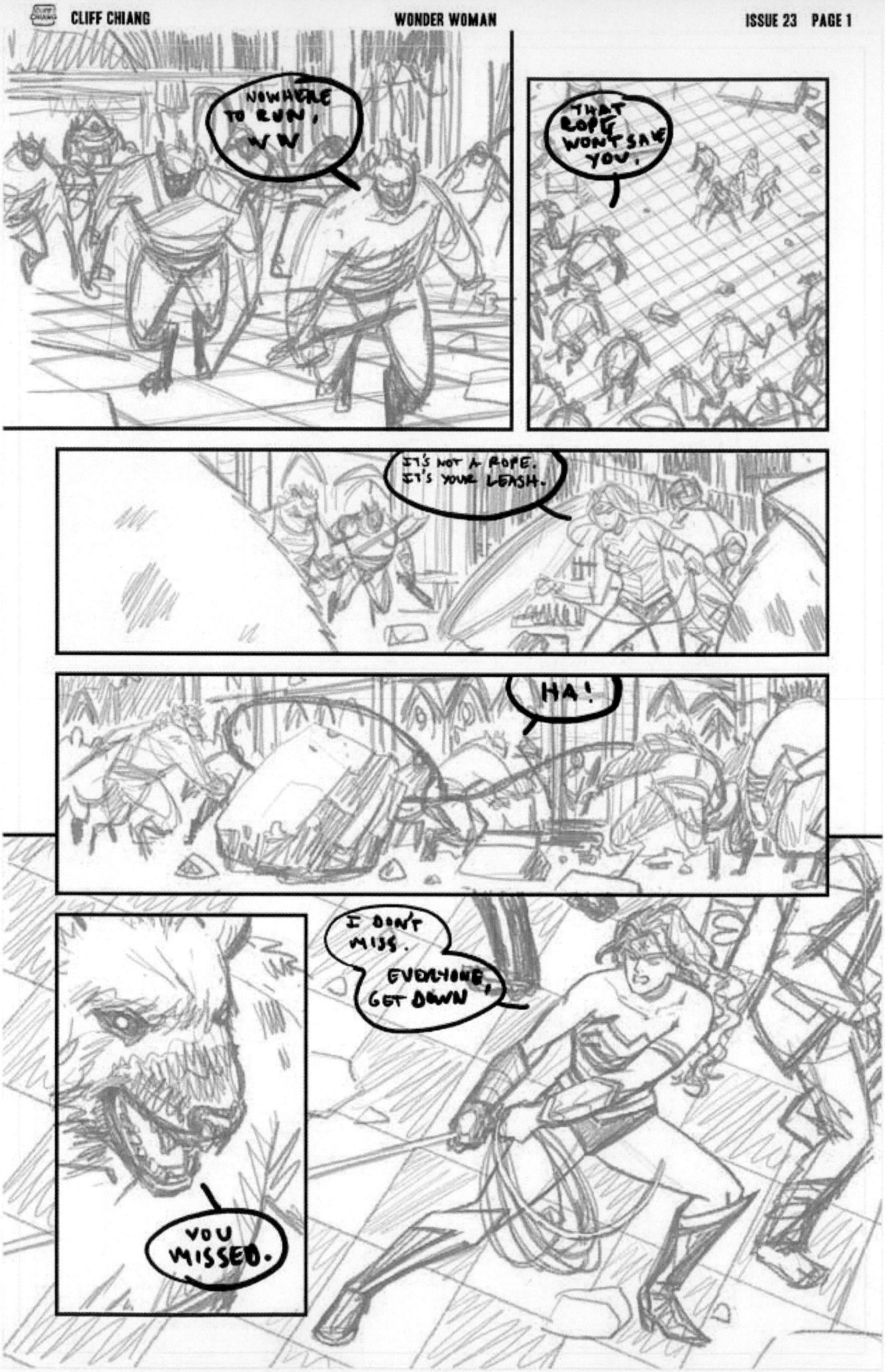
CLIFF CHIANG
WONDER WOMAN
ISSUE 23 PAGE 1
NOWHERE TO RUN, WW
THAT ROPE WON'T SAVE YOU.
IT'S NOT A ROPE. IT'S YOUR LEASH.
HA!
YOU MISSED.
I DON'T MISS.
EVERYONE, GET DOWN

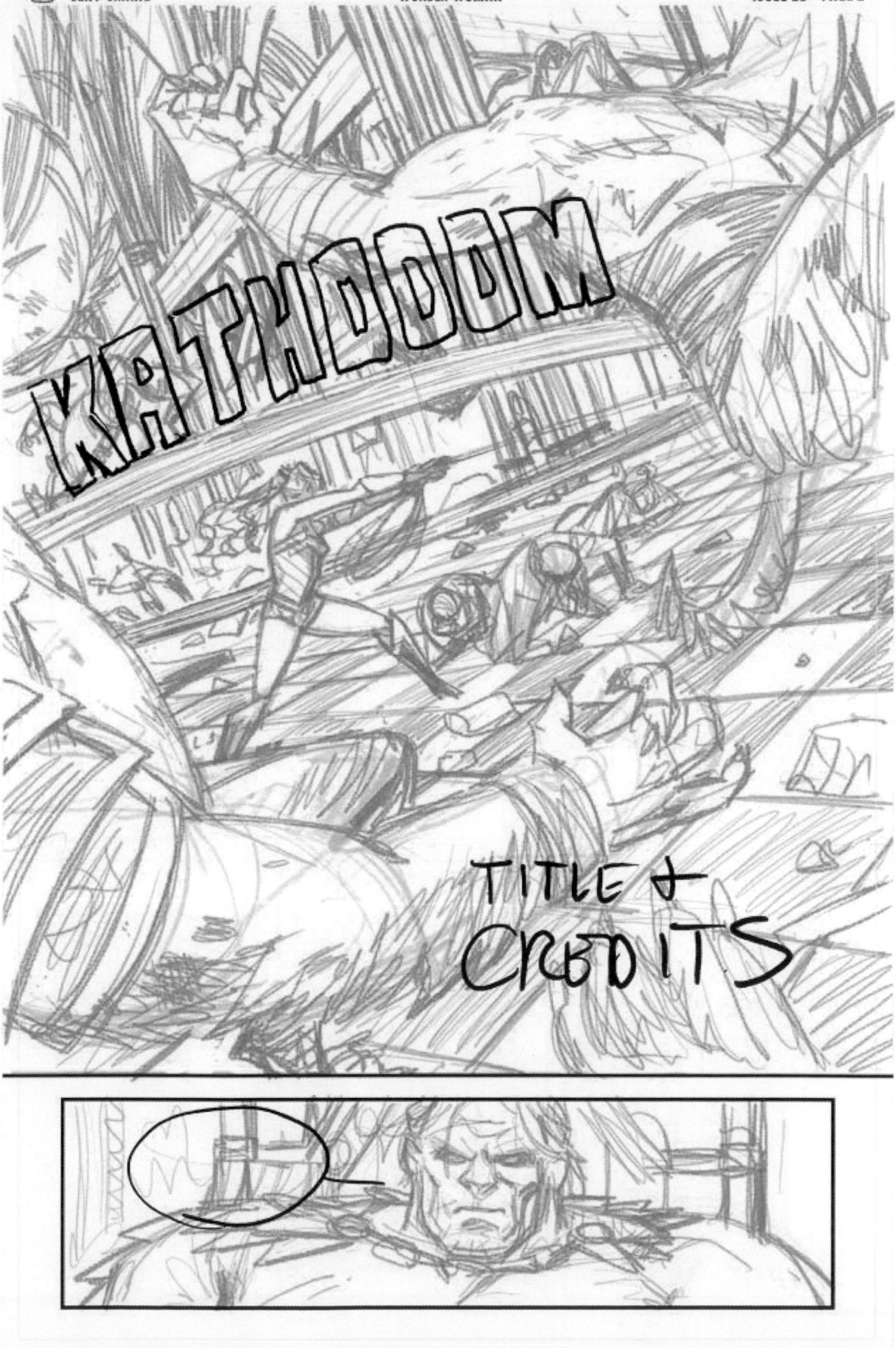
KATHOOOM
TITLE &
CREDITS

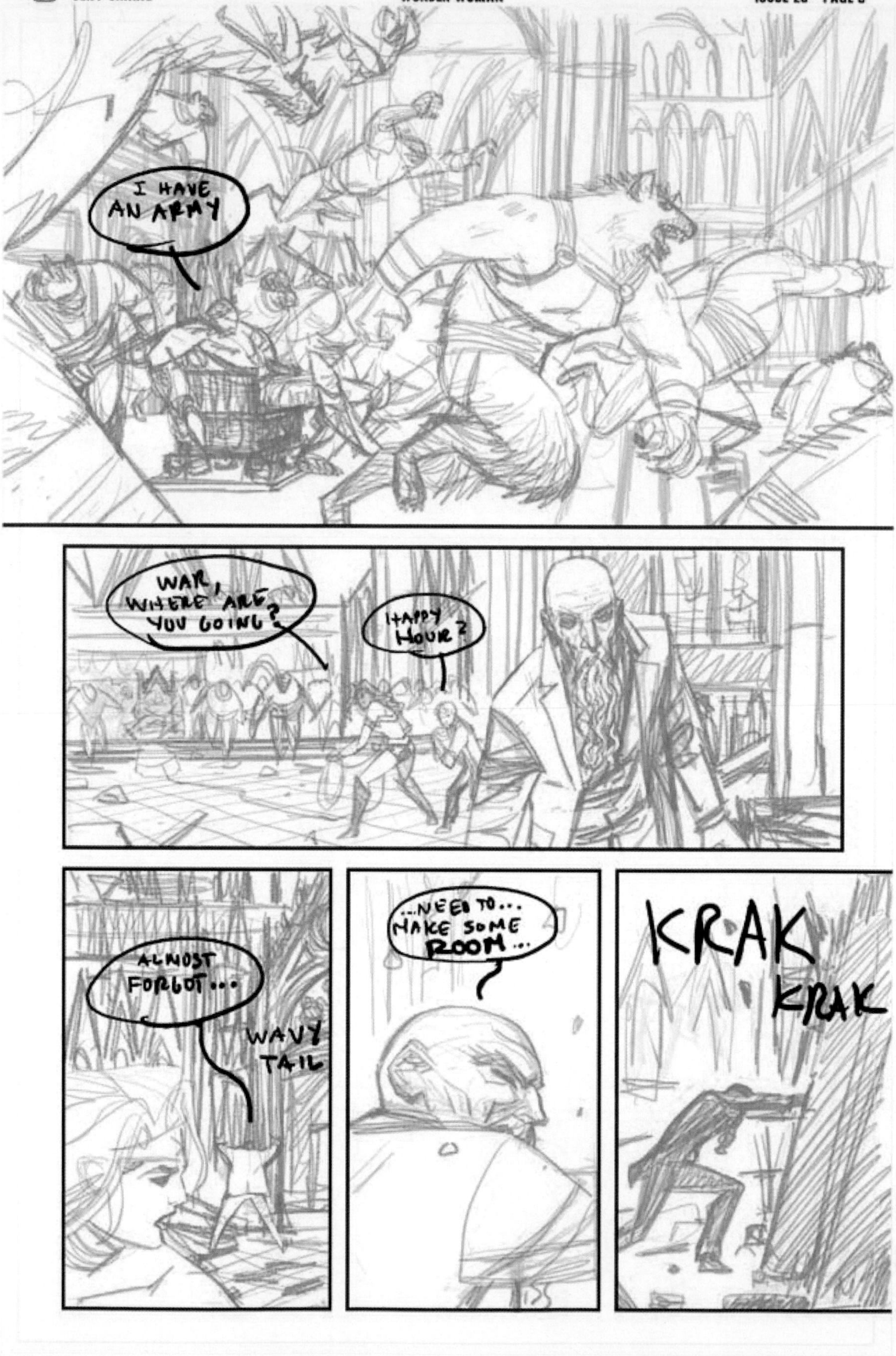
I HAVE AN ARMY
WAR, WHERE ARE YOU GOING?
HAPPY HOUR?
ALMOST FORGOT...
WAVY TAIL
...NEED TO... MAKE SOME ROOM...
KRAK
KRAK

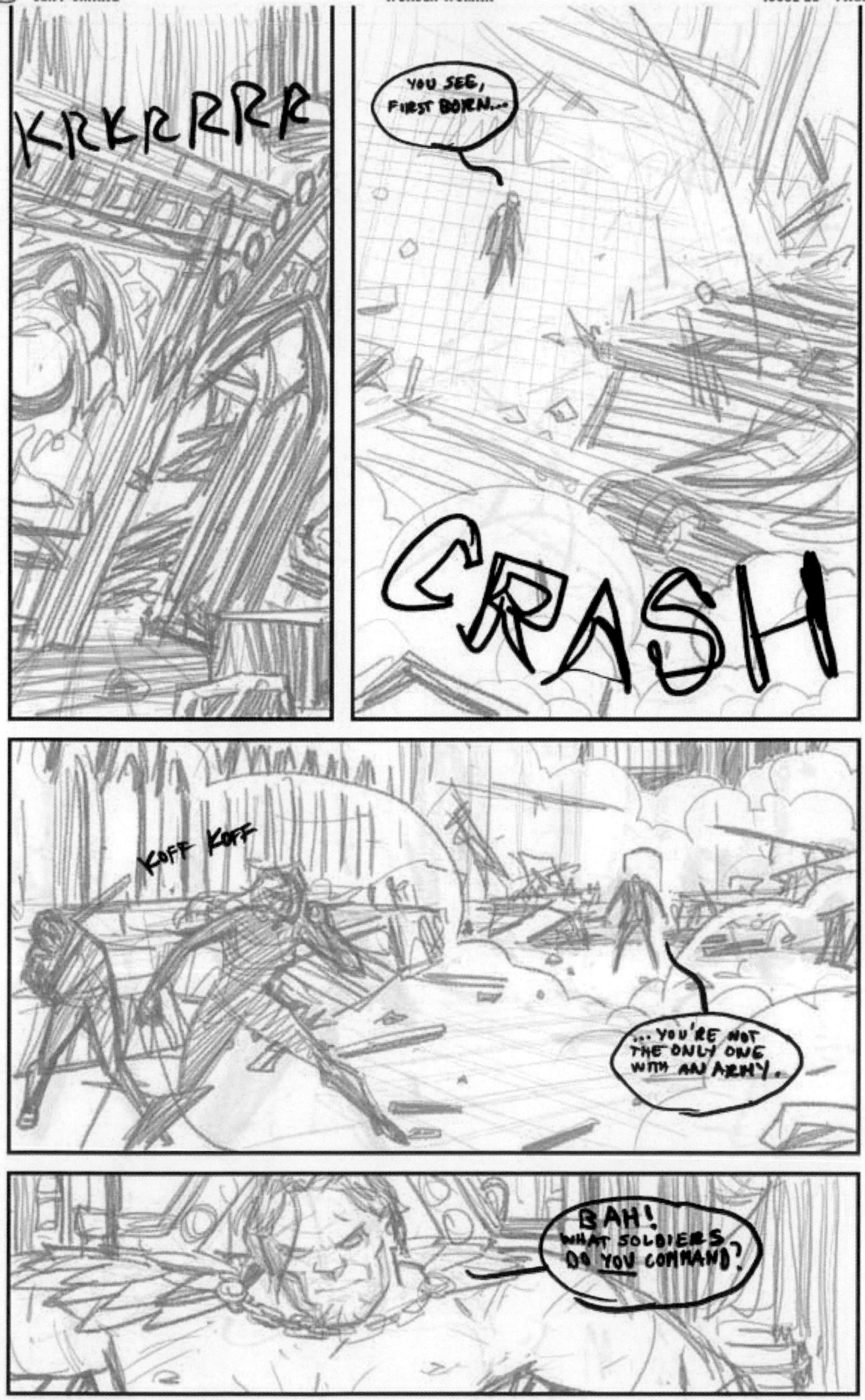
KRKRRRR
YOU SEE, FIRST BORN...
CRASH
KOFF KOFF
...YOU'RE NOT THE ONLY ONE WITH AN ARMY.
BAH! WHAT SOLDIERS DO YOU COMMAND?

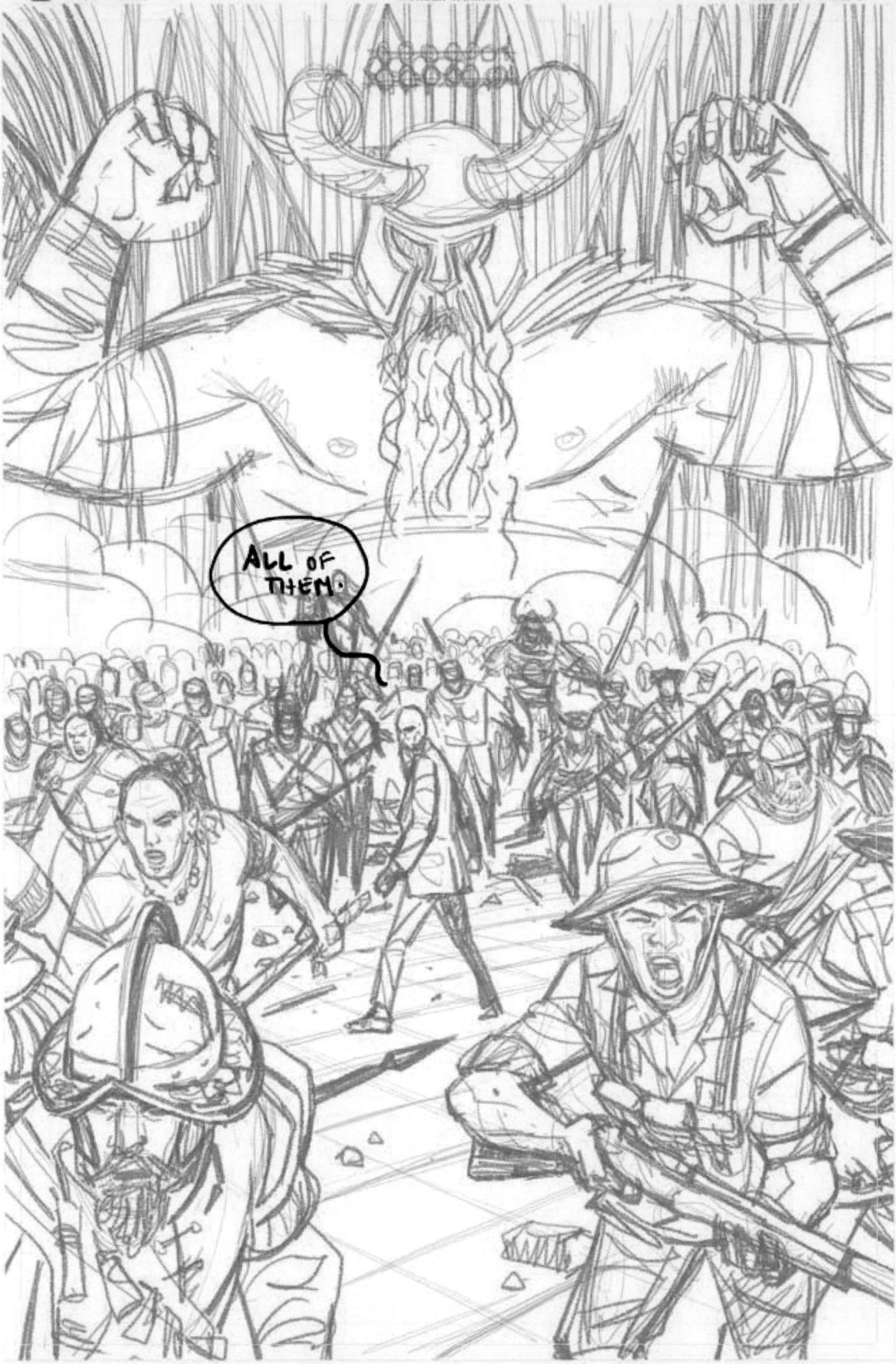
ALL OF THEM.

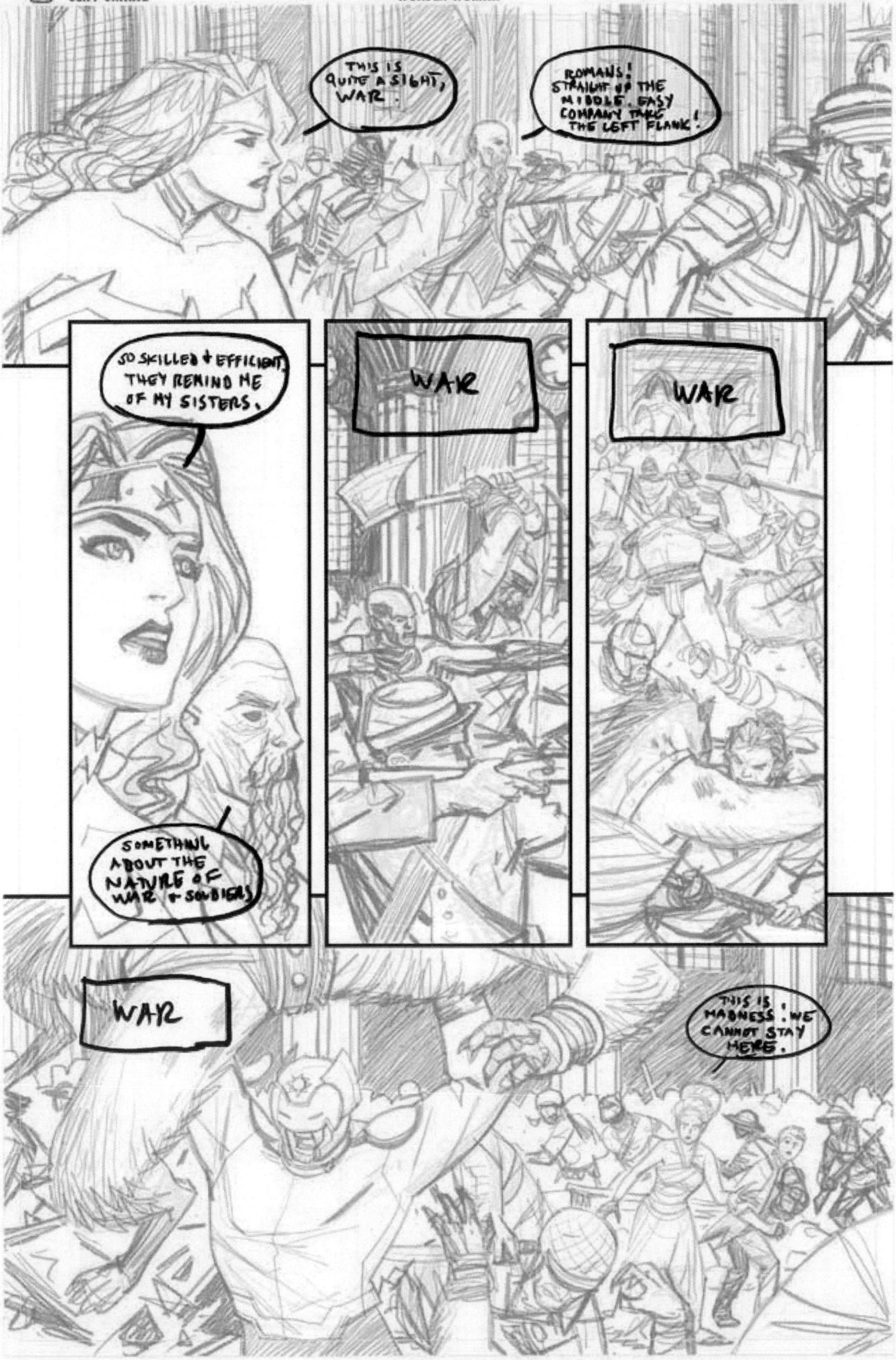
THIS IS QUITE A SIGHT, WAR.
ROMANS! STRAIGHT UP THE MIDDLE. EASY COMPANY TAKE THE LEFT FLANK!
SO SKILLED + EFFICIENT, THEY REMIND ME OF MY SISTERS.
SOMETHING ABOUT THE NATURE OF WAR + SOLDIERS
WAR
WAR
WAR
THIS IS MADNESS! WE CANNOT STAY HERE.

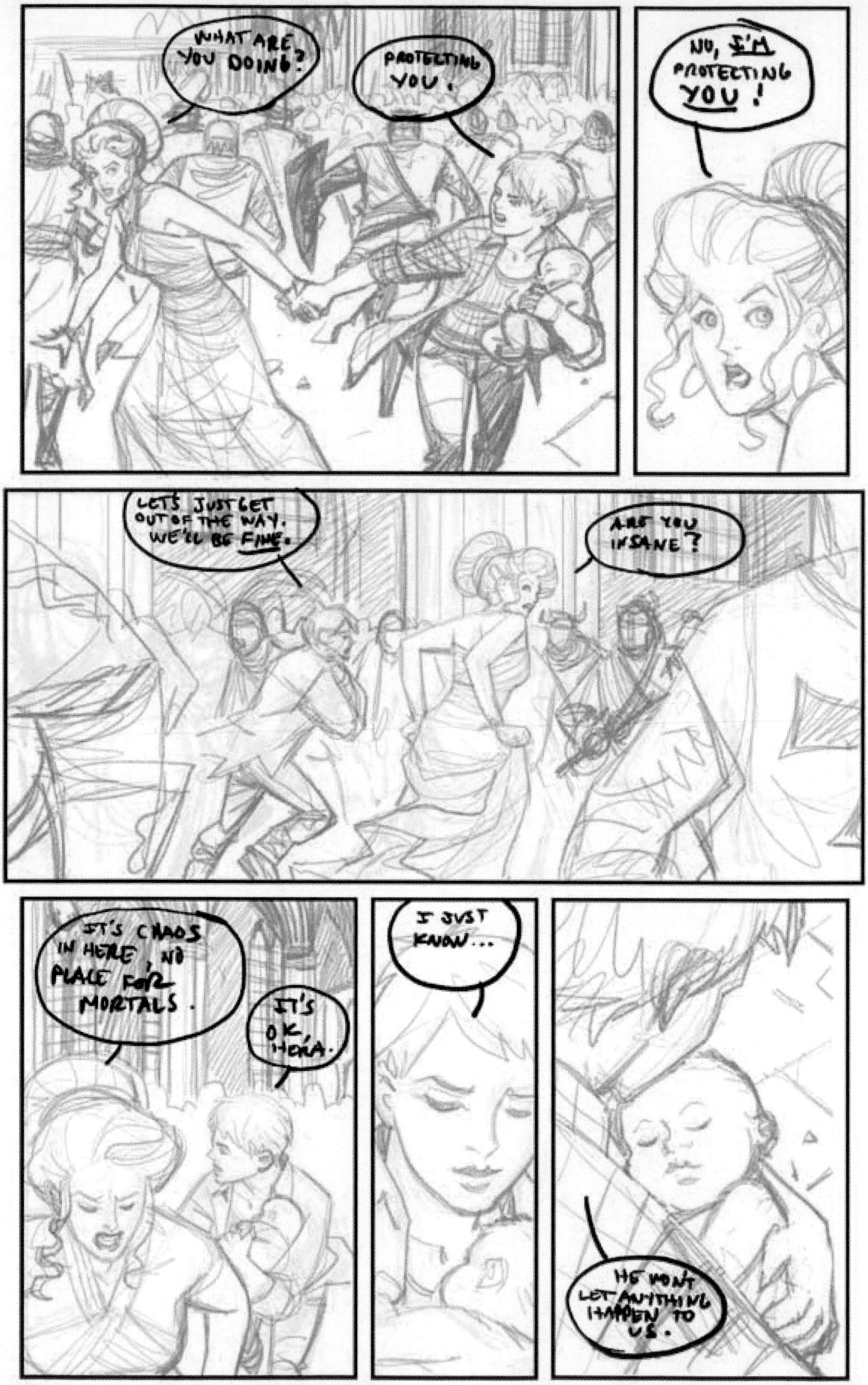
WHAT ARE YOU DOING?
PROTECTING YOU.
NO, I'M PROTECTING YOU!
LET'S JUST GET OUT OF THE WAY. WE'LL BE FINE.
ARE YOU INSANE?
IT'S CHAOS IN HERE, NO PLACE FOR MORTALS.
IT'S OK, HERA.
I JUST KNOW...
HE WON'T LET ANYTHING HAPPEN TO US.

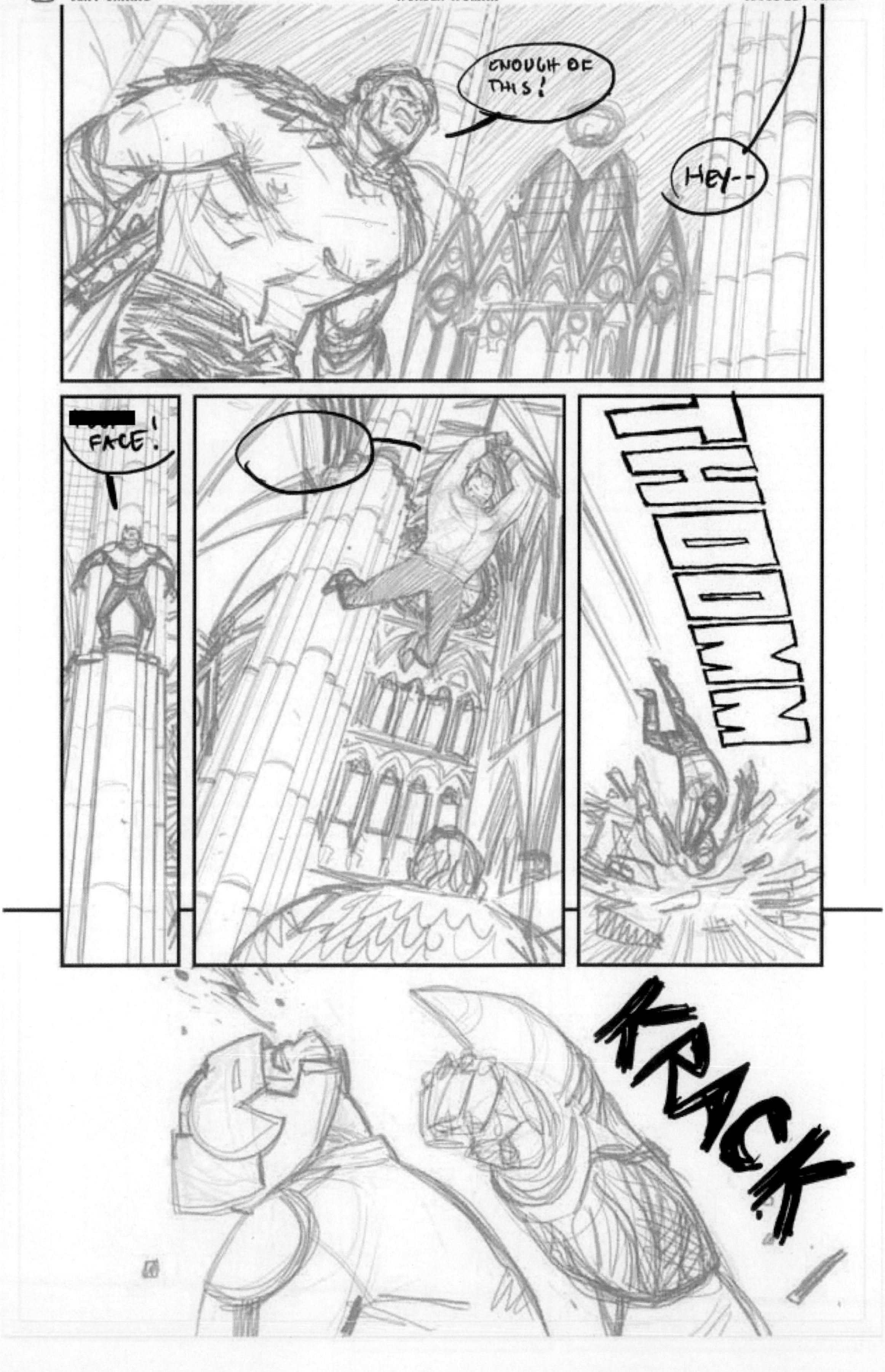
ENOUGH OF THIS!
HEY--
[redacted] FACE!
THOOMM
KRACK

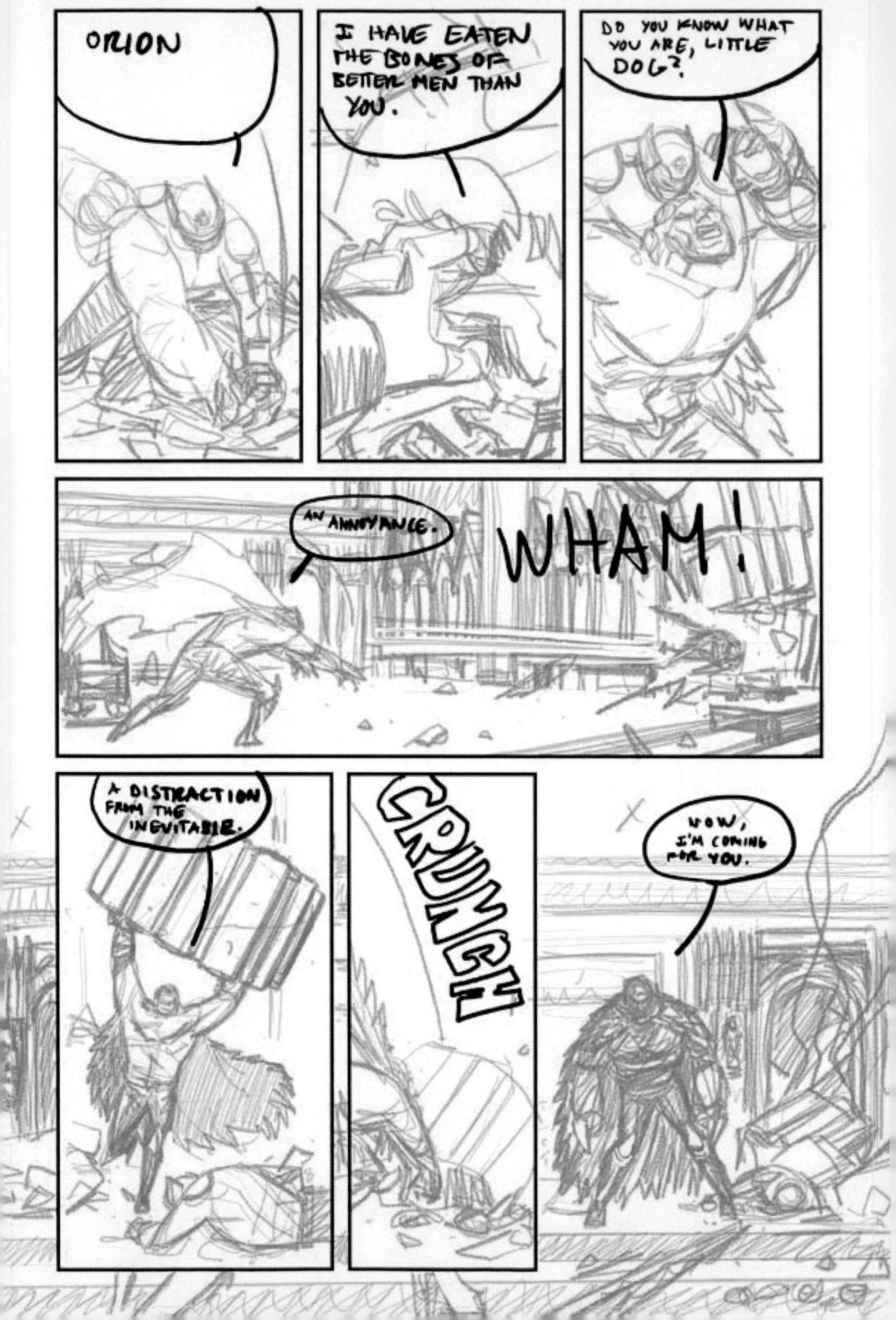
ORION
I HAVE EATEN THE BONES OF BETTER MEN THAN YOU.
DO YOU KNOW WHAT YOU ARE, LITTLE DOG?
AN ANNOYANCE.
WHAM!
A DISTRACTION FROM THE INEVITABLE.
CRUNCH
NOW, I'M COMING FOR YOU.

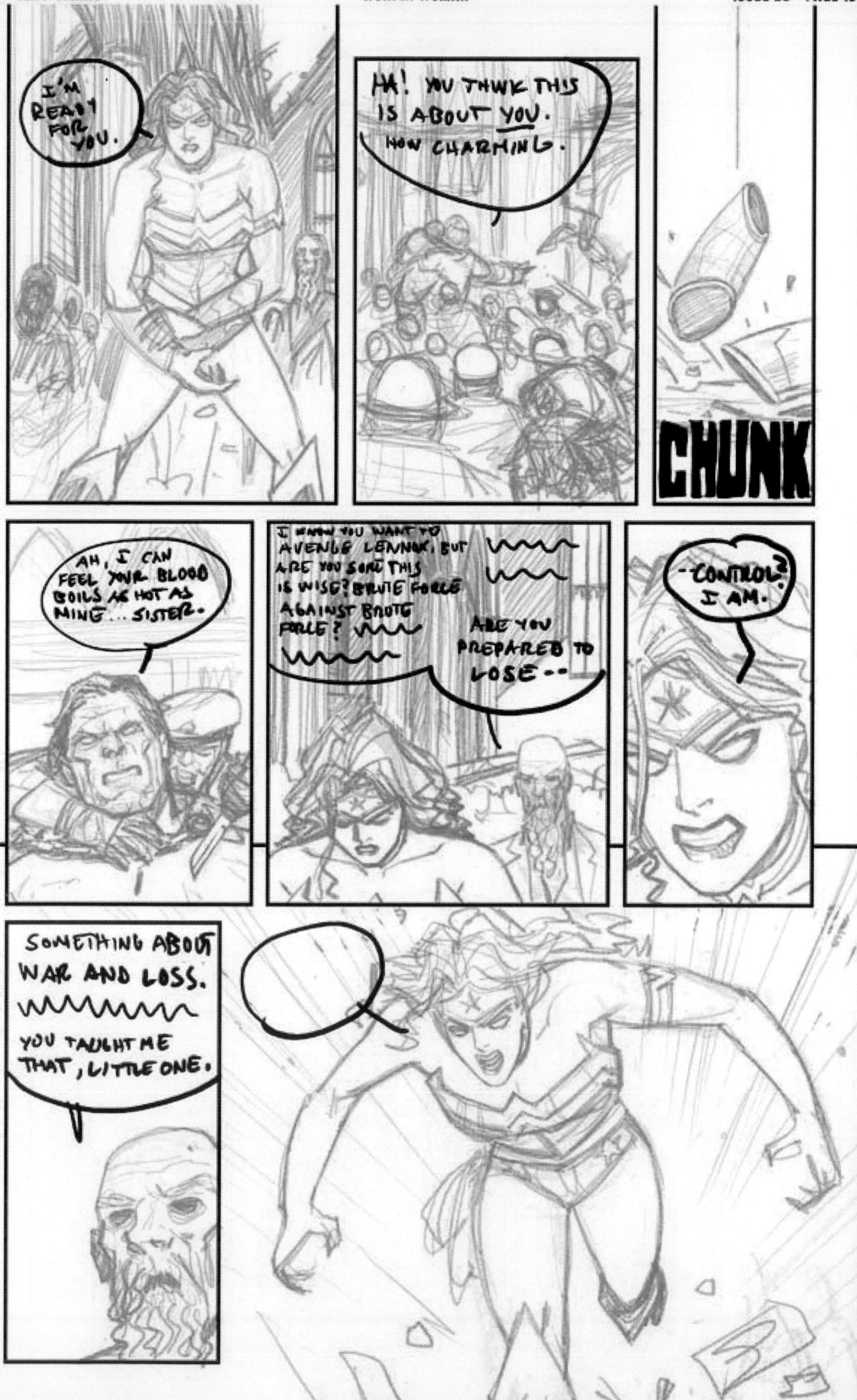
I'M READY FOR YOU.
HA! YOU THINK THIS IS ABOUT YOU. HOW CHARMING.
CHUNK
AH, I CAN FEEL YOUR BLOOD BOILS AS HOT AS MINE... SISTER.
I KNOW YOU WANT TO AVENGE LENNOX, BUT ARE YOU SURE THIS IS WISE? BRUTE FORCE AGAINST BRUTE FORCE?
ARE YOU PREPARED TO LOSE--
--CONTROL? I AM.
SOMETHING ABOUT WAR AND LOSS.
YOU TAUGHT ME THAT, LITTLE ONE.

ANGRY!
ANGRIER!
CRAZY ANGRY!!!

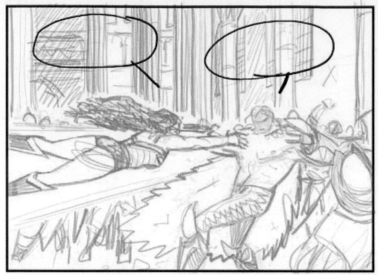

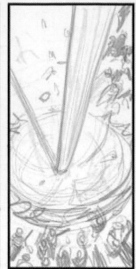

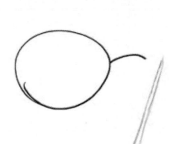

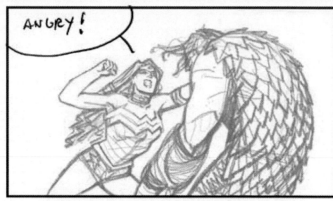

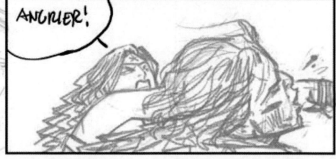

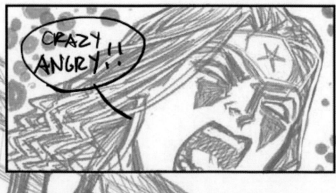

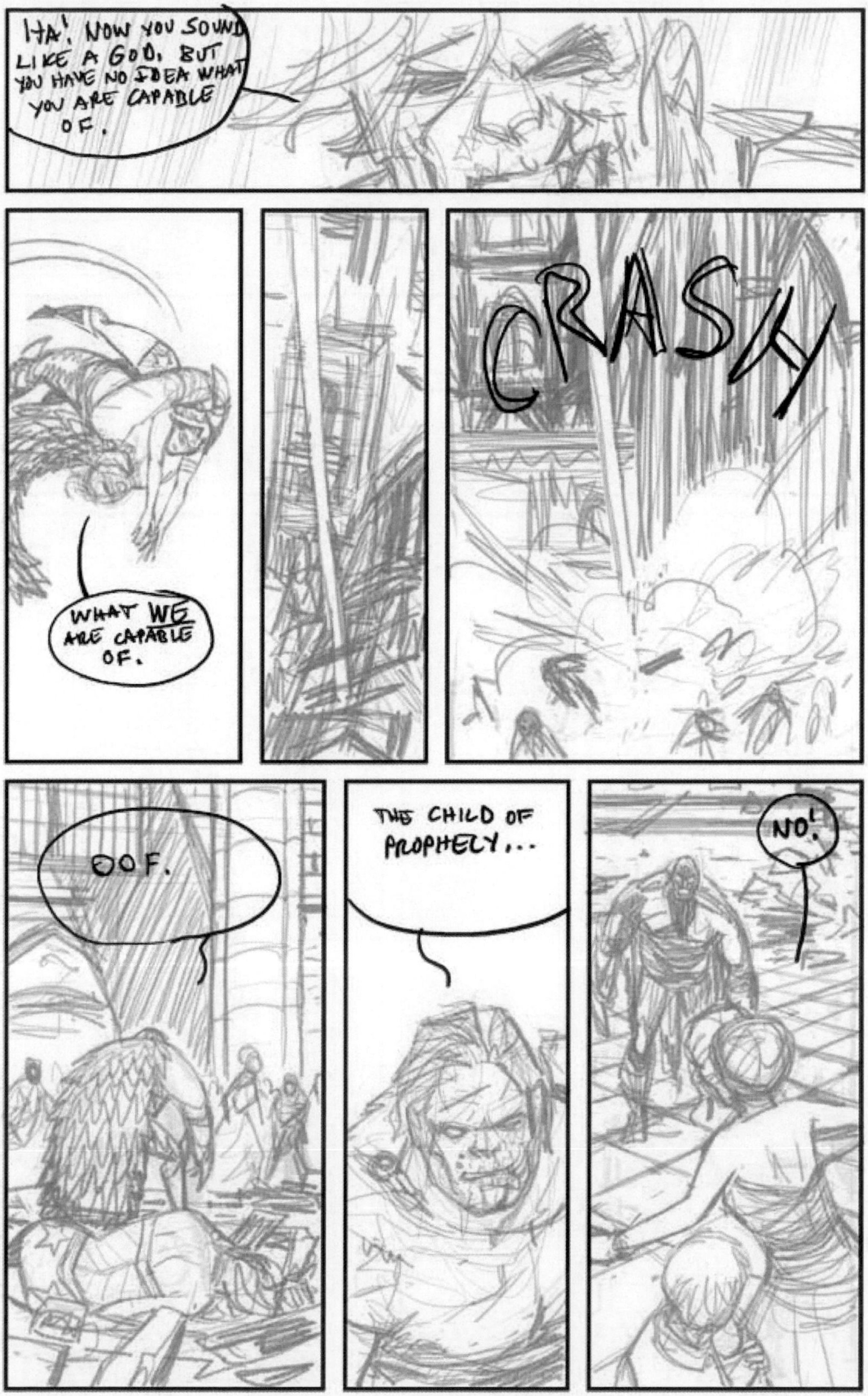
HA! NOW YOU SOUND LIKE A GOD. BUT YOU HAVE NO IDEA WHAT YOU ARE CAPABLE OF.
WHAT WE ARE CAPABLE OF.
CRASH
OOF.
THE CHILD OF PROPHECY...
NO!

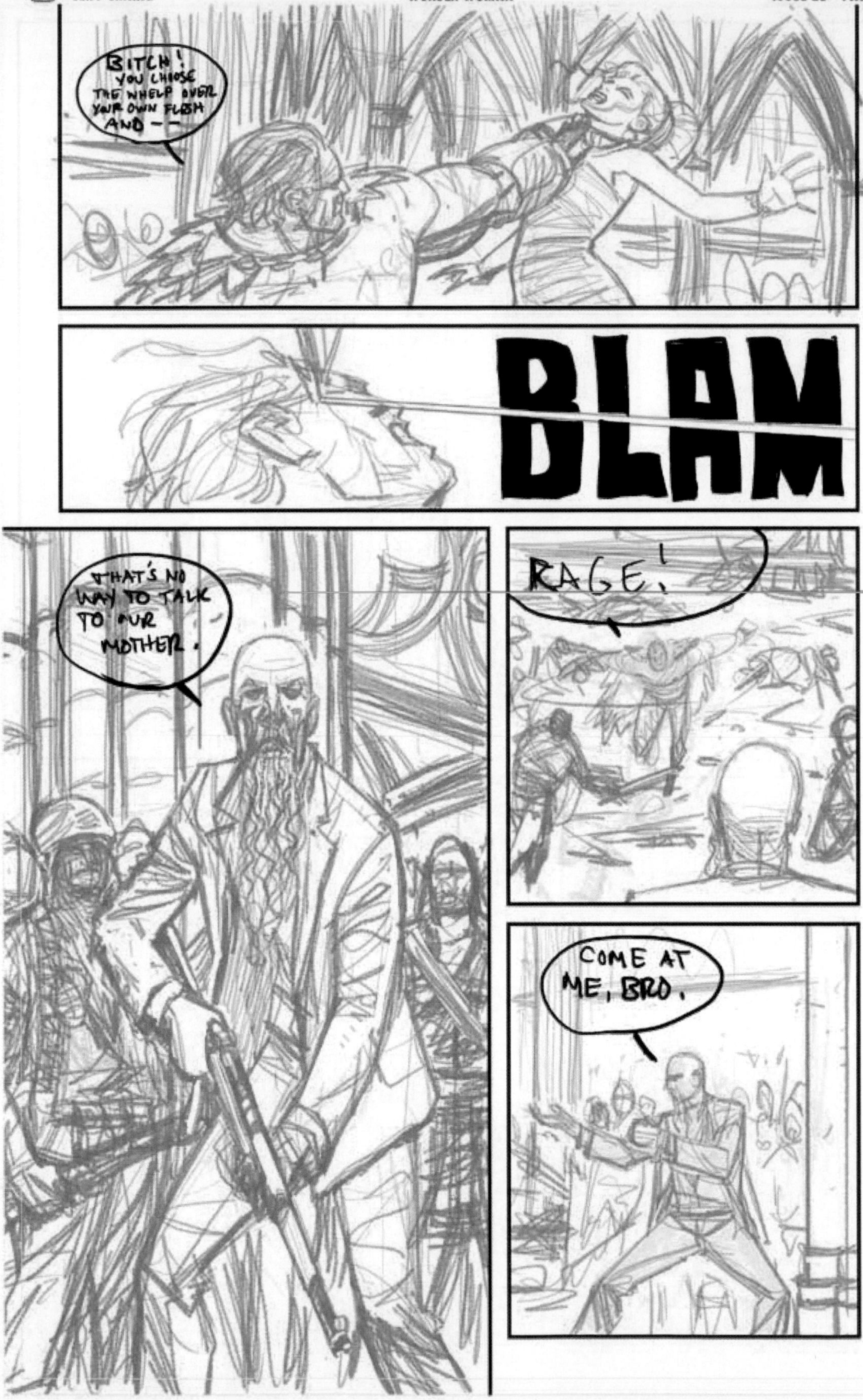
BITCH! YOU CHOSE THE WHELP OVER YOUR OWN FLESH AND --
BLAM
THAT'S NO WAY TO TALK TO OUR MOTHER.
RAGE!
COME AT ME, BRO.

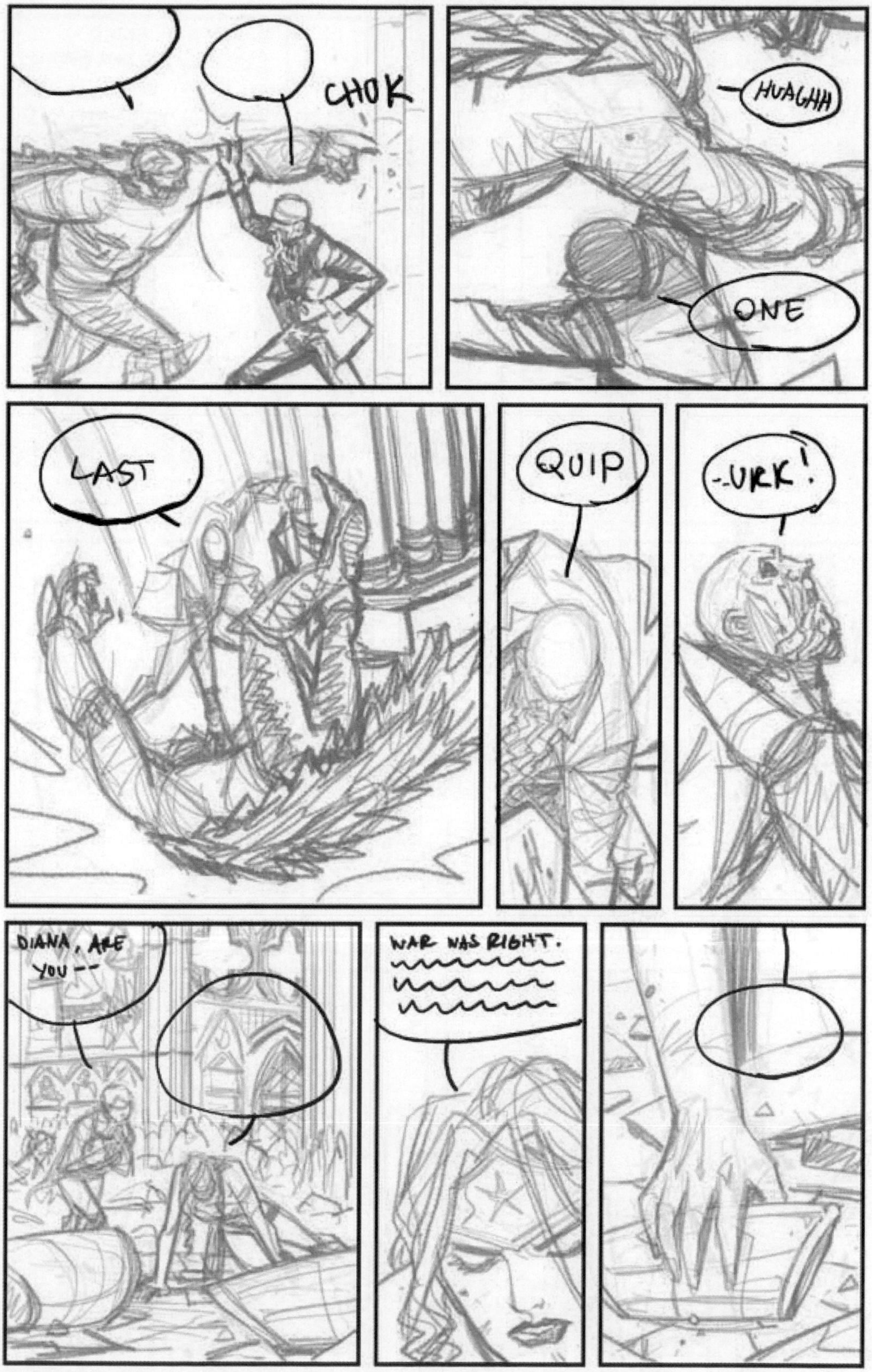
CHOK
HUAGHH
ONE
LAST
QUIP
--URK!
DIANA, ARE YOU --
WAR WAS RIGHT.

HA! HOW FOOLISH OF ME. I BELIEVED THE CHILD TO BE THE KEY TO OLYMPUS...

KAK

BUT THERE'S ANOTHER WAY...

IF I BUT ENTER OLYMPUS, I CAN DESTROY IT FROM WITHIN. AND IF ONLY THE OLYMPIANS CAN TRAVEL BETWEEN THE REALMS, THEN I MUST BECOME ONE.

I WILL BECOME THE GOD OF WAR. BY KILLING YOU.

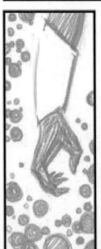

AND ALL I NEED TO DO IS SQUEEZE...

HUUAAYZGHHH

NO!

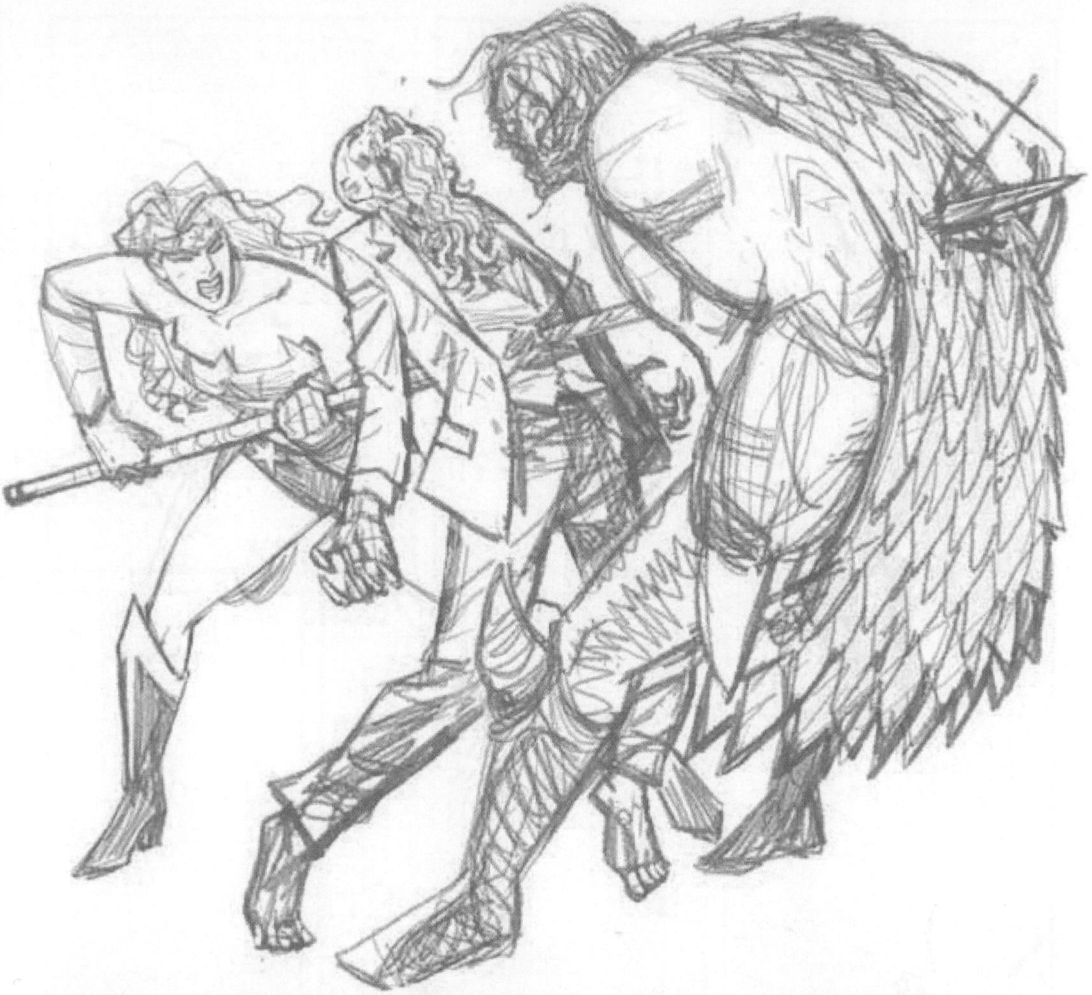

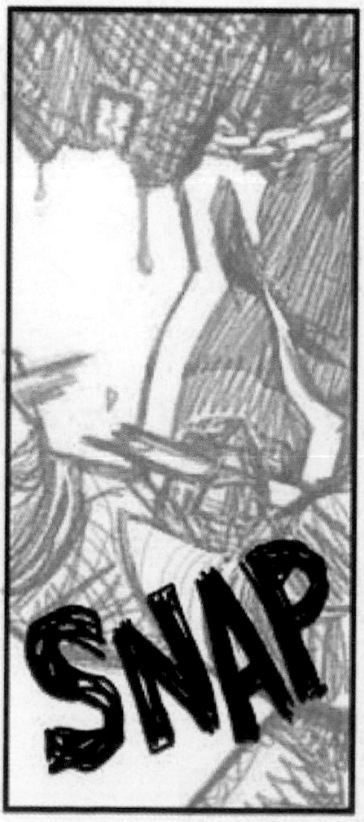
SNAP

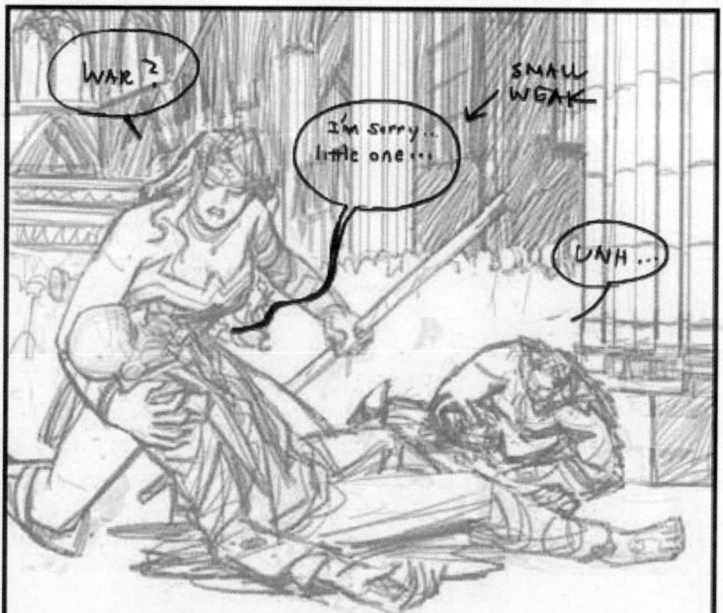
WAR?
SMALL
WEAK
I'm sorry...
little one...
UNH...

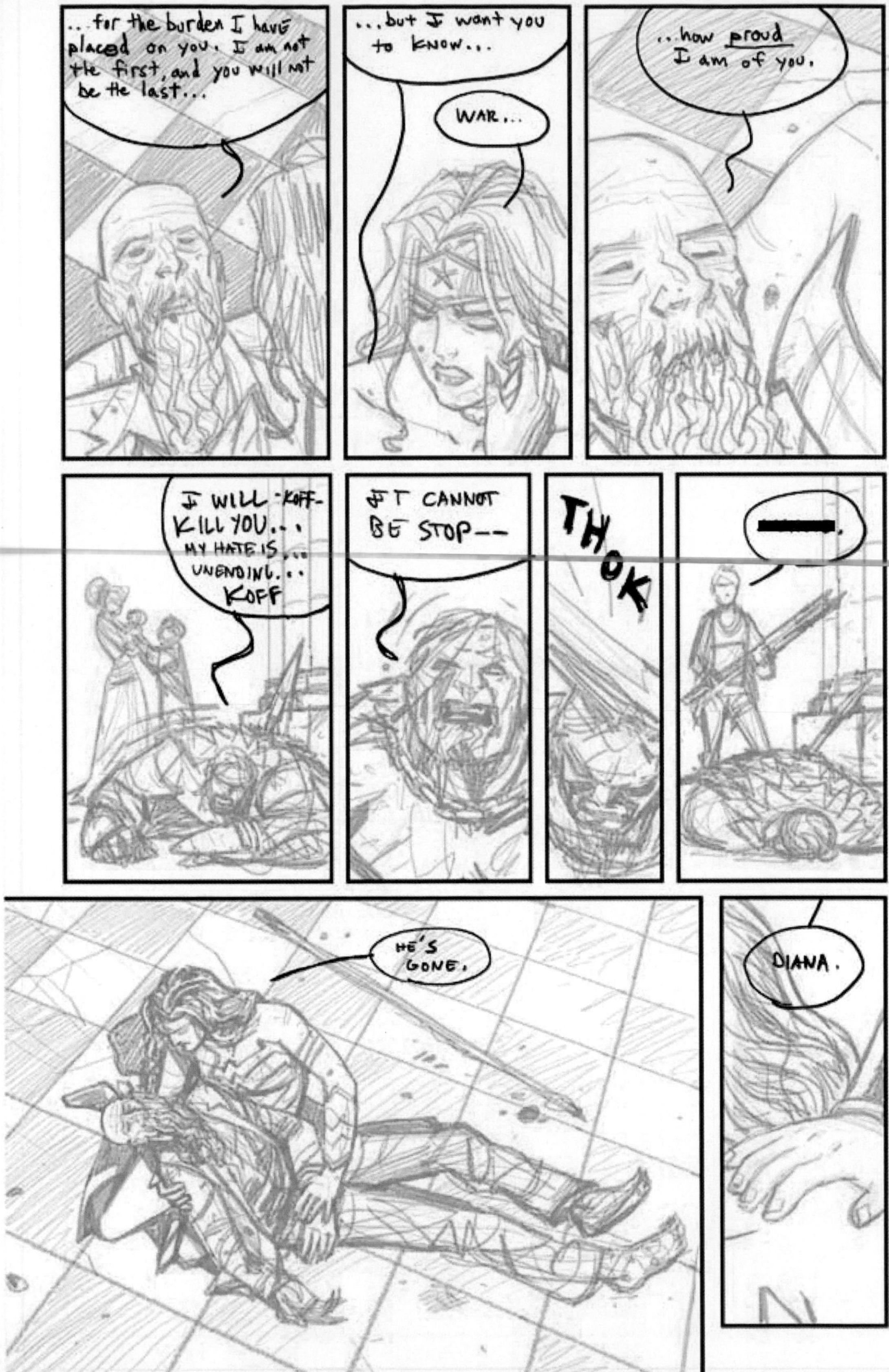
...for the burden I have placed on you. I am not the first, and you will not be the last...
...but I want you to know...
WAR...
...how proud I am of you.
I WILL -KOFF- KILL YOU... MY HATE IS... UNENDING... KOFF
IT CANNOT BE STOP--
THOK
HE'S GONE.
DIANA.

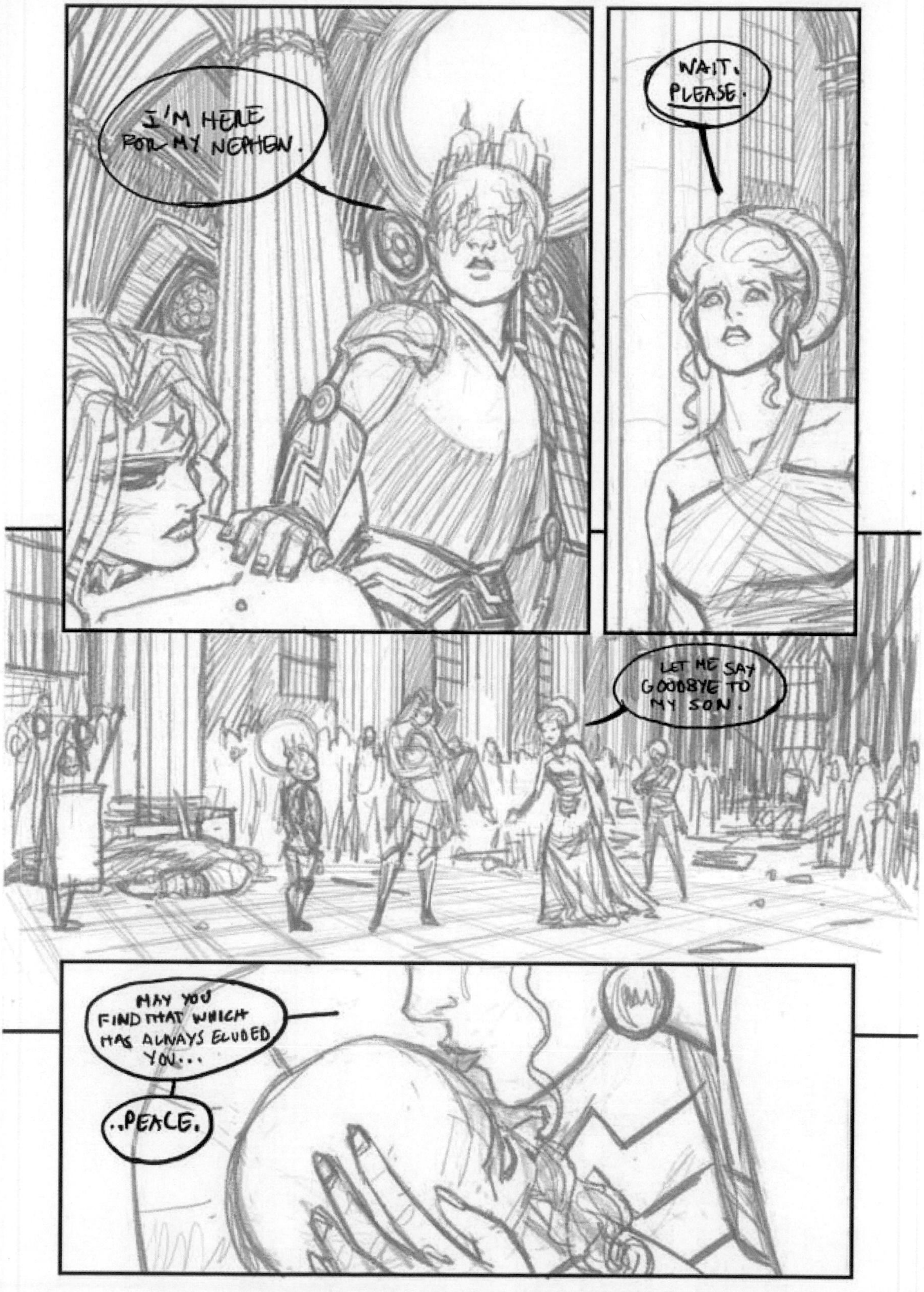
I'M HERE FOR MY NEPHEW.
WAIT. PLEASE.
LET ME SAY GOODBYE TO MY SON.
MAY YOU FIND THAT WHICH HAS ALWAYS ELUDED YOU...
..PEACE.

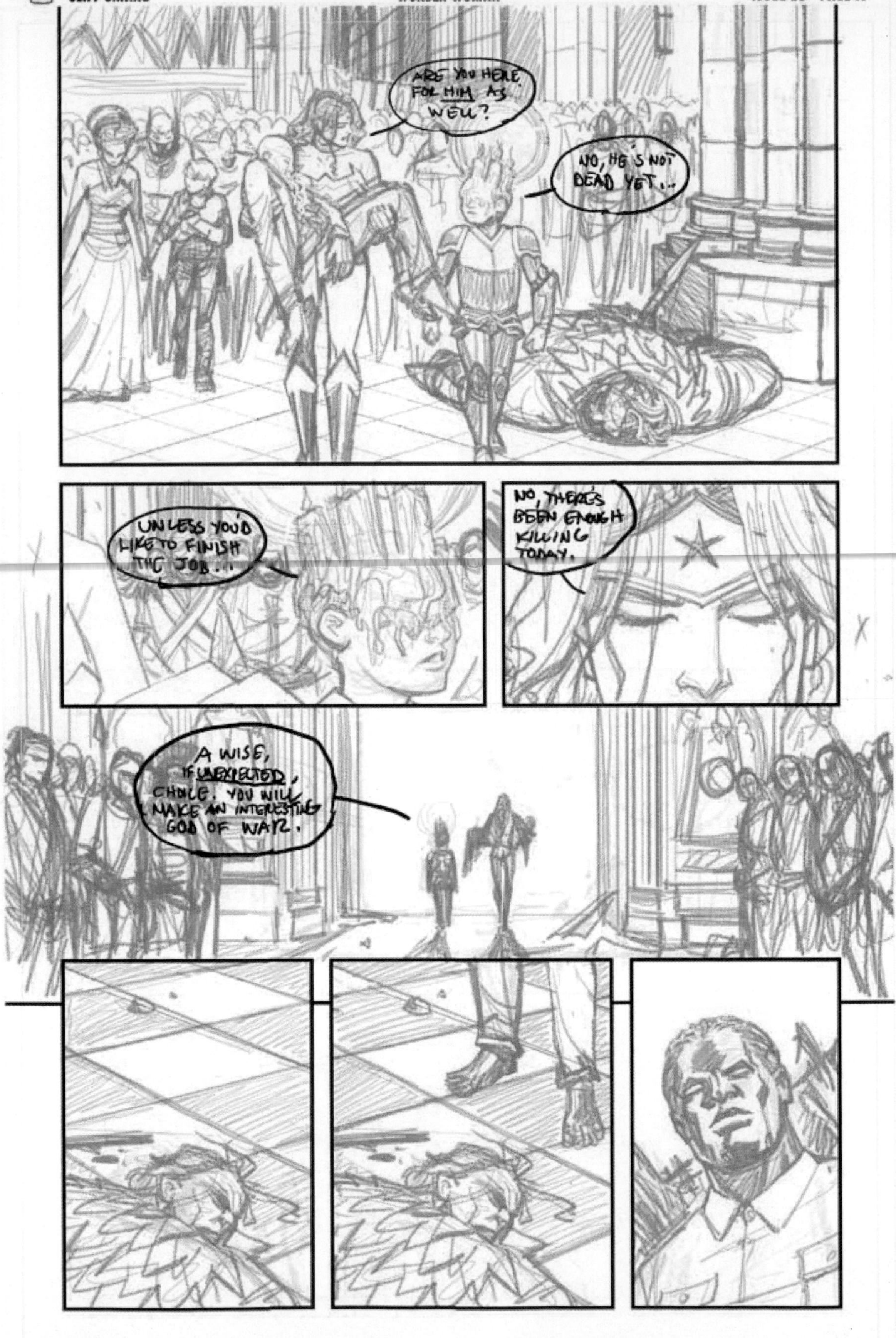
ARE YOU HERE FOR HIM AS WELL?
NO, HE'S NOT DEAD YET...
UNLESS YOU'D LIKE TO FINISH THE JOB...
NO, THERE'S BEEN ENOUGH KILLING TODAY.
A WISE, IF UNEXPECTED, CHOICE. YOU WILL MAKE AN INTERESTING GOD OF WAR.

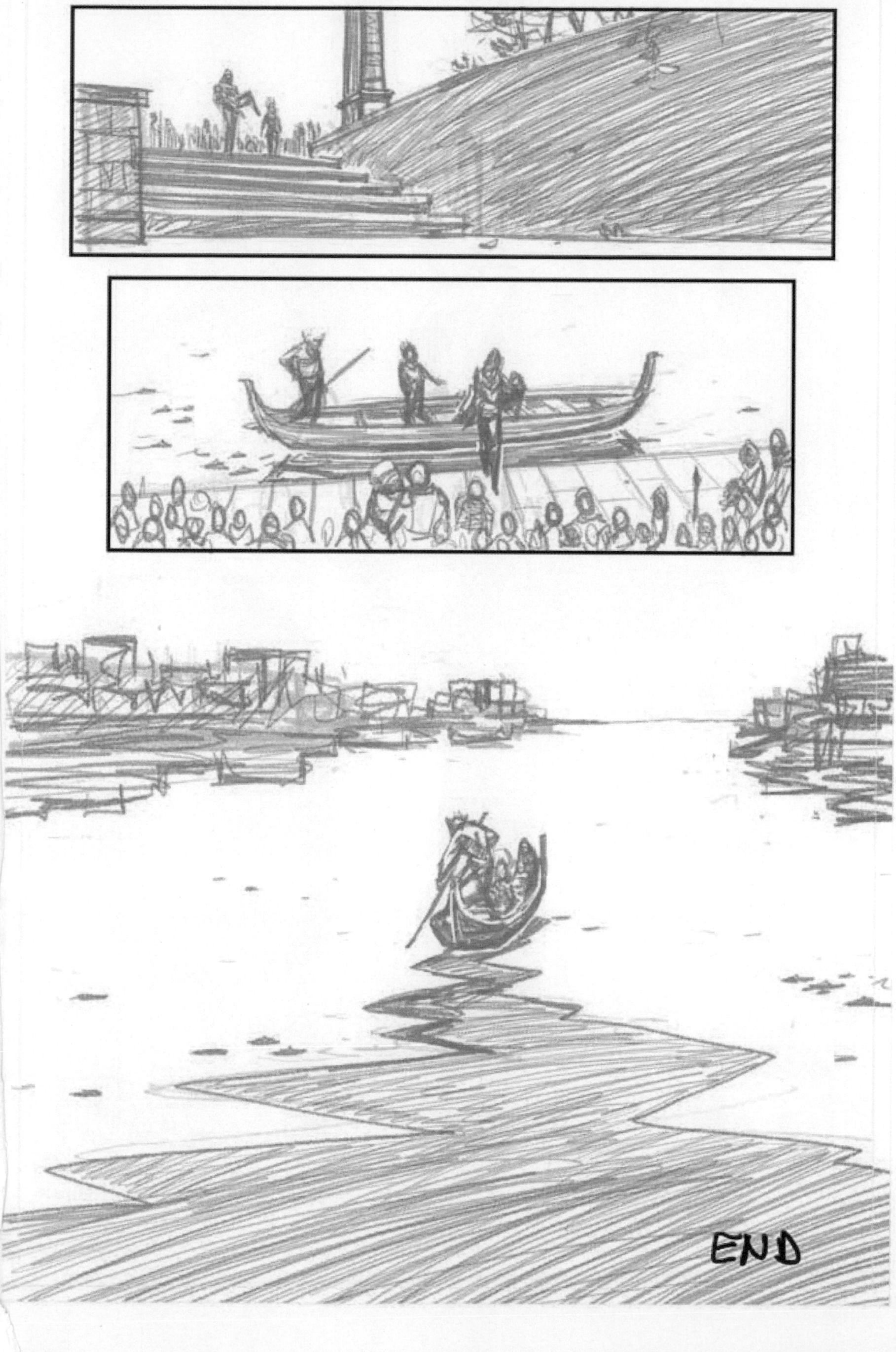
END

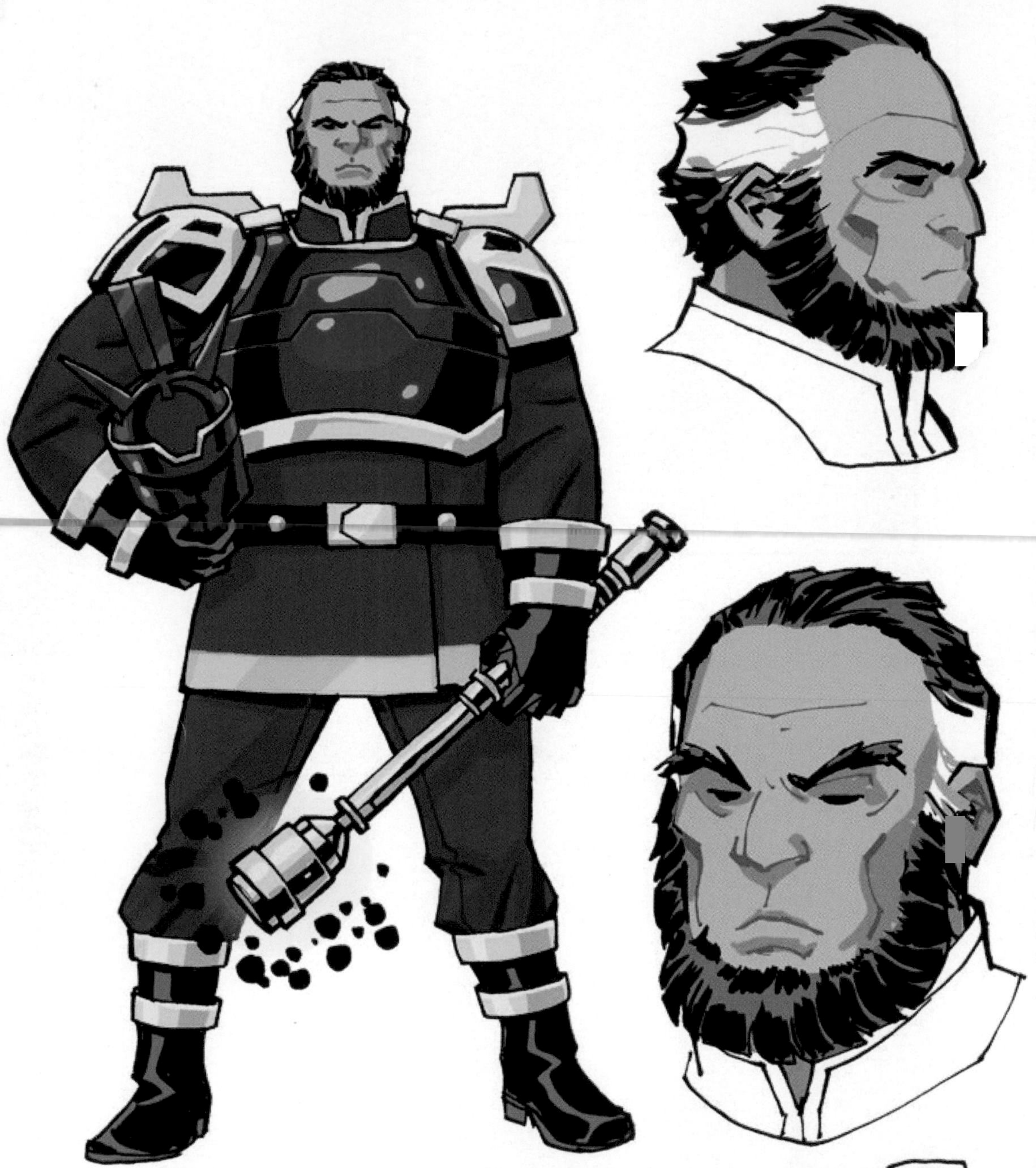
CLIFF CHIANG 2013
GENERAL IZAYA
"HIGHFATHER"